ISLAM AND THE
DIVINE COMEDY

ISLAM AND THE DIVINE COMEDY

By MIGUEL ASIN

Professor of Arabic at the University of Madrid
and Member of the Academia Española

TRANSLATED AND ABRIDGED

By HAROLD SUNDERLAND

First publised in London 1926
© Goodword Books 2008
Reprinted 2001 (twice), 2002, 2008

Goodword Books
1, Nizamuddin West Market
New Delhi - 110 013
email: info@goodwordbooks.com
Printed in India

www.goodwordbooks.com

INTRODUCTION

By the Duke of Alba

The Spanish original, of which the present is an abridged translation, appeared six years ago under the title of *La Escatología musulmana en la Divina Comedia* (Madrid, Imprenta de Estanislao Maestre, 1919).

Its author, Miguel Asín y Palacios, a Catholic priest and Professor of Arabic at the University of Madrid, is the disciple of another Arabic scholar of Spain, Julián Ribera, by whom he was initiated in Oriental studies and the methods of historical research. Asín has devoted over twenty-five years of his life to the investigation of the philosophic and religious thought of mediæval Islam—the Islam of the Orient as well as that of Spain—and its influence on the culture of Christian Europe. His training in Arabic philology and his mastery of mediæval scholastics had enabled him several years before to make important discoveries regarding the influence in theology of Averrhoes on St. Thomas Aquinas, of Ibn Arabi of Murcia on Raymond Lull, and of the *Ikhwan as-safa* on Fr. Anselmo de Turmeda, and so forth. His most important discovery, however, and the one on which his fame is chiefly based, was his discovery of Islamic models the influence of which on the Divine Comedy of Dante forms the subject of the present work. From the very date of its publication in Spanish the book aroused the curiosity of the general public and caused a great stir among the critics of literary history. The Italian Dantists particularly could with difficulty bring themselves to recognise that Moslem sources should have formed the basis for the Divine Comedy, the poem that symbolises the whole culture of mediæval Christian Europe. The book at once became the subject of lively and passionate controversy. Over a hundred articles and pamphlets have been written and lectures delivered in favour of, or against, the thesis propounded by Asín Palacios. The principal reviews devoted to literature and literary history, those both of a general and special character, have published articles from the pens of Dantists and Romance and Arabic scholars of note in Europe and America, expounding or criticising the thesis. Asín has intervened in the controversy to sum up the judgments, favourable, adverse or doubtful, and finally refute his opponents ; this he has done in different publications,[1] and the present is a translation of the work containing the original thesis. The balance of opinion is strongly in his favour. Apart from a score or so of adverse critics, mainly of Italian nationality, whose attitude is to be accounted for on the grounds of national or pro-Dante prejudice, an immense majority of critics of all nations, whose competence, whether as Romance or Arabic scholars˙ and whose impartiality are beyond all question, has opted in favour of Asín Palacios' theory.

Both parties to the controversy have been unanimous and unstinting in their praise of the book.

Pio Rajna, the chief of the Italian Dantists, writing in *Nuova Antologia*, admits that the importance of the thesis is so far-reaching that " if it were true, it would lead to a conception of Dante differing considerably from that hitherto formed by the Dantists."

Parodi, another leading figure among the Dantists of Italy, in the *Bulletino della società dantesca italiana* confesses that " this book has had a more than flattering reception, it has roused a feeling of curiosity mingled with astonishment in all who have read it and has won the approval and assent of not a few."

Nallino, Professor of Arabic at the University of Rome,

---

[1] Asín Palacios has published this summary, under the title of *Historia crítica de una polémica*, simultaneously in four reviews : *Boletín de la Real Academia Española* (Madrid, 1924) ; *Il Giornale Dantesco* (Florence, 1924) ; *Revue de littérature comparée* (Paris, 1924) ; *Litteris* (Lund, Sweden, 1924).

stated in the *Rivista degli studi orientali* that the book was
" of great value as a contribution to mediæval studies in
general, as proving the hitherto unsuspected infiltration of
Islamic conceptions of the after-life into the popular beliefs
of Western Christendom ; and, especially, as one of the
most important works on the religion of Islam that have
of late appeared."

Bonucci, Professor at the University of Sienna, in the
Rivista di Studi filosofici e religiosi, affirms that " a book
such as this does more to advance the history of, and
comment on, Dante's thought than a whole century of the
minutiæ of the Dantists."

Friedrich Beck, the famous Romance scholar of Germany,
writes in the *Zeitschrift für romanische Philologie :* " No
book on Dante of such importance has appeared for years ;
we wonder whether the Italians, in their patriotic pride, can
find a work of theirs to equal that of the learned Spaniard.
Asín has given a great impulse to the study of Dante and
has opened up vistas so startlingly new that the students
will be bound to seek new bearings and adopt fresh points
of view."

Söderhjelm, Professor of Romance languages at the University of Helsingfors, in *Neuphilologische Mitteilungen,* says :
" This book is a revelation and an event ; it will doubtless
be regarded as one of the most notable, perhaps the most
notable of all, literary productions that have marked the
Jubilee of Dante."

The review *Analecta Bollandiana* states : " The author of
this book is universally known. There is scarcely any
example of a work on Oriental philology having attracted
so great attention. The audacity of the thesis could not
fail to rouse the most lively interest in all who are initiated
in the problems of literary history. The analogies shown
by the author to exist between the Divine Comedy and
Islam are so numerous and of such a nature as to be dis-
quieting to the mind of the reader, who is forced to picture
to himself the great epic of Christianity as enthroned in the

world of Moslem mysticism, as if in a mosque that were closed to Islam and consecrated to Christian worship. At all events, there will always remain to the author of this book the honour of having started one of the most memorable debates in the history of universal literature."

Caballera, Professor of Ecclesiastical History at Toulouse, although disagreeing with the thesis, admits in the *Bullétin de littérature ecclésiastique* that "the reader is bewildered by the prodigious learning of the author, his logic, his talent for argument, which are nothing less than astounding ; the clearness of his statements makes a profound impression."

Lastly, the learned Romance scholar Van Tieghem, in the *Revue de littérature comparée*, states that " this is an honest, objective book, as clear and well arranged as it is rich in matter, which will remain on record as one of the most daring and fruitful attempts to open up new vistas in the history of European literature."

I need not refer to the flattering opinions this book has earned from the critics in England and America, as they will be known to the English-speaking public. Both Romance and Arabic scholars, such as Arnold, Browning, Cumming, Guillaume, Jordan, Leigh, Macdonald, and Ryan, have expressed themselves frankly in favour of Asín Palacios.

The almost universal applause which this book has gained, has induced me to contribute towards its diffusion by making it available to the English-speaking peoples. The idea was first suggested to me by Lord Balfour, whose interest in matters of philosophy and literature is universally known. Animated by his advice, I have now had the book translated into English, in the hope that it may reach a wider circle of readers, who, whilst finding difficulty in reading Spanish, may be curious to know of a problem that is of interest for the study of literary history in general and particularly of the Divine Comedy of Dante, who has ever counted so many fervent admirers among the English-speaking peoples.

The translation has been carefully and faithfully made by Mr. Harold L. Sunderland, who is at home both in the Spanish language and in the subject of the book. In order, however, to attain its diffusion among a wider public. the translator has, in agreement with the author, cut out the documentary evidence and critical apparatus that goes to swell the Spanish original—a complete translation of the Spanish original into French will also be published shortly by Paul Geuthner, of Paris—and is useful and intelligible to the specialists only. Thus, the Arabic texts and the tercets of the Divine Comedy that are compared with them, as well as some of the notes and paragraphs of secondary importance for the argument are not contained in the present translation. The essence of the book remains intact, however, with all its dialectic vigour and literary charm.

If the English reader should concur with my opinion, my aims in promoting the translation of the Spanish book will have been fully achieved.

August, 1925.

AUTHOR'S PREFACE TO THE ORIGINAL SPANISH EDITION

In my recent work on the neo-Platonic mysticism of the Spanish Moslem philosopher Ibn Masarra,[1] I had already hinted that his doctrines, filtering through into Christian scholasticism, had not only met with acceptance at the hands of theologians of the Franciscan or pre-Thomist school, but had even influenced a philosopher-poet of such universal renown as Dante Alighieri, whom all critics and historians had hitherto held to be an Aristotelian and Thomist.[2] After enumerating briefly the fundamental reasons underlying my vague surmise, I ventured to call the attention of specialists to the close resemblance that I found between the general outlines of the ascension of Dante and Beatrice throughout the spheres of Paradise, and another allegory of the ascension of a mystic and a philosopher, in the *Futuhat*, written by the great Sufi of Murcia, Ibn Arabi, who was undoubtedly a follower of Ibn Masarra.[3]

The question so raised was of obvious interest : for if not merely the neo-Platonic metaphysics of the Cordovan Ibn Masarra and the Murcian Ibn Arabi, but the allegorical form in which the latter cast his Ascension may have exercised an influence as models, as they certainly existed as forerunners, of the most sublime part of the Divine Comedy,

---

[1] Asín, *Abenmasarra*, p. 120. The complete bibliography of all books consulted will be found in the Appendix.

[2] When making this assertion I was unaware of the works published two years before in Italian reviews by the erudite Dante critic, Bruno Nardi, the first and only writer to attribute a neo-Platonic affiliation to the philosophy of the Florentine poet. We shall refer to the works of Nardi in Part IV, chap. IV, § 7.

[3] Cf. Asín, *Abenmasarra*, p. 163.

Dante's conception of Paradise, then Spain may be entitled
to claim for her Moslem thinkers no slight share in the world-
wide fame enjoyed by the immortal work of Dante Alighieri.
And again, the absorbing influence exercised by the latter
over our allegorical poets, from the end of the fourteenth to
the sixteenth century, from Villena to Garcilaso, not to
mention Francisco Imperial, Santillana, Mena and Padilla,
would be balanced in a measure by the antecedent influence
of our Moslem mystics in the complex genesis of the Divine
Comedy.

Such was the starting-point of my research, but soon the
horizon opened out unexpectedly before me. On closer
study of Ibn Arabi's quasi-Dantesque allegory I found that
it was itself no more than a mystical adaptation of another
ascension, already famous in the theological literature of
Islam : the *Miraj*, or Ascension, of Mahomet from Jerusalem to the Throne of God. As this *Miraj* was preceded
by an *Isra*, or Nocturnal Journey, during which Mahomet
visited some of the infernal regions, the Moslem tradition at
once struck me as a prototype of Dante's conception. A
methodical comparison of the general outlines of the Moslem
legend with those of the great poem confirmed my impression
and finally quite convinced me : the similarity had
extended to the many picturesque, descriptive and episodic
details of the two narratives, as well as to what is called the
" architecture of the realms," that is to say, the topographical
conception of the infernal regions and of the celestial abodes,
the plans of which appeared to me as drawn by one and the
same Moslem architect. But on reaching this stage of my
research, a new doubt arose. How if these resemblances
between the Divine Comedy and its hypothetical Moslem
model should be due to the fact that both derived from some
common source ? In other words, might not the features of
Dante which appeared foreshadowed in Moslem sources, be

traced to mediæval Christian legends that preceded his great
work ?   At this juncture, therefore, it became imperative, in
the first instance, to turn to those legends, and to make sure
that I were not ascribing a Moslem origin to anything in
Dante that might be adequately accounted for by those
Christian legends.

This further process of inquiry and comparison held in
store an even more unexpected conclusion. It not only
confirmed that in Moslem sources there were to be found
prototypes of features in the Divine Comedy hitherto
regarded as original because nothing similar to them had
been discovered in the Christian legends, its predecessors ; it
further revealed the no less Moslem origin of many of those
mediæval legends themselves ; it let in a flood of light
upon the whole problem. The Moslem element thenceforth
appeared as a key to much that had already been accounted
for, and to what was still obscure, in the Divine Comedy.
The conclusion was consonant with what students of
Dante had hitherto ascribed to the influence of Christian
precursors, and it explained what, as being inexplicable,
they had attributed solely to the creative genius of the
poet himself.

The above is, in outline, my thesis.[1]   It will sound to many
like artistic sacrilege, or it may call an ironic smile to the lips
of those—and they are not a few—who still conceive an
artist's inspiration as something preternatural, owing nothing
to any suggestion outside itself. This is a very common
attitude towards works of such universal renown as the
Divine Comedy. Ozanam, in his inquiry into its poetic

---

[1] When writing the third part of my book, dealing with the Moslem
elements in the pre-Dante Christian legends, I discovered from TORRACA
(*Precursori*, 331) that the influence of the Mahometan ascension over
Dante had previously been suspected by Blochet. But, Blochet, in his
essay, *Les sources orientales de la Divine Comédie*, failed to state the
problem in its real terms and his hypothesis, being unsupported by documentary evidence, remained a mere surmise. Accordingly, Torraca
easily disposes of it, saying :—

sources, had already brought out this point.[1] For a long time—he says—this poem was considered as a solitary monument, standing in the midst of the mediæval desert. When, a century ago, Cancellieri pointed to some passages of Dante's Inferno and Paradiso as being closely modelled upon the *Vision of the monk Alberic*, the devotees of Dante rose up in wrath at the sacrilege of supposing the Master capable of servile imitation of an obscure monk of the twelfth century : they, who were none too ready to admit even the undeniable fact of his imitation of classic models.

But time has passed and the nineteenth century, the age of cold dispassionate criticism, has peopled the deserts of the Middle Ages with living realities. Labitte, Ozanam, D'Ancona, Graf, a whole host of scholars and labourers in research have studied the legends of the after-life, both classical and Christian, which explain the genesis of Dante's poem ; and the lovers of Dante no longer resent the more sober and more scientific view of poetic inspiration which has gained acceptance. It is now admitted that the essential trait of genius does not lie in the absolute novelty or originality of the work of art ; neither can it consist in the power—the prerogative of God alone—of creating both Form and Matter out of nothing.[2]

The greater equanimity of the modern school of Dantophiles encourages me to hope that they will not be moved to ire by the suggestion of Moslem influences in the Divine Comedy. D'Ancona, in his inquiry into its Christian and classical sources,[3] remarks that Dante showed himself ever

"Egli ragiona così; Dante conobbe le narrazioni occidentali di altri viaggi al mondo di là ; ma queste narrazioni derivano dalla leggenda orientale (i.e. the *Miraj*) ; dunque essa è la fonte prima della Divina Commedia."

The difference between this argument and the one on which the present work is based will be readily apparent to the reader.

[1] OZANAM, p. 373.   [2] OZANAM, p. 498 *et seq.*

[3] D'ANCONA, *Precursori*, pp. 108 and 113.

keen to study and to learn, with a receptive mind towards the ideas and sentiments of his age ; and surely it will not be denied that his century was steeped in the learning and art of Islam. In the opinion of D'Ancona it may always be difficult to affirm specifically that any one legend was the actual and original model that Dante had in his mind, the pregnant germ from which his divine poem was to grow Yet I venture to think that the difficulty will not be found insuperable, if only the Moslem originals be considered, to wit : the above-mentioned legends of the Nocturnal Journey and Ascension of Mahomet, completed and adorned as they were with a mass of topographical and episodic detail, whether derived from other Islamic legends of the Life beyond the grave, from the Apocalyptic scenes of the Day of Judgment, or from the theories and conceptions of certain of the Moslem mystics in respect of Heaven and the Beatific Vision, which in spirituality and idealism were not unworthy of Dante's own conception of Paradise. To throw into relief such resemblances and analogy, as conducive to the imitation which they suggest, is of necessity the main task of the present work. To complete the demonstration, render the conclusion unavoidable, and forestall all reasonable objection, it will finally outline and enumerate the coincidences of the Christian mediæval legends that preceded the Divine Comedy, with Moslem legends of a remoter date.

MADRID, 1919.

CONTENTS

PART I

THE LEGEND OF THE NOCTURNAL JOURNEY AND ASCENSION OF MAHOMET COMPARED WITH THE DIVINE COMEDY

CONTENTS

PART I—*continued*

PART I—*continued*

PART II

THE DIVINE COMEDY COMPARED WITH OTHER MOSLEM LEGENDS ON THE AFTER-LIFE

PART II—*continued*

PART III

MOSLEM FEATURES IN THE CHRISTIAN LEGENDS
PRECURSORY OF THE DIVINE COMEDY

PART III—*continued*

PART III—continued

PART IV

PROBABILITY OF THE TRANSMISSION OF ISLAMIC MODELS
TO CHRISTIAN EUROPE AND PARTICULARLY TO DANTE

PART IV—*continued*

PART I

*THE LEGEND OF THE NOCTURNAL JOURNEY
AND ASCENSION OF MAHOMET COMPARED
WITH THE DIVINE COMEDY*

ISLAM AND THE DIVINE COMEDY

PART I

THE LEGEND OF THE NOCTURNAL JOURNEY AND ASCENSION OF MAHOMET COMPARED WITH THE DIVINE COMEDY

I

THE ORIGIN OF THE LEGEND

1. THE Moslem legend of Mahomet's nocturnal journey and ascent to the spheres of after-life originated and developed like most religious legends. Born of a brief passage in Revelations, in its very obscurity it defied theological interpretation. But what baffled the sages in their agnosticism kindled the imagination of the faithful masses, and the details of a story founded upon the sacred text were readily conceived.

One brief allusion only appears in the Koran : " Praised be He [the Lord] "—runs the first verse of the seventeenth chapter—" who called upon His servant [Mahomet] to travel by night from the sacred temple [of Mecca] to the far-off temple [of Jerusalem] whose precinct We have blessed, in order to show him Our wonders."

2. The mysterious allusion seems from the first to have aroused the curiosity of pious Moslems. A rich crop of legends sprang up as if by magic. The vivid imagination of the East had been fired, and the myth of the nightly journey was soon clothed with a wealth of detail and set in a wonderful variety of episode and scenery.

The entire records of the evolution of the legend in all its ramifications would fill volumes. Around an insignificant verselet of the Koran a plot was woven, and the story

3

developed in the form of *hadiths* or traditions of the Prophet, who was supposed to describe the wonders he saw on that memorable night. In the following pages an endeavour has been made to lay before the reader some of the principal versions extant. These have been divided into three cycles or groups, which begin with the simple, fragmentary types, and end with those in which Oriental fantasy reaches its climax.

II

FIRST CYCLE—VERSIONS OF THE " ISRA," OR NOCTURNAL JOURNEY

1. The simplest cycle seems to be one of the ninth century that is formed of six *hadiths,* in each of which, with slight variations, Mahomet is made to tell the story of an *Isra,* or journey by night on earth. Few topographical details, however, are given, and no mention is made of an ascent to celestial spheres.

In the following summaries the two main versions are compared with the Divine Comedy.

Version A of Cycle I

2. Mahomet relates to his disciples how he was awakened from sleep by a man who leads him to the foot of a steep mountain. To climb this, as he is urged to do, seems impossible ; but, heartened by his guide, he begins the ascent and eventually reaches the high table-land at the top of the mountain. Proceeding on their way, Mahomet and his guide witness six scenes, one after another, of horrible torture. Men and women with lips torn asunder ; others whose eyes and ears are pierced by arrows ; women hanging by their heels while vipers sting their breasts ; others, both men and women, that likewise hanging suck up in agony the stagnant water from off the ground ; then, wretched creatures in filthy clothes who reek as of latrines ; and lastly, corpses in the last, abominable stages of putrefaction. These punishments, the guide explains to Mahomet, are meted out in turn to liars ; those that have sinned with eyes or ears ; to mothers who have refused to suckle their children ;

to violators of the fast ; adulterers ; and to unbelievers.
Continuing their journey, the travellers suddenly find themselves enveloped in a cloud of smoke ; and they hear a
confused noise as of mingled cries of pain and fury. Gehenna
is there ; and Mahomet is urged to pass on.

Men sleeping peacefully in the shade of trees are now
designated as the bodies of those who died in the faith.
Children at play are the offspring of true believers. The
men with the white, godlike features, who are robed in fine
clothes and are exquisitely perfumed, are the true friends of
God, His martyrs and saints. On they go, and now Mahomet
descries three well-known figures drinking wine and singing
psalms. One is Zayd, the son of Haritha, a slave who for
love of Mahomet sacrificed his freedom. Had he not fallen
in the battle of Muta, when a general in the Prophet's
armies, he would assuredly have been Mahomet's successor.
The second is Jafar, son of Abu Talib and cousin to Mahomet,
who was killed in the same battle, after having preached
the faith of Islam in Abyssinia. The third is Abd Allah,
the son of Rawaha, the scribe and intimate friend of the
Prophet, who also died at Muta. The three greet Mahomet
with cries of love and allegiance. At the final stage Mahomet
raises his eyes to Heaven and beholds Abraham, Moses, and
Jesus, who, gathered around the Throne of God, await his
coming.

3. This embryonic version, simple though it may be, has
its points of coincidence with Dante's poem.[1] In each case
it is the protagonist himself who recounts his adventures.
Each makes the journey by night, led by an unknown guide
who appears to him on awaking from a profound sleep. In
both legends the first stage comprises the ascent of a steep
mountain. Purgatory, hell, and paradise are by both visited
in succession, although the sequence and detail differ. The
first five torments witnessed by Mahomet represent the
purgatory of Islam. The sixth, as also Gehenna, which
follows it, is the hell of unbelievers. The remaining episodes
deal with the paradise of children, and the heavens of the
faithful, of saints, martyrs, and prophets. Both stories end

[1] Reference to the Divine Comedy will be omitted when the resemblance
is one that affects the whole of a scene spread over several pages. For such
the reader may consult any of the summaries of Dante's poem.

with the vision of the Divine Throne. The sins or virtues
of the dwellers of each abode are explained by the guide,
and from time to time the visitor attempts to converse with
the souls of men once known to him.

4. Apart from the general outlines, there are few features
in common. Even between the torments there is little
similarity. With the introductions to the two stories, however, it is different. The description in the Islamic legend of
the lofty mountain ; Mahomet's dismay at having to climb
it ; his guide's assurance of help ; and, finally, the ascent
itself, when Mahomet follows in his guide's footsteps ; all
are features bearing a striking resemblance to Dante's
Inferno, and, especially, his Purgatory.[1] Moreover, Dante is
warned of the approach to hell by the same sign as Mahomet
—a confused noise as of " parole di dolore, accenti d'ira."[2]

Version B of Cycle I[3]

5. Mahomet is suddenly awakened by two persons ; who,
taking him by the arm, call upon him to rise and follow them.
On reaching the outskirts of Jerusalem, the visions of the
after-world begin. The guides, in this version, refuse to
answer any questions, bidding Mahomet wait until the end
of the journey for an interpretation of what he sees. The
first five visions correspond, as in Version A, to the purgatory
of Islam.

The Prophet sees a man supine at the feet of another—
man, angel or demon. The latter hurls an enormous boulder
down upon his victim's head, crushing his brain. The rock
rolls on and, when the torturer recovers it, he finds his
victim whole as before ; and so the torture is renewed without
end. Mahomet stands aghast and asks what crimes the
wretch has committed. But his guides hurry him on to
where another tormentor is forcing an iron javelin into the
mouth of another sufferer, lacerating his cheeks, eyes and
nostrils. Farther on, Mahomet sees a man struggling in a
river red with blood and seething like boiling pitch. Vainly
does he strive to gain the shore, for at each effort a fiend

---

[1] *Inf.* I ; *Purg.* IV.   [2] *Inf.* III, 26, 28.
[3] Of Version B there are four varieties which, to avoid repetition, are
here reduced to one by the elimination of details common to A and B.

forces red hot stones down his throat, obliging him to swim
back into the middle of the stream. This torture, like the
previous one, is everlasting. Still farther, they come to a
tubular structure, broad at the base and narrow at the top ;
and through the walls comes an uproar as of human voices.
The interior, Mahomet finds, is like a glowing oven, where
men and women ceaselessly writhe, now being flung upwards,
now sinking to the bottom, as the heat of the flames increases
and diminishes. The scene recurs again and again, and the
horror is accentuated by the shrieks of the victims. At
length, Mahomet reaches the summit of a dark hill, where
men, raving like madmen, exhale, through their mouths,
nostrils, eyes and ears, the fire that has been infused into
them.

Here, the tortures end. A few steps further on is a garden,
green with eternal spring. At the entrance two men, one
repulsively ugly, are feeding the flames of a fire with wood.
Within, at the foot of a spreading tree and surrounded by
lovely children, they see a venerable old man, so tall that
his head touches the sky. Ascending by the tree, Mahomet
comes to a beautiful abode, like a city of silver and gold,
inhabited by men, women and children ; some, white and
handsome, others black and ugly. A mighty river, whose
water is clearer than crystal, separates this from another,
larger city. In this river, at the bidding of Mahomet's
guides, the black and ugly bathe and from it emerge purified
and transformed into beings of beauty. Mahomet drinks of
the water and, again ascending by the tree, reaches an even
more beautiful place, inhabited by men both young and old.

At this juncture Mahomet rebels against the silence of his
guides, and at last they consent to explain each vision to him.
The wretch whose head was being crushed is the hypocrite
who, though outwardly professing to honour the holy book,
fails to abide by its precepts. He whose mouth is being
torn asunder is the liar, backbiter and violator of the fast.
The swimmer in the river of blood is the usurer. Those
writhing in the furnace are adulterers. The men on the black
hill being consumed by fire are Sodomites. The man of
repulsive aspect is the steward of hell, who appoints to each
his torture. The venerable old man is Abraham, who gathers
to his bosom children who die before reaching the age of
reason. The first abode is the paradise of true believers ;
and Moslems, who have sinned but die repentant, must wash

3

away their sins in the river before they can enter heaven.
The second is the mansion of the martyrs. All the visions
explained, the guides, who make themselves known as
Gabriel and Michael, call upon Mahomet to raise his eyes, and
in amazement he beholds afar off a castle like a white cloud.
This, his guides tell him, is the celestial mansion that awaits
him, close to the throne of God. Mahomet would fain enter
it at once, but his guides dissuade him, bidding him await
his time.

6. This version shows an advance in its descriptive
features, which are more suggestive of Dante's scenes. As
in the Divine Comedy, the four spheres of after-life—
purgatory, Abraham's bosom, hell, and paradise—are
staged separately, although on one plane until paradise is
reached by means of a tree that leads, not as in later versions,
to several celestial spheres, but to one only. Neither is
Mahomet led, as formerly, by one guide ; although the two
are angels and not, as in Dante, humans. For the first time,
too, mention is made of the steward who, like Dante's Minos,
awards the tortures to the damned.[1] But these details are
of less importance than other characteristic features. As in
Dante,[2] Jerusalem is the starting-point in this version of the
Moslem myth. Again, Dante's commentators are agreed
upon the correlativity of the punishments with the sins committed, which is also a feature in the Moslem Versions A
and B—the sinner suffers in the members or organs that
served the deed.[3]

7. But coincidence between Version B and Dante's text
is most marked in the torture of adulterers and usurers.
The naked men and women writhing in a furnace inevitably
suggest the adulterers in Dante who are incessantly swept
on by the gale of hell.[4] Even more striking is Dante's
adaptation of the Moslem punishment of usurers to those
who committed violence and deeds of blood. Submerged in

---

[1] *Inf.* V, 4 *et seq.*   [2] *Inf.* XXXIV, 114 ; *Purg.* II, 3.
[3] See ROSSI, I, 146, who summarises the *contrapasso* in the Divine
Comedy, and compare with the tortures described in Versions A and B.
[4] *Inf.* V, 31 *et seq.* It should be added that, at the approach to this
region, Dante, like Mahomet in Version B, hears the cries of the damned
(Ibid. 25 *et seq.*).

the deep waters of a river of blood, they, like the usurers,
strive to gain the shore, only to be forced back by the Centaur
archers (who take the place of the simpler stone-throwers in
the Moslem legend).[1] So strikingly alike are these two
features that other instances of resemblance lose by comparison ; as the torture of the Sodomites, burnt inwardly in
the Moslem story, and rained upon by fire, in Dante [2]; or
the rivers that in both legends separate purgatory from
paradise and of whose sweet waters both Dante and Mahomet
drink.[3]

III

SECOND CYCLE—VERSIONS OF THE "MIRAJ"
OR ASCENSION

1. The legends of the second cycle date as far back as those
of the first. They are, however, grouped apart, for, whereas
the former are concerned almost exclusively with the *Miraj*
or ascension, the latter have as their main theme the Isra or
nocturnal journey on earth.

2. There are three main versions of the legends forming
this second cycle. The first and most authentic comes to us
on the authority of Bukhari and Muslim and must, therefore,
be considerably older than the ninth century. Of the second
version only one fragment is quoted. Here the authorship is
doubtful, although it is attributed to Ibn Abḥas, a kinsman
of Mahomet, and may thus have been the work of an
Egyptian author of the ninth century, Ishac the son of
Wahab. The third version is generally regarded as apocryphal ; it may have been the work of a Persian of the eighth
century, Maysara son of Abd ar-Rabihi, or of Omar son of
Sulayman, who lived in Damascus in that century. Summaries of the three versions are as follows :—

---

[1] *Inf.* XII, 46 *et seq.* The coincidence may extend to the crime, for the
Arabic text of Version B reads : " those who ate of usury," while Dante
says literally (*Inf.* XII, 104) that " Ei son tiranni, che dier nel sangue e
nell' aver di piglio."
[2] *Inf.* XIV and XV.
[3] *Purg.* XXXI, 102. Cf. *Purg.* XXXIII, 138.

Version A of Cycle II

3. In his house (or, according to other versions, in the Mosque) at Mecca Mahomet is awakened by Gabriel, who, either alone or helped by angels in human form, prepares the Prophet for the ascension. His breast is opened and his heart extracted and washed in water brought in a golden cup from the well of Zemzem ; his breast is then filled with faith and wisdom. Thereupon Gabriel takes him by the hand, and the ascent begins, either from the Mosque of Mecca itself or, as in other versions, the Temple of Jerusalem Descriptions of the ascension differ, but, generally, Mahomet, holding Gabriel's hand, is made to rise through the air in flight. In some versions (as in B of the first cycle) the two are raised to heaven by the miraculous growth of a tree ; in others, a celestial animal, larger than an ass but smaller than a mule, carries Mahomet, or Mahomet and his guide, from Mecca to Jerusalem, the gates of paradise and, lastly, the Throne of God. Of the ascension proper there are ten stages.

The first seven correspond to the seven heavens of the astronomers, but are numbered and not named after their respective stars. The scene at each is repeated with true Oriental monotony. Gabriel knocks, and is asked by the guardian who is without and, upon Gabriel's answering, the guardian asks whether he is alone. When the guardian is satisfied that God has really sent Mahomet as His Prophet, he welcomes the travellers and bids them enter. In each heaven one or more prophets are presented to Mahomet, who is acclaimed Holy Prophet and, at times, holy son or brother.

The order in which the prophets appear is generally : Adam, Jesus and John, Joseph, Idris (or Enoch), Aaron, Moses, and Abraham. Of these characteristic descriptions at times are given. Adam is seen between two hosts of men, now smiling now weeping, as he glances to the right and left alternately. Mahomet learns from Gabriel that these hosts are the blessed and the damned. The cousins Jesus and John appear together ; Jesus, of medium stature, with a fair complexion, and fresh as if just coming from his bath. Joseph is of wonderful beauty. Moses, with flowing curls, tall and of stately appearance, bursts into tears when he is reminded that more Islamites will find salvation than those of

his faith. Lastly, Abraham, to whom Mahomet bears a
greater resemblance than any son, is seen leaning against the
temple wall of the celestial Jerusalem, a replica of the earthly
city. Every day seventy thousand angels visit this temple,
which in the *Koran* is known as the *House of Habitation*.[1]
The visit to this temple occupies the eighth stage of the
ascension, or the ninth in those versions that introduce the
vision of a gigantic tree of paradise, called in the *Koran* the
Lotus-tree of the Boundary[2] ; for neither man nor angel may
pass beyond it when nearing God. Of fabulous size, its
leaves are as large as the ears of an elephant and its fruit,
like pitchers. From its root spring four rivers : two hidden
that water Paradise, and two visible, the Euphrates and the
Nile, that irrigate the earth. Here, or previously, Mahomet
is proffered glasses of wine, milk, and honey ; he chooses the
milk and is applauded by Gabriel for so doing, inasmuch as
his religion is based on nature. The last stage has now been
reached, Mahomet beholds the Throne of God, and the
Almighty Himself reveals to him His mysteries.

Among these revelations is God's commandment, to be
transmitted by Mahomet to his people, ordaining fifty
prayers each day. On his descent the Prophet communicates
this commandment to Moses, who urges him four times to
return and beseech the Almighty to reduce the number ; and
the prayers finally are reduced to five. Again Moses calls
upon him to return, but Mahomet is loth to do so, and the
descent is completed without further incident.

4. In this version there is no allusion to hell or purgatory,
so that it is only to the *Paradiso,* or third part of Dante's
poem, that any resemblance exists. The general lines of
action in both stories are, however, strikingly similar.
Mahomet, purified like Dante, rises through the air holding
Gabriel's hand just as Dante is led by Beatrice. In both
stories there are as many stages as astronomical heavens.
The difference in number and designation merely denotes the
superior scientific knowledge of a cultured poet whose work
appeared five centuries later than the tales of those inerudite
Moslem dreamers. Apart from this, it is clear that the
seven heavens traversed by Mahomet are identical with
those that Dante names after the seven stars of the Ptolemaic

[1] Cf. *Koran,* LII, 4.   [2] *Koran,* LIII, 14.

system ; the Moon, Mercury, Venus, the Sun, Mars, Jupiter, and Saturn, to which he adds the sphere of the Fixed Stars, the Crystalline heaven and the Empyrean. The counterparts of these in the Mahometan story are the three final stages : the Lotus-tree, the House of Habitation, and the Throne of God. In each ascension there are thus ten stages. Not that there is any need to labour the point of numbers, for the poet's licence alone would have admitted of his moulding the scheme of the Moslem creation to his own ideas. What is obvious is, that in none of the so-called precursors of the Divine Comedy could Dante find so typical a model as the Moslem legend of Version A. Beatrice, human indeed, but rendered angelic through the Beatific Vision, descends from heaven with divine permission to conduct Dante to the Throne of God. Through space they fly ; and likewise Gabriel leads Mahomet. In both ascensions the travellers pass through the astronomical heavens, tarrying awhile in each to converse with the blessed and receive enlightenment on theological problems. The prophets in the Moslem heavens are the saints in Dante's poem. The literary artifice in both works is identical, no matter how they differ in art and spiritual detail.

5. Version B, given below, belongs to this cycle inasmuch as the Ascension forms the main theme. It differs from Version A, however, in that it contains the vision of hell ; and for this reason it may be regarded as a first attempt to link the *Isra* with the *Miraj*. It introduces into the *Miraj* a description of hell, which, as a rule, is peculiar to the *Isra* or Nocturnal Journey. The parts already given in Version A need not, therefore, be repeated ; an analysis of the more typical features of B will suffice.

Version B of Cycle II

6. Mahomet, accompanied by Gabriel, ascends to the third heaven, where he sees a gigantic angel, hideous and terrible to behold, and incandescent as if a being of fire. Seated on a bench of flame, he is intent upon forging instruments of torture out of solid fire. Terrified, yet curious, Mahomet

learns from Gabriel that this is the Keeper of Hell. So
fierce is the Keeper's response to Mahomet's greeting that
the Prophet, mindful of the smiling welcomes in the other
heavens, is overcome by terror. His fears allayed by
Gabriel, who explains that the angel has been created by
the Almighty to wreak vengeance on sinners, Mahomet
ventures to ask the Keeper to let him see the regions of hell.
" Thou mayst not see them," refuses the Keeper angrily ;
whereupon a voice is heard from on high, commanding :
" Oh, Angel, beware lest thou deny him aught." Then the
Keeper opens the door so that Mahomet may peep through ;
and from the opening fire and smoke burst forth, as if to
warn the Prophet of the awful sights that await him. Hell,
he sees, is formed of seven floors, one underneath the other.
The uppermost, which is reserved for deadly sins, is subdivided into fourteen mansions, one close above the other,
and each a place of punishment for a different sin.

The first mansion is an ocean of fire comprising seventy
lesser seas, and on the shore of each sea stands a city of fire.
In each city are seventy thousand dwellings ; in each
dwelling, seventy thousand coffins of fire, the tombs of men
and women, who, stung by snakes and scorpions, shriek in
anguish. These wretches, the Keeper enlightens Mahomet,
were tyrants.

In the second mansion beings with blubber lips writhe
under the red-hot forks of demons, while serpents enter
their mouths and eat their bodies from within. These are
faithless guardians, devoured now by serpents even as they
once devoured the inheritances committed to their trust.
Lower down usurers stagger about, weighed down by the
reptiles in their bellies. Further, shameless women hang by
the hair that they had exposed to the gaze of man. Still
further down liars and slanderers hang by their tongues
from red-hot hooks lacerating their faces with nails of copper.
Those who neglected the rites of prayer and ablution are now
monsters with the heads of dogs and the bodies of swine and
are the food of serpents. In the next mansion drunkards
suffer the torture of raging thirst, which demons affect to
quench with cups of a liquid fire that burns their entrails.
Still lower, hired mourners and professional women singers
hang head downwards and howl with pain as devils cut their
tongues with burning shears. Adulterers are tortured in a
cone-shaped furnace, as described in Version B of Cycle I ;

and their shrieks are drowned by the curses of their fellow damned at the stench of their putrid flesh. In the next mansion unfaithful wives hang by their breasts, their hands tied to their necks. Undutiful children are tortured in a fire by fiends with red-hot forks. Lower down, shackled in collars of fire, are those who failed to keep their word. Murderers are being knifed by demons in endless expiation of their crime. Lastly, in the fourteenth and lowest mansion of the first storey, are being crucified on burning pillars those who failed to keep the rule of prayer ; as the flames devour them, their flesh is seen gradually to peel off their bones.

At the request of Mahomet, now horror-stricken and on the verge of swooning, the Keeper closes the door, bidding the Prophet warn his people of what he has seen. Other more terrible tortures, he enjoins him, are inflicted in the six other floors, the cruelty increasing with the depth. This closes the scene, and Mahomet, as in Version A of Cycle II, continues his ascent.

7. At first sight there would seem to be no likeness between this episode and the Divine Comedy. The two essential parts, the visions of paradise and hell, appear, not as in Dante in separate settings and at different times, but illogically intermingled. It is in the third heaven that Mahomet witnesses the tortures of hell—not, as in former versions, before his ascent. But, if this circumstance is overlooked and the episode of hell considered apart from the ascension, a singular likeness to the Inferno will be apparent.

8. Above all, this version unquestionably provides the prototype of Dante's architecture of the realm of pain. How he mapped out his Inferno everybody knows[1] : a huge, funnel-shaped chasm down into the centre of the earth, with nine tiers of steps, stages, or strata, each a prison and place of punishment for a separate class of sinners. The greater the depth of the mansion, the greater the sin and the torture inflicted. Some of the circles are subdivided into three or more tiers, which correspond to as many grades of sin. The resemblance to the legend will be at once apparent. The Moslem hell is similarly formed of floors or tiers that get

[1] Cf. Rossi, i, 140, 142, 143 ; Fraticelli, 47, n.8 and Porena, p. 9.

lower as the sin is greater. Each floor is the mansion of one class of sinner ; and each has its tiers, one above the other, that correspond to the various subcategories of the sin. True, the number of main floors in each story differs, but this is of little moment when compared with other striking similarities in matters where a merely artistic imitation would not have required so strict an adherence to the model. Any other plan could have been adopted by Dante, but he preferred to follow the Moslem model, with its great divisions and subdivisions. This scheme admirably served his purpose for what Dante students term the moral architecture of the Inferno ; that is to say, the distribution and punishment of the souls in accordance with their crimes. On one point only do the topographies differ—no mention is made of the Islamic hell's being situated below the earth. But the legend merely states that Mahomet *saw* hell from the third heaven, not that hell *was* there itself. For the present, however, this point is of secondary interest and will be dealt with at greater length in later chapters.

Suffice it to have established the fact that the architecture of the Inferno had its counterpart in the religious tales of Islam as far back as the ninth century. The other features of resemblance between this version and Dante's poem are of minor interest.

9. Mahomet's meeting with the Keeper of Hell, however, obviously has its parallel in the scene where Dante is refused passage by the boatman Caronte and grim Minos.[1] The poet has merely reproduced the Moslem scene in a more artistic form, adapted from the classical mythology. The Moslem Keeper, wrathful and glowing like red hot coal ; his curt refusal to open the door ; and the imperious command from on high—all seem like rough sketches of Dante's boatman, a " demon with eyes like red hot coals, shooting forth flames," whose voice is raised in anger as he exclaims : " I will not pass thee to the other shore," and who ultimately yields at the command from heaven, rendered by Virgil : " Fret not, Caronte, so is it willed up yonder, where

[1] *Inf.* III, 82–100 ; V, 4–24.

every will is law ; question no more." A further analogy is
afforded by the scene where " dread Minos," the Keeper of
Hell itself, at the entrance mercilessly appoints the tortures
to the damned. In a fury he drives the poet away until
Virgil intervenes saying : " Hinder him not ; his journey is
ordained by fate." The words would seem to be an echo
of the heavenly warning in the Moslem legend : " Beware
lest thou deny him aught."

This dual scene is introduced by Dante, under various
disguises, into other circles of the Inferno. At the entrance
to the fourth circle Plutus assumes the role of Caronte and
Minos.[1] In the fifth circle Phlegyas, and later the devils at
the gates of Dis, repeat the scene with the self-same parleys.[2]
On this last occasion it is an angel from heaven who trans-
mits the order that allows the travellers to pass.[3] In the
seventh circle Minotaurus offers the resistance, which again
is overcome by Virgil.[4] In the fifth pit of the eighth circle
demons for the last time vainly strive to bar their way.[5]

10. Meantime, there are other actual features of resemblance. The violent burst of flame that meets Dante at the
entrance to the first circle of the Inferno [6] compares with the
fire that escapes through the door as Mahomet is about to
scan the first stage of hell in the Moslem legend.

Here again the first of the fourteen tiers is evidently the
model of Dante's city of Dis. On reaching the shores of the
Stygian Lake,[7] Dante " clearly distinguishes its towers . . .
glowing with the heat of a fiery furnace ; and the eternal
fire which consumes the city from within spreads over all
a reddish hue."

Dis, therefore, is a city of fire, as is the city in the Moslem
hell. Again, once within its walls,[8] Virgil and Dante see the
countless tombs, each a bed of fire, wherein, in coffins of red
hot iron, lie the arch-heretics crying aloud in agony. This
is undeniably a copy of the vision where Mahomet sees an
ocean of fire, on whose shores stand cities aflame with

---

[1] *Inf.* VII, 1–15. [2] *Inf.* VIII, 13–24 ; 82 *et seq.* [3] *Inf.* IX, 79–106.
[4] *Inf.* XII, 11–27. [5] *Inf.* XXI, 58 *et seq.* [6] *Inf.* III, 133–4.
[7] *Inf.* VIII, 67–75. [8] *Inf.* IX, 109 *et seq.*

thousands of red hot coffins in which tyrants in agony expiate their crimes.

11. A minute examination of the tortures described in the fourteen minor stages of the Moslem hell will also show that the Florentine poet with no great imaginative effort might well have used these as plans for his great images. Thus, the picture of the reptiles stinging the tyrants, the faithless guardians and the usurers in the various tiers of the Moslem hell recurs in the circles of the Inferno where gluttons and thieves are so tortured.[1] The torture of maddening thirst, suffered by drunkards in the seventh stage of the Moslem hell, is applied to forgers in the tenth pit of Dante's eighth circle[2]; and the latter with their swollen bellies have their prototype in the Moslem usurers. In the same circle Griffolino of Arezzo and Capocchio of Sienna scratch the scales off their leprous sores,[3] like the slanderers of the fifth Moslem stage who lacerate their faces with finger-nails of bronze. The undutiful children whom Mahomet sees in the eleventh tier, suffer a similar torture to the *barattieri* in the fifth pit of circle eight, who are kept squirming in a lake of burning pitch by demons armed with spears.[4] Lastly, the Moslem torture of murderers (in the thirteenth tier), who are being perpetually knifed and resuscitated, is clearly the model of Dante's punishment, in the ninth valley of the eighth circle, of the authors of schism.[5] Here, indeed, in sarcastic vein, he places Mahomet, the very protagonist of the legend upon which he probably based his work.

12. Closely related to this version and belonging to the same cycle is Version C. Here again the main theme is the ascension, although an abortive attempt is made to introduce the vision of hell into the ascension. The last episodes of the *Miraj*, which in A and B are merely alluded to, are mainly dealt with. Version C is chiefly characterised by hyperbole and repetition. The fantastic depiction of the heavenly scenes and persons is in striking contrast to the

---

[1] *Inf.* VI, 13–33 ; XXIV, 82 *et seq.* : XXV, *passim.*
[2] *Inf.* XXX, 49–57 , 81–84 ; 102 ; 106–7 ; 119 ; 123.
[3] *Inf.* XXIX, 79–87.   [4] *Inf.* XXI, *passim.*   [5] *Inf.* XXVIII, 22–42.

gross materialism shown in the Koran. For his images the author relies almost exclusively upon light, colour and music.

The following is an epitome of this version, the text of which *in extenso* makes tedious reading.

Version C of Cycle II

13. (a) In the first heaven Mahomet, with Gabriel, sees a gigantic cock, with a body of bright green and plumage of dazzling white, whose wings stretch across the horizon and whose head touches the Throne of God. Ever and anon it beats its wings and chants a song of praise to God, a song that is taken up by all the cocks on earth.[1]

(b) He then beholds an angel, half of snow and half of fire, who calls on all creatures of heaven and earth to unite in a bond of fellow love, symbolised in his own body by the blending of the two contrasting elements.

(c) Proceeding, he sees, seated and holding the universe on his knees, another angel gazing fixedly on a beam of light upon which writing can be seen. This, Gabriel tells him, is the Angel of Death who wrests the soul from the body. The guide describes the anguish of the soul at death and its exodus from the body ; the preliminary judgment by the angels Munkar and Nakir and the fate of the soul up till the last day of judgment. He then presents the Prophet to the Angel, who moves Mahomet to tears by his description of the part played by him at the hour of death.

(d) Continuing their journey, Mahomet and his guide come upon the Keeper of Hell. This angel's description is identical with that in Version B ; and the same episode is repeated almost literally, with one exception : when the door of hell is opened, Mahomet recoils from the flames and beseeches Gabriel to have the angel close the door. Mahomet's visit to hell thus comes to nought in this version.

(e) Farther on, they meet hosts of angels, with countless faces on their breasts and backs, who chant unending hymns of praise to God.

[1] The cock was to some extent revered by the primitive Moslems. Its crowing at dawn announced the time for prayer, and the more pious among the masses were wont to set to its notes words exhorting the faithful to pray. This might have given rise to the belief that the crowing of all the cocks on earth could only be simultaneous by being the echo of the crowing of a celestial cock. Some *hadiths* indeed attribute an angelic nature to this heavenly cock. Cf. DAMIRI, I, 388-9.

(Here the legend goes on to describe the ascension up to the sixth heaven but omits the scenes of the spheres depicted in versions A and B. The author's intention seemed to be the completion of the other versions by adding the visions that followed after the heavens of the astronomers.)

(*f*) Another multitude of angels is encountered in the sixth heaven. The body of each angel is studded with wings and faces, and all their members have tongues with which in fear and humility they sing songs of praise to God. These, Gabriel explains, are the cherubim, destined to remain eternally in the same attitude of obeisance to God. They may not look at or speak to one another ; neither may they look upwards or downwards to the heavens below. Mahomet's greeting they acknowledge by gestures, with eyes downcast. When Gabriel tells them who Mahomet is, they bid him welcome and renew their song of praise to the Almighty.

(*g*) Wrapt in admiration, the Prophet is led by Gabriel to behold in the seventh heaven other still more marvellous angels. But here Mahomet states that " he dare not relate what he saw there nor describe those angels " ; he merely states that " at that moment God gave him a strength equal to that of all the beings on earth, and a new power which seemed to be of God Himself, that enabled him to turn his eyes upon those angels, the dazzling light of whom would otherwise have blinded him." Gabriel explains to him the origin of those marvellous creatures, but again Mahomet " may not relate " what his guide has told him.

(*h*) Gabriel now leads him by the hand up to the heaven of theology, the Divine Dwelling itself. A description of this abode occupies the greater part of the version. Seventy rows of gigantic angels appear before him, bearing, like the others, innumerable wings and faces. " The dazzling brilliance of the light with which they shone would have blinded all who endeavoured to behold them." Mahomet is stricken with terror, but is comforted by Gabriel, who assures him that he has yet to see still greater marvels ; for God has vouchsafed to him alone of mortals the privilege of ascending to mansions even more sublime. In a flash they rise to a height that in the ordinary course could only be attained in fifty thousand years. Here, other seventy rows of angels, similar to the former, chant sweet choruses of divine praise. The scene is repeated until a total of seven

throngs, each numbering seventy rows of angels, is reached.
So close to one another are they that they would seem to
form one mighty heavenly host. Mahomet is awed, and
at this point he interrupts his story to exclaim : " It seemed
to me then as if I had lost all memory of the other marvels of
creation. True, it is not meet that I should speak of what I
saw ; but even might I do so, I were not able to convey it by
words. But, had it been that I was to die of terror before
my allotted span was o'er, I surely would have died when I
beheld these angels, the marvel of their forms and the rays
of light emitted by them, and hearkened to the murmur of
their voices. But God in His great mercy comforted me and
renewed my strength, so that I might listen to their hymns
of praise ; He gave power unto my eyes, that I might behold
their light." Mahomet sees that those seven throngs
" surround the Throne of God, Whose praises they sing."

(i) The seven stages that follow are monotonous in the
recurrence of exactly the same scenes and the simile of the
sea in each. Mahomet and his guide are wafted into " a
boundless sea of light irradiating with such intensity that
his vision becomes blurred and all creation appears flooded
with the refulgence and consumed in flame." Purblinded
and terror-stricken, Mahomet proceeds, now to cross a sea
of utter darkness. The violent contrast adds to his fears,
and he fancies that the whole universe is wrapt in darkness.
His guide appears to have forsaken him ; but Gabriel,
taking him by the hand, explains that these scenes are but
the portents of their approach to God. In the next stage a
sea of fire, whose waves of flame emit sparks and crackle
loudly, again strikes terror into the Prophet's heart. " I
verily thought "—he then exclaims " that the entire universe
had caught fire ; in terror I raised my hand to my eyes to
blot out the sight and turned to Gabriel."

(j) Again reassured by his guide, he now traverses " a
range of immense mountains of snow, whose lofty peaks tower
one above the other as far as the eye can reach and whose
intense whiteness sheds a light as bright as the rays of the
sun " ; and again the Prophet stands lost in amazement.
When he sees beyond the snowy heights another sea of fire
burning still more fiercely than the first and that the flames of
the two seas cannot be quenched by the snowy barrier, his
terror grows, and Gabriel redoubles his effort to calm him.
The next stage brings them to an immense ocean of water,

whose mighty waves rise like lofty mountains to break
ceaselessly one upon the other. Amidst the waters Mahomet
sees angels with myriad wings who shed a light of such
intensity as to baffle description. " Had it not been,"
Mahomet confesses, " that God gave me strength . . . , their
light had surely blinded my eyes and my body had been
scorched by the fire of their faces." Dumbfounded, the
Prophet sees that the enormous waves do not even touch
the knees of these angels, whose heads, Gabriel explains,
reach up to the Throne of the Most High, to Whom their
voices are ever raised in harmonious adoration.

(k) The last stage is again a sea of light, the refulgence of
which Mahomet paints in terms of extreme hyperbole, at the
same time regretting that " he could not describe it, were he
to make the utmost effort." " The rays," he says, " so
nearly blinded me that I saw nothing." A fervid prayer,
offered up by his angel guide, saves him from blindness.
" God," he insists, " gave strength and clearness to my
vision, so that I might behold these rays . . . and scan the
whole expanse with my eyes. But . . . it seemed to me as
if the heavens and earth and all the things therein glittered
and burned, and again my vision was dimmed. The red light
changed to yellow, then white, and then green, and at length
the colours were blended in one luminous mass, so lustrous
that once more my vision failed me." Another prayer from
Gabriel and Mahomet's sight is restored and strengthened.
Then does he see, " encompassed by that sea of light and
drawn up in one serried row, other angels circling round the
Throne of God." The loveliness of these visions defies
description, and here Mahomet falls back on his wonted
subterfuge that, even were it lawful, he could not tell a
hundredth part of what he saw. He merely observes that
those angels, with eyes downcast, sang sweet hymns of
praise ; and " as they sang, a flame of light which enveloped
the Divine Throne shone as fire from out their mouths."
Aghast, Mahomet learns from Gabriel that these, with all
other angels in the realms above the sixth heaven, are
Cherubim.

(l) The main and final stage of the ascension now begins.
In the words of the Prophet : " Higher and higher through
the celestial ether we rose, faster than the arrow speeding
from the bow, yea, swifter than the wind. And at last we
reached the Throne of the Glorious, Supreme and Almighty

One ; and, as I gazed upon it, all the works of creation sank
into insignificance. The seven heavens, the seven earths,
the seven hells . . . the whole of creation, compared to
that throne, was like a tiny ring of the mesh of a coat of mail
lying in the midst of a boundless desert."

(*m*) As, lost in wonder, Mahomet stands before the
Throne, a green wreath descends, and the Prophet is carried
by it into the presence of God Himself. Astounded at the
marvellous vision before him, he again and for the last time
confesses his inability to describe it. " I saw a thing so
great that neither tongue could tell of nor mind conceive
it. So dazzled were my eyes that I feared I should lose
my sight. However, endowed by God with a spiritual
vision, I began to contemplate all that I had in vain tried
to see before ; and I saw a light so bright . . . but it is not
meet that I should describe the majesty of His Light. I
then beseeched the Lord my God to bestow upon me steadiness of vision, and by His grace this came to me. Then
only were the veils drawn aside, and I beheld Him seated
upon His Throne in all His majesty and glory, irradiating
a sublime brilliance . . . but more it is not meet that I should
tell of Him." God now deigns to draw the Prophet nigh to
Him ; and, when Mahomet feels the Divine hands upon his
shoulders and looks upon the radiance of His face, he is
thrilled to the core. Intense delight pervades his soul, and,
as if by enchantment, his fears are dispelled. " Methought,"
he says, " when I looked upon my Master that all creatures
in heaven and earth had vanished, for lo I saw nothing else,
neither did I hear the voices of the angels. When at length
it pleased Him to break the Divine spell, it seemed to me as
if I had awakened from a deep sleep, and I had to ponder
before I came to understand where I was and to what
height God in His great mercy had chosen to exalt me."
In an intimate discourse God now reveals to the Prophet
that he has been chosen as His messenger to all the peoples
of creation and that his nation shall be the greatest of all
nations upon earth. Enraptured, Mahomet listens to the
Deity's words, when suddenly a curtain of flaming light is
drawn before his eyes and the Almighty is hidden from his
view.

(*n*) The wreath that had borne him to the Throne now
carries Mahomet to where Gabriel is waiting, and disappears
on high. It is at this juncture that Mahomet becomes aware

of the marvellous change the Beatific Vision has wrought in his being. " Lo, my God and Master had so strengthened my spiritual power of sight that with my heart I now saw what lay behind me as with my eyes I could see what was in front." He is astounded, but Gabriel explains the phenomenon and calls upon him to exercise his powers of vision, in order that, from their sublime height, he may embrace in one sweeping glance the splendour of the whole universe. With ease he can now behold all the marvellous and glittering lights that had well-nigh blinded him before : the Divine Throne, the curtain around it, the oceans and the mountains of the theological heaven, the cherubim, and, finally, the astronomical heavens shining in all their radiance underneath. He can even see the surface of the earth.

(o) Lost in contemplation, Mahomet hearkens to the harmony of the angels. " Lo," he says, " I heard the voices of the cherubim as, around the Throne of God, they chanted hymns of praise to the Almighty. Each note could I distinguish : the clear trebles ; whisperings as of leaves stirring in the wind ; soft, plaintive notes like the cooing of the dove ; gentle murmurs like the humming of bees ; and ever and anon loud bursts as of thunder." The solemnity of the angelic music is reflected in the Prophet's mind. Perturbed, he is again heartened by Gabriel, who impresses on him that he is the chosen of the Lord, Who to him alone has shown the mercy of allowing him to rise to His Almighty Throne ; soon will he see the heavenly mansion that awaits him. Gabriel now strives to interpret to the Prophet the marvels he has witnessed : the seas of light, darkness, fire, water, pearls and snow are the veils shrouding the glory of the Throne of God ; and the angels in the spheres down to the sixth heaven are the guardians of the Throne. The duty of the angels in the lower heavens is to sing praises to God. The spirit (Gabriel himself) ranks above all these ; and next to him comes Israfil. The angels in the highest sphere who encircle the Throne are cherubim ; and so strong is the light they emit that no angel in the lower spheres dare raise his eyes towards them lest he be blinded ; and so it is with the angels in the circles lower still ; they dare not look at those above them lest blindness overcome them.

(p) Gabriel's explanations finished, the descent begins, and " swifter than the arrow and the wind " is their flight. The

4

description of the gardens of paradise in this legend is merely a detailed reproduction of the paradise of the Koran. The Lotus-tree of the Boundary reappears here as a tree of fabulous magnitude, whose branches, laden with leaves, whereon dwell the celestial spirits, extend throughout paradise. The portrayal of the Kauthar, the river of paradise, is also based on the Koranic description.[1] Another tree, the Tree of Happiness,[2] also from the Koran, gives the inspiration for the picture of the mansions of the blessed—a picture in which the spiritual tone, predominant in other visions, is absent. The last stage of the journey is through the astronomical heavens, and on their way Mahomet tells the prophets he meets of the marvels he has seen. At the same place on earth where he had called upon him to undertake the ascension, Gabriel leaves Mahomet. The legend ends with Mahomet's astounding assertion that he accomplished the whole journey in a single night.

14. The monotonous style, the excessive hyperbole and the constant repetition, coupled with the entire absence of spiritual effect in the last episode, make it difficult to associate this version with the artistic poem of Dante. The most idealistic part of the Divine Comedy is undoubtedly the Paradiso ; and it would, therefore, be as well, before attempting to compare the two works, to remind the reader that the final episode of Version C must be regarded as an addition cleverly introduced by the author to invest the legend with a semblance of authenticity and orthodoxy. For at bottom the tale reflects little of the mind of Mahomet, a polygamist and warrior who led men to battle. It would rather seem to betray a Moslem with leanings towards neo-Platonism, or a follower of the *Ishraqi* and pseudo-Empedoclean school, so addicted to the usage of similes of light and geometrical circles in the illustration of metaphysical ideas.[3] It should also be borne in mind that, in the tenth century, the authorship of this legend was attributed, not to an Arab, but a Persian, by name Maysara, the son of Abd ar-Rabihi. It is possible that, living in the eighth century, this Persian had retained some traces of the

---

[1] *Koran*, CVIII, 1.   [2] *Koran*, XIII, 28.
[3] See my work, *Abenmasarra*, ch. IV, V and VIII.

Zoroastrian creeds of his native country, which had just been forcibly converted to Islamism.

The reader, then, before attempting to compare the two works, should cast one more glance at the Paradiso. Let him divest the poem of its discourses and dialogues, the theological doctrine it breathes, its philosophical and astronomical lore and the allusions to Italian history with which it is replete, and he will be able, with both works thus reduced to their simplest outline, to proceed with a methodical comparison.

15. The most striking analogy between the two works is the idealistic tone of the general description of paradise. Dante students have emphasised the gulf that divides his paradise in this respect from any previous conceptions.[1] Departing from the beaten track of a material heaven, the poet made use of the intangible, the most delicate phenomena of nature. In his celestial spheres life is a feast of light and sound, and his paradise, the realm of mind emancipated from the body.

And light and song also figure largely in the descriptions of paradise of this Version C. Apart from the sea of darkness, introduced as a contrast to the seas of light and fire, the scenes and personal descriptions in the principal stages of Mahomet's Ascension are drawn in a perspective of light, just as are those of Dante. The twenty odd scenes of the main action, and more especially Mahomet's progress through the seventh astronomical sphere, are set in the most vivid colours. The angels, too, although at times shown in human form and at others, as monstrous shapes, irradiate a splendour that dazzles the eyes of the spectator. A comparison of these with numerous similar descriptions in the Paradiso makes it clear that in both stories the element of light reigns supreme.[2] Beatrice grows in brilliance at each stage of the Ascension. The spirits of the blessed in each sphere and in the Empyrean appear to Dante as resplendent lights,

[1] Cf. ROSSI, I, 165, 168.

[2] To quote all these passages would be tantamount to writing out the entire *Paradiso*. See mainly Cantos V, VII, VIII, IX, X, XII, XIII, XIV, XV, XVIII, XXII, XXIII, and XXVII–XXXIII.

at times assuming the shape of a crown or wreath, at others, appearing in the allegorical form of the iris, the cross, the eagle and so forth. God Himself is a light of ineffable brilliance, and the choirs of angels around him are brilliant orbs of light. A luminous effect likewise marks each stage of Dante's journey. But a more detailed comparison of the employment of light in the two legends will be made later on.

And as with light so it is with sound. Excepting the Angel of Death and the Keeper of Hell, all the angels Mahomet meets sing songs of praise to the Lord. The words of these anthems, taken from the Koran, are at times transcribed literally by Mahomet. On completing the ascension, he again hears the angels in a symphony that he seeks to describe by similes taken from the sounds of nature. In Dante's poem also the celestial spirits sing hymns of praise from the Holy Scriptures, and the poet attempts to convey the majesty of the harmony by comparing it with sounds of nature and music.[1]

16. But these are general features of resemblance. Many of the actual passages are either similar or identical, which still further proves the close relationship between the two legends.

On various occasions Mahomet dwells upon the speed of his flight, and twice he likens it to the wind and the shaft sped from the bow. The latter simile is used by Dante in telling of his ascent to the heaven of the Moon and of Mars [2]; the former, when he describes the flight of the souls that come to meet him in the sphere of Venus. Again, he compares the ascension of the souls in the heaven of Saturn to the rush of a whirlwind.[3]

Inability to describe what he sees is an expedient to which Mahomet often has resort. Dante affects this hyperbole in his prologue and in five other Cantos : in the sphere of the Sun ; in the heaven of Gemini ; in the Empyrean ; when he

---

[1] Compare chiefly the following passages of the *Paradiso* : VII, 1–6 ; X, 139–144 ; VIII, 28–31 ; XII, 7–9, 22–30 ; XIV, 118–126 ; XX, 73–75, 142–144 ; XXI, 139–142 ; XXIV, 112–114 ; XXV, 97–99, 130–135 ; XXVI, 67–69 ; XXVIII, 94–96 ; XXXII, 94–99, 133–135. [2] *Par*. II, 23–24 ; V, 91–92. [3] *Par*. VIII, 22–24 ; XXII, 99.

beholds the Virgin Mary; and in his last episode when he deals with the mystery of the Holy Trinity.[1]

It will further be noted that Mahomet's pretext, " that it is not lawful that he should tell of what he saw," is found to recur frequently in the Paradiso.[2]

The feature, however, that shows most conclusively the affinity between the two stories is the one that is repeated *ad nauseam* in the Mahometan Ascension. At each stage of heaven Mahomet is dazzled by the lights, and each time he is fearful of being blinded. Repeatedly he raises his hands to his eyes to shield them from the intense radiance, and in the end he becomes dazed. Gabriel then intercedes with God and Mahomet is granted a new, preternatural vision, that enables him to look freely upon the lights that before had dimmed his sight.

This scene is reproduced, often with the same words, in more than ten episodes of Dante's Paradiso. In the sphere of the Moon it is the splendour of Beatrice[3]; in Mars, the image of Our Lord surrounded by the Martyrs[4]; in the sphere of the Fixed Stars, the light of the Apostle James, when the poet exclaims[5]: " As who doth gaze and strain to see the sun eclipsed a space, who by looking grows bereft of sight, so did I to this last flame."[6] In the eighth sphere the refulgence of Christ in the image of a sun blurs the poet's vision[7]; at the instance of Beatrice, however, he again tries his eyesight and finally discerns amid the shadows a brilliant star, the symbol of the Archangel Gabriel; the movements of this star his eyes have not the strength to follow.[8] In the ninth sphere the brilliance of the Divine Essence is such that he has to close his eyes.[9] In the tenth sphere the Triumph of the Blessed calls forth from the poet[10]: " As a sudden flash of lightning which so shattereth the visual spirits as to rob

---

[1] *Par.* I, 4–9; X, 43–47; XXIII, 55–59; XXX, 19–22; XXXI, 136–138; XXXIII, 55–56, 106.   [2] *Par.* XXXIII, 90, 121–3, 139, 142.
[3] *Par.* III, 128–9.   [4] *Par.* XIV, 77–8; 82.   [5] *Par.* XXV, 118–121.
[6] The quotations on this and the following pages are from the English version by the Rev. P. H. WICKSTEED, M.A. " The Temple Classics." Edit. J. M. Dent, London.   [7] *Par.* XXIII, 28–33.
[8] *Par.* XXIII, 76–84; 118–9.   [9] *Par.* XXVIII, 16–18; XXIX, 8–9.
[10] *Par.* XXX, 46–51.

the eye of power to realize e'en strongest objects ; so there
shone around me a living light, leaving me swathed in such
a web of its glow that naught appeared to me." But his
fears are assuaged by Beatrice, and he adds[1]: " So soon as
these brief words came into me I felt me to surmount my
proper power ; and kindled me with such new-given sight
that there is no such brightness unalloyed that mine eyes
might not hold their own with it." In the Ninth Canto, when
he beholds the apotheosis of the Divine Essence, he introduces a still more far-fetched hyperbole. St. Bernard,
guiding Dante in the place of Beatrice, pleads with the
Virgin to grant Dante the favour of being raised to the
Divine Light. His eyes, strengthened, slowly take in the
immense, trinal light, but he says[2]: " I hold that by the
keenness of the living ray which I endured I had been lost
had mine eyes turned aside from it. And so I was the
bolder, as I mind me, so long to sustain it as to unite my
glance with the Worth infinite. Oh grace abounding, wherein
I presumed to fix my look on the eternal light so long that
I consumed my sight thereon."

17. The principal part played by Gabriel in the ascension
is to guide Mahomet and act as his adviser and comforter ;
and this very role is assigned by Dante to Beatrice. Gabriel,
however, at times plays a further part, as, for instance, when
he prays to God to help Mahomet and calls upon the Prophet
to thank the Lord for allowing him to visit heaven. A
parallel scene appears in the Tenth Canto of the Paradiso.
In the sphere of the sun, Beatrice exclaims[3] : " Give thanks,
give thanks to the sun of the angels, who of his grace hath
to this sun of sense exalted thee." And in the ensuing
verses Dante pours forth heartfelt thanksgivings and effusions
of divine love. The prayers offered up for Dante are too
well known to call for special mention.[4] The most striking
analogy, however, is seen in the following. In the Paradiso
Beatrice leads Dante only as far as the Empyrean, where
St. Bernard takes her place[5]. In the Moslem legend, Gabriel

---

[1] *Par.* XXX, 55–60.   [2] *Par.* XXXIII, 52–54 ;   76–84.   [3] *Par.* X, 52–54.
Cf. *Par.* II, 29–30.   [4] *Par.* XXXI. XXXIII.   [5] *Par.* XXXI, 58–60.

leaves Mahomet to accomplish the last stage alone ; and he is conveyed to the Divine Throne by a luminous and spiritual wreath. And herein lies another noteworthy similarity. The wreath which descends from on high and bears Mahomet up to the Divinity has its parallel in the " facella, formata in cerchio a guisa di corona " that Dante sees in the eighth heaven descending from the Empyrean, whither it returns escorting the Virgin Mary.[1]

The solutions furnished by Beatrice, or as on occasion the blessed, to Dante's problems of theology and philosophy, have each an equivalent in the Mahometan ascension. Here, although occasionally it is an angel, such as the Angel of Death and the angel guarding hell, that gives the interpretation, it devolves chiefly upon Gabriel to explain the riddles of the Moslem hereafter. Especially remarkable is the likeness between the final episode of the Moslem ascension, when Gabriel in the highest heaven explains to Mahomet who the angels inhabiting the celestial spheres are, and Beatrice's long dissertation in the ninth heaven on the nature and being of the various angelic hosts. Further, Beatrice and Gabriel are agreed upon assigning to the cherubim a place in the circles nearest to God and the other circles to angels of lesser rank.[2] True, the Christian angelology, although derived from the same Hebrew theology and Alexandrine metaphysics, differs from the Islamic on several points ; but, considered from a literary point of view, this does not affect the analogy in episode.

18. Let the reader now turn to some of Dante's angelic visions and, first, to that of the gigantic eagle formed of thousands of angels that the poet sees in the Heaven of Jupiter.[3] All Dante students have admired its beauty and originality ; and yet it is surely admissible to proffer the suggestion that the picture was inspired by Mahomet's vision of the gigantic cock, at the outset of his ascension. If the unpoetical nature of this domestic fowl, when comparing it with the eagle, the king of the air and, in classical

---

[1] *Par.* XXIII, 94 *et seq.*   [2] *Par.* XXVIII, 94, 98–101, 118–120.
[3] *Par.* XVIII–XX.

mythology, the attribute of Jove, be disregarded, it will be seen that there is a strong resemblance between the two conceptions. To begin with, Dante's eagle is a being of innumerable spirits with wings and faces. These, the spirits of the blessed, emit an irridescent light and chant in harmony hymns calling upon mankind to lead a righteous life. As it chants, the eagle flaps its wings and then comes to rest.[1]

The cock of the Moslem legend is also a gigantic bird that beats its wings as it chants religious songs, calling mankind to prayer, and then sits at rest. Version C certainly makes no allusion to the spiritual nature of the bird, but other versions and various authentic *hadiths* expressly state that it is an angel. In addition, in the Moslem legend, visions of gigantic angels, each comprising a monstrous agglomeration of wings and faces, repeatedly recur ; and these angels too, resplendent with light, chant with their innumerable tongues hymns of praise. So consummate an artist as Dante might very well have combined these two images to produce the hybrid and yet most beautiful picture of the eagle.

The angels with wings of gold that fly over the mystic rose, by which the abode of bliss in the Paradiso is symbolised,[2] also appear to be copied from Mahomet's vision in the first heaven, where an angel of snow and fire appears. For these angels also : " had their faces all of living flame . . . and the rest so white that never snow reacheth such limit."

19. But the similarities extend even to the general outlines of entire passages. In the sphere of the Fixed Stars, Beatrice calls upon Dante to cast his eyes downwards and endeavour to see how many worlds lie beneath his feet, in order to prove whether his vision has been strengthened. Dante exclaims : " With my sight I turned back through all and every of the seven spheres, and saw this globe such that I smiled at its sorry semblance." " And all the seven were displayed to me, how great they are and swift, and how distant each from other in repair." " The thrashing-floor

---

[1] *Par.* XVIII, 100–101 ; 103–108. XIX, 1–6 ; 34–35 ; 37–39 ; 95–97. XX, 73–74. XVIII, 76–77 ; 85–86 ; 91, 93. XIX, 10–12 ; 20–21.
[2] *Par.* XXXI, 13–15.

which maketh us wax so fierce, as I rolled with the eternal twins, was all revealed to me from ridge to river-mouth."[1]

It is surely obvious that the general scheme of this passage is at once a faithful copy and skilful combination of two episodes of Version C : when Mahomet beholds the Divine Throne, whose magnificence makes all former visions pale into insignificance, and compares its infinite grandeur with the now dwarfed appearance of the universe ; and when, his spirit having experienced the ecstasy of the Beatific Vision, he is asked by Gabriel to cast his eyes downwards and test his supernatural power of sight. With one wondering glance—the legend runs—he embraces the whole universe, his eyes penetrating the celestial and astronomical spheres beneath his feet right down to the surface of the earth.

20. A final and irrefutable argument, however, may be based on the last episode crowning the Paradiso, when Dante beholds the Beatific Vision of the Divine Essence in all its splendour. An examination of this vision will prove of interest. The Divine Essence is the luminous centre of nine concentric circles of angelic spirits who, revolving unceasingly around it, sing Hosannahs to the Lord. Each circle comprises countless angels.[2] The two first circles are those of the seraphim and cherubim. Dante is unable to fix his gaze on the light but soon his sight is strengthened and he can behold it steadily. He admits that he is powerless to describe the vision, for the ecstasy of the moment effaced all memory of it but, even were he able to recall the vision, 'twere not possible for mortal to describe it. Dante's attempts to picture the Trinity and the Incarnation need not be taken into consideration. His description of the vision is reduced to a vague recollection of the subjective phenomena : steady and progressive mental contemplation, a trance in which he is wrapt in admiration, and a feeling of intense delight and spiritual sweetness that pervades his soul.[3]

[1] *Par.* XXII, 133–135 ; 148–153.
[2] *Par.* XXVIII, 16–18 ; 25–34 ; 89–93.   XXX, 100–105.
[3] *Par.* XXXIII, 57–63 ; 93–94 ; 97–99.

Dante students have long and in vain sought the origin of this sublime apotheosis, for none of the religious legends, so critically studied by the great scholars, Labitte, D'Ancona, Ozanam and Graf, furnishes the least resemblance in geometrical conception to these concentric circles of angels who ever revolve around the Divine Light. Nevertheless, the striking likeness between Dante's poem and the Moslem legend conclusively proves the strength of our argument. In the latter, too, rows of angels, each row representing a different rank, with the Cherubim nearest, surround the Divine Throne. These angels also chant anthems in honour of the Lord and radiate streams of light; and the number of rows again is nine. Thus do they also in nine concentric circles revolve unceasingly around the Throne of God— a God who in both stories is depicted as a focus of ineffable light. Again, both protagonists describe the Beatific Vision twice—Mahomet, when, before undertaking the last stage of his Ascension and still accompanied by Gabriel, he first discerns the Divine Throne, and again when Gabriel has left him; and Dante, when, with Beatrice, he beholds the Divine Apotheosis from the ninth heaven and a second time in the final Canto. The psychological effects on both are also similar. Mahomet, too, is dazzled and fears lest he be blinded; then God bestows upon him steadiness of vision, so that he can fix his eyes upon the Divine Light; he also is incapable of describing the Throne and can only recall that he experienced a rapture of the soul, preceded by a sensation of intense delight.

The stories have many other minor points in common, but the chief features of resemblance as given above will perhaps suffice to establish proof of the affinity between the two.

IV

THIRD CYCLE—FUSION OF THE VERSIONS OF THE "ISRA" AND THE "MIRAJ"

1. The legends of this cycle really form a synthesis of those of the first two cycles, and their episodes are for the

greater part repetitions of previous ones. Nevertheless, although from our point of view they are of minor import- ance, they represent a distinct stage in the evolution of the legend. In the former cycles the *Isra*, or Nocturnal Journey, and the *Miraj*, or Ascension, were related separately ; but here the two are fused into one continuous story. One version will suffice to illustrate the earliest type of non- Christian mediæval legend that related, as in Dante's poem, in one uninterrupted story the visit to hell and purgatory and the ascension to paradise. This version may be called the earliest, for it has been handed down to us in the voluminous *Tafsir*, or commentary on the Koran, by the celebrated historian Tabari, who lived in the 9th century. Briefly summarised, the legend runs as follows :—

Sole Version of Cycle III

2. The introduction is identical with that in Version A of Cycle 2. Mahomet, either in his house or the Mosque at Mecca, is suddenly awakened by Gabriel, alone or accom- panied by other angels. He is purified and led on a Nocturnal Journey to Jerusalem and thence to heaven. The episodes are as follows : At the outset Mahomet meets an old woman who, decked in finery, from the roadside endeavours to entice him to tarry with her ; but Mahomet turns a deaf ear and passes on unheeding. Gabriel explains that this woman is an allegory of the world. Her tinsel represents the allure- ments of the world, which like her is effete, for so short is life on earth that it resembles the brief years of old age. Immediately after this vision—or before it in some versions —Mahomet is called upon to halt by two voices, one from either side of his path. These are the voices of the Jewish and Christian faiths, that would fain convert him to their creeds. Proceeding, he encounters the Devil, who in turn tries to lure him from his path ; but, at Gabriel's warning, he hastens on. At last, freed from all temptations, he arrives at a stage where he is welcomed by Abraham, Moses and Jesus.

The visions that follow either represent allegories or depict the tortures of hell, some of the latter resembling and others differing from the punishments of the previous versions. Firstly, Mahomet beholds men cutting corn sown but the day before, and, in amazement, he sees the stubble grow as fast as the corn is cut. These, Gabriel informs him, are symbolic of the Moslems who devote their all to the spreading of the faith and whom God rewards seven-hundredfold. Then follows the torture of the crushed head, as in Version B of Cycle 1, and thereafter, the punishment of those who failed to make the offerings required by rite. Clothed in rags, these graze like beasts, chewing fetid herbs. Further on, the adulterers sit at a table bearing both wholesome meat and raw and putrid flesh. The latter they devour in du e punishment for their lewdness, which led them to reject their wives and seek the embraces of loose women. At this juncture the travellers' path is barred by the trunk of a tree, and in surmounting it their clothes get torn. This obstacle is a symbol of the bad Moslems who lead their brothers off the path of virtue. An aged wood-cutter, who toils to heap still higher the pile of wood he has collected, although his strength forbids his carrying his loads away, next comes into view, symbolising the rich miser who hoards the wealth he cannot use. Proceeding, they witness the torture of the hypocritical preachers, who, like the liars in Versions A and B of Cycle 1, have their tongues and lips torn. A huge bull, which, rushing out of a narrow shelter, is now vainly trying to re-enter it, is figurative of the torment undergone by the conscience of those who speak hasty words they afterwards regret. The travellers now pass through a valley, where Mahomet, breathing in the soft perfumed air, listens in rapture to a song whose words he cannot catch. The valley, Gabriel explains, represents heaven, and the voice he hears sings to the Lord, beseeching Him to fulfil His promise to the faithful. God hearkens to the prayer and renews His covenant to save all Moslems. A parallel scene in antithetic setting is now introduced. Mahomet traverses another valley, which, reeking abominably, represents hell. Another voice is heard invoking the Lord to punish all sinners, and from on high God answers that He will wreak His vengeance.

Leaving the valley of hell behind, the travellers reach the Mosque of Jerusalem, the goal of their Nocturnal Journey. The scenes laid here are of little interest. Mahomet, surrounded by angels, prays, and in turn he is greeted by the spirits of Abraham, Moses, David, Solomon and Jesus. Offered glasses of milk, water and wine, he drinks of the milk and water, and, as in Version A of Cycle 2, Gabriel applauds his choice. The story of the ascension is told in terms that are almost identical with those of that version. When he reaches the seventh heaven, however, the passage of Version B of the first cycle, depicting Abraham, is inserted with slight variations. Abraham is seen as a venerable old man, seated at the entrance to paradise between two hosts of men, the one with white, the other with spotted faces. The latter bathe in three rivers, emerging from the third with faces as white as those of the other host which they now join. The one host, Gabriel explains, are the believers of unspotted soul and the other, penitent sinners. The three rivers are symbolic of the mercy, loving-kindness and glory of God. The final stage, as in Version A of Cycle 2, is the visit to the Lotus-tree of the Boundary. The legend ends with the familiar intimate colloquy between God and the Prophet.

3. As already suggested, this version is interesting, not from a comparative point of view, but because it constitutes a fusion of the versions of Cycles 1 and 2. As the date of the version is not later than that of the fragmentary tales, it would seem as if the Moslem traditionists had decided upon such fusion at an early period. This decision, no doubt, was based on considerations of art rather than theology, the object being more to satisfy, with one complete story, the curiosity of the faithful than to justify the existence of so many fragmentary and often contradictory versions of one and the same event. That this latter object, implying the necessity of accepting as authentic all those different versions, influenced the theologians of a later epoch, will be seen further on. In this version there is no trace of it. Tabari, by whom the version has been handed down to us, although himself an eminent theologian, merely records it as the work of story-tellers and omits all mention of the authenticity or otherwise of the different fragments and versions.

4. Of the two main parts of the legend, the second (the ascension) contains little that is new either in descriptive feature or episode. The first part, on the other hand, could easily be regarded as a reading of the *Isra* of a different cycle

from those hitherto considered. Its many new episodes are precisely the visions that do not deal with realities, but are symbols of abstract ideas, of vices and virtues. A new element, moral allegory—so marked a feature of Dante's poem—is thus introduced. Vossler[1] has pointed out how successfully Dante combines the two imperfect forms of mediæval visionary style—the religious or apocalyptic, and the profane or allegorical ; and he lauds Dante's originality, for, as he truly remarks, his allegories are not derived from Capella, Prudentius, or Alan of Lille.[2] The free use of allegory in this version of the Nocturnal Journey is, therefore, of interest. No doubt few of the visions can be regarded as models of the scenes in the Divine Comedy ; but their mere occurrence in such number in a Moslem legend that in other respects has been shown to have had so great an influence on Dante, is significant. It may reasonably be supposed that the origin of other allegories of the great poem which, in Vossler's opinion, cannot have been derived from its Christian or classical precursors, can be traced back to Moslem literature.

5. A systematic investigation in this direction will be made later on. Let it here suffice to cite one typical instance of the adaptation to the Divine Comedy of Moslem symbols. The resemblance between the vision of the old woman appearing at the outset of Mahomet's journey as a symbol of the temptation of the world, and the vision seen by Dante when he reaches the fifth circle of purgatory, is obvious. The old woman, whom Mahomet sees, concealing under splendid adornments the ravages that time has made upon her charms, endeavours to draw him from the path by flattery and alluring gestures. Not until later does Gabriel interpret the vision. The old seductress is a symbol of the world, decked in finery to entice the Prophet. Had she succeeded, the Moslem people had likewise preferred worldly well-being to eternal bliss.

Dante, having traversed the fourth circle of purgatory,[3] dreams of a woman who stammers and squints, is lame,

---

[1] VOSSLER, II, 216.   [2] *Ibid*, 211.   [3] *Purg.* XIX, 7–36 ; 55–60.

one-armed, and jaundiced. Yet so skilfully does she hide her
defects that it is with difficulty that Dante resists her
fascination. Virgil exposes the hideousness beneath her
clothes, but not until later does he interpret the vision.
The woman is the eternal sorceress, as old as mankind, who
ruins men with her allurements, although it is given to all to
free themselves, even as Dante had done.

The general outlines of the two episodes are clearly
identical ; although in the detail Dante introduces classical
allusions,[1] which are lacking in the Moslem picture. And
indeed all commentators of the Divine Comedy agree that
this vision is symbolic of the false felicity of the world,[2] just
as Gabriel interpreted it to Mahomet as being an allegory of
the fleeting pleasures of earth.[3] The coincidence is significant.

6. Lastly, the resemblance of one of the descriptive features
of the garden of Abraham in this version to Dante's purgatory is remarkable. Before entering the celestial mansions,
Dante has to be purified thrice in three different streams :
firstly, when he leaves hell and Virgil, on the advice of Cato,
washes away the spots that disfigure his face after his visit to
the infernal regions, restoring the natural colour to his tear-
stained cheeks[4] ; and a second and a third time before
he leaves purgatory, when Matilda and Statius in turn
immerse Dante in the Lethe and Eunoe, the waters of which
efface from the mind the memory of sin and renew the
supernatural power of the soul for good, thus preparing it for
the bliss of heaven.[5]

The idea of this threefold purification would seem to be
taken direct from the scene where the souls of penitent
sinners are washed in the three rivers of the garden of
Abraham. The effects, here also, are both physical and
moral : the natural colour is restored to their faces, and their

---

[1] The fable of Ulysses and the syrens.
[2] Cf. FRATICELLI, 310, n. 7. LANDINO, fol. 269, SCARTAZZINI, 536 and 539.
[3] In Moslem oneirology the vision, seen in a dream, of a woman, a
prostitute with naked arms, is interpreted as a symbol of the world.
[4] *Purg.* I, 94–99 ; 124–9.
[5] *Purg.* XXXI, 100–103. XXXIII, 127–129 ; 142–145.

souls, cleansed from sin by repentance, are by the grace of God made fit to enter into the glory of heaven.

V

THEOLOGICAL COMMENTARIES ON THE LEGEND

1. To trace step by step the evolution of this legend would be a task beyond the scope of this work, even if it were possible with our restricted knowledge of the bibliography of this branch of Moslem literature. In any case, the resultant gain, so far as our argument is concerned, would be but slight. Religious literature is essentially conservative, and the literature of Islam, pre-eminently so. In the comparatively brief period of two centuries the legend of the ascension had assumed a multiplicity of forms, and each version was authenticated, even by relations of the Prophet himself. Such testimony went unquestioned by the masses ; and thus it came about that the legend ultimately became crystallised in one definite form; into which the main versions regarded as authentic were fused. This fusion was the work of theologians and interpreters of the Scriptures in an endeavour, chiefly, to harmonise a number of apparently contradictory tales. The earliest version of the legend in its new form was the one of Cycle 3, and this version remained final. All that appeared later were either *commentaries* upon it or *allegorico-mystical adaptations* and *literary imitations* of it. Certainly, an abundant literature, such as was induced in Europe a few centuries later by Dante's poem, grew around the legend. A brief review of the three aforementioned categories will reveal how, following upon its definite crystallisation, theologians and men of letters elaborated the story of the ascension.

Commentaries by theologians preponderated over all the other forms. The many exegetical works on the Koran all deal with the completion and interpretation of the first verse of the seventeenth chapter, in which the ascension is alluded to. The various traditional versions of the legend are discussed on the evidence of the most authoritative theologians. The collections of authentic *hadiths* also devote pages to the legend in its different forms. To the same category belongs a profusion of historical works on Islam and biographies of Mahomet and the prophets. Each book has its chapter on the ascension, which, it must be remembered, is regarded by all true Moslems as an historical fact and not unnaturally forms an integral part of the story of the life of Mahomet.[1]

But the most interesting of these commentaries are the treatises written by theologians who collated their data from the above-mentioned works. One such treatise appeared as early as the tenth century. This, the work of Abu Laith of Samarcand, dealt in particular with the Prophet's colloquy with God.[2] Not until the twelfth century, however, did this form of literature reach its culminating point ; at all events, no works of an earlier date have come down to us in such profusion.[3]

The authors of almost all these treatises are mainly concerned with the co-ordination of the various versions of the *Isrà* and the *Miraj* ; and they solve the problem either by uniting all the forms into one or by assuming that several ascensions were made. Other questions, such as the date of the ascension, the spot whence Mahomet set out, and so forth, also, however, occupy their attention. Indeed they went farther and introduced among a host of other points, the mystical meaning of the purification of the Prophet's

---

[1] VICTOR CHAUVIN has compiled a complete list of the biographies of Mahomet in his *Bibliographie des ouvrages arabes ou relatifs aux Arabes*, IX, *passim*. For the special literature of the *Miraj* v. ibidem, X, 206–8.
[2] Cf. BROCKELMANN, I, 196.
[3] Reference to the works quoted by CHAUVIN shows that of the better-known treatises on the *Miraj* one is of the 10th century, another of the 13th, two of the 14th, one of the 15th, four of the 16th, two of the 17th, four of the 18th, and one of the 19th. As in all literatures, the more modern drive the older treatises out of circulation. Thus the treatise on the *Miraj*, now printed in Cairo in preference to all others, is that of Ghiti (16th century), which is sometimes published with the glosses of Dardir (18th century). For the purposes of the present work, in addition to the two printed treatises, others as yet unedited and contained in the Gayangos Collection have been consulted, viz. MS 105, fol. 70–93 (16th century), cf. BROCK, II, 304; fol. 94–166 (17th century), cf. BROCK, II, 317; fol. 211–250, dated 1089 Heg.

5

heart ; the composition and sequence of the mansions above the astronomical heavens ; and the visibility of God. However, so far as our comparison is concerned, this literature reveals one curious coincidence alone : the Divine Comedy of Islam—like that of Dante at a later date—had a host of enthusiastic admirers, who studied it in all its phases. The meaning of every word was investigated and an explanation for the most insignificant details sought with a scrupulousness arising more from religious than literary motives.

2. This coincidence is only natural, however, and in itself does not constitute a proof. What is of more moment is that these exegetical treatises supplement the traditional text of the legend. For in the fused version there appear many new scenes and episodes, which, as regards their authenticity and age, can only be attributed to those versions of the three cycles already examined or to others contemporaneous with them.[1] Of these new episodes only those that distinctly resemble scenes in Dante need be considered here.[2]

3. At the outset of his Nocturnal Journey—before his visit to the infernal regions—an afrite, armed with a firebrand, bars Mahomet's way. Attacked and pursued by the demon, the Prophet is comforted by Gabriel, who teaches him a prayer, by repeating which he is enabled to extinguish the demon's torch.[3]

As Dante and Virgil reach the fifth pit of the eighth circle of hell, a similar scene unfolds itself.[4] The two poets are pursued by a horde of demons armed with javelins and led by a fierce and swarthy devil. Virgil calms Dante's fears and utters a brief command, whereupon the devil's fury subsides and his weapon falls at his feet.

---

[1] Indeed, the authors of these works invariably, by the testimony of the oldest traditionists and companions of the Prophet, seek to establish the authenticity of these episodes. The author of the first treatise in MS 105, quoted above (see p. 39, footnote 3), gives in the form of an appendix (fol. 92, recto) a complete list of the thirty-eight companions of the Prophet who are supposed to have narrated the *Miraj* in whole or in part.

[2] The episodes are taken from the printed and unedited treatises mentioned above. Reference to the actual passages will be made in each case.

[3] Cf. GHITI, 41, and DARDIR, 7. Also MS 105, Gayangos Collection, fol. 120.

[4] *Inf.* XXI, 22-33 ; 58-105.

4. But few new episodes are introduced into the ascension proper. The first and main one is the scene of the ladder stretching from the Temple of Jerusalem to heaven. Its rungs are of gold, silver, and emerald. By it the souls of the blessed rise, and on either side angels stand in line. By means of this ladder Mahomet, with Gabriel, reaches heaven in less time than it takes to tell.[1]

The similar scene in the Twenty-first and Twenty-second Cantos of the Paradiso is familiar to all. In the heaven of Saturn the poet sees a golden ladder that leads to the last of the celestial spheres. The spirits of the blessed descend by its rungs. Beatrice calling upon him to ascend, he finds himself at the top in less time than it would take to withdraw the hand from fire.[2]

5. The prophets inhabiting the heavens visited by Mahomet seldom appear alone, as in the previous versions; but each is surrounded by a group of the blessed, their disciples on earth. Thus, in the fifth heaven, Aaron tells Biblical stories to a group of Jewish unbelievers; others, like Enoch, Moses, and Abraham, discuss theology with Mahomet.[3] The Prophet also meets other Biblical and Moslem characters. In the fourth heaven he sees Mary, the mother of Moses, with the Virgin Mary[4]; and in the seventh heaven, two hosts of Moslems, the one clad in white and the other in grey.[5] With the light of the Divine Throne shining upon him, a man unknown to him is seen by Mahomet. This man, Gabriel explains, is a symbol of the glory that awaits the contemplative souls.[6] Between heaven and earth he beholds the prophet Ezekiel begirt by a circle of light and prostrate in prayer.[7] Bilal, too, he sees, the first Moslem to hold the sacred office of Muezzin and call the faithful to prayer.[8] Again, one of his dearest companions, Abu Bakr, appears to him in fantastic form to act as his guide, when Gabriel leaves him in the final stages of the ascension.[9] Lastly, a heavenly maiden, the destined bride of his disciple Zayd, the son of Haritha, reveals her identity and that of her intended spouse.[10]

[1] Ghiti, 44, and Dardir, 14. Likewise MS 105 of the Gayangos Collection, fol. 123 and 232 v°. [2] Par. XXI, 28–33; 136–7; XXII, 68–9; 100–111.
[3] Ghiti, 44 et seq.; Dardir, 14 et seq.
[4] MS 105 Gayangos Coll. fol. 124 v°, line 7. [5] Ibid, fol. 126 v°.
[6] Ibid, fol. 127 v°. [7] Ibid, fol. 232 v°. [8] Kanz, VI, 293, No. 5.079.
[9] MS 64 Gayangos Coll. fol. 115 v°. [10] Tabari, Tafsir, XV, 12.

Thus, by their wealth of incident and profusion of secondary characters, these versions offer a plan of the Moslem legend that, unlike the plans of previous versions, is not so far removed from that of the Divine Comedy. Dante also imagined the celestial spheres to be peopled by the blessed, who were allotted to the various heavens according to their virtues or the profession they followed. The persons in each group discourse among themselves or with Dante on religion or philosophy. For the greater part they are Christians, but Hebrews and even Pagans are also introduced. Further, both sexes are represented. Some are famous characters of olden times, but the majority are either friends or relations of the poet, who, with the memory of them on earth still fresh in his mind, depicts their moral traits in masterly, yet measured, terms.

It is, of course, not claimed that the Moslem legend, at this, the final stage of its evolution, can compare in its poetical technique with the Divine Comedy. But in the general scheme of action, as well as in the roles of the protagonist and other characters, the resemblance between the two can hardly be said to be either remote or accidental.[1]

VI

ADAPTATIONS FROM THE LEGEND, MAINLY MYSTICAL ALLEGORIES

1. The religious authorities of Islam having at last determined upon a version that was to be regarded as authentic and as the accepted revelation, the legend may be said to

---

[1] One detail in the description calls for mention. Over the gate of paradise Mahomet sees an inscription extolling the virtues of almsgiving and lending free of interest (GHITI, 86, and DARDIR, 20). It will be remembered that in the version of Cycle 3 Mahomet hears a voice from hell describing the torments prepared and calling upon God to deliver up the sinners. In addition, there is the inscription branded on the forehead of the sodomite and the murderer in the Moslem hell, saying that they have "despaired of God's mercy" (Corra, 31, and Kanz, VII, 2,086, No. 3,173), which is similar to the "Lasciate ogni speranza, voi ch' entrate." If Dante was indeed acquainted with these features, it would be easy for him to combine and embody them in his inscription over the gate of hell; for the spiritual conception of his paradise precluded all idea of material gates and inscriptions.

have crystallised into a definite form. The imagination of the faithful could now no longer indulge in further inventions or additions. Nevertheless, the loss of new episode thus incurred was amply compensated for by another and more fertile mode of elaboration ; in its final form the legend underwent considerable literary alteration.

The glosses originally added in explanation of obscure words and ellipses become merged in the text. The simplicity of the primitive versions is lost in figurative language and other literary adornments. The ascension is the theme of legends in versified prose and even poems, works in which the rich fancy of the East is given full play. The lesser characters, as well as the two protagonists, and even God Himself, engage in lengthy discourses, interspersed with rhyme and replete with metaphors and abstruse conceits. At times inanimate objects, such as the Divine Throne, are represented as living beings ; heavenly animals, like the serpent that encircles the Throne and the beast that carries Mahomet, are personified and made to hold long speeches. Again, the abodes of the beyond are described with a wealth of detail taken from the Koran and the *hadiths* of the Prophet dealing with heaven and hell.[1]

2. This first attempt at elaboration merely expanded the text of the legend. Followed a host of adaptations, allegorical or mystical, in which the ascension—supposed to be an historical fact—is applied to other physical and spiritual beings, that are either real or symbolical and earthly or heavenly. These ascend to the regions of bliss in practically the same stages as Mahomet did in his *Miraj*. Brief mention can be made of only a few of these tales.

3. The most popular is that of the ascension of the soul at death. On leaving the body, it is led by its guardian angel up through the astronomical heavens to be judged before the Throne of God. The following is a short summary of the ascension :—

[1] Cf. MS 105 of the Gayangos Coll., fols. 216, 218, 223 v°, 225, 245 and 246, in which fragments in rhymed prose and verse are inserted dealing with the *Miraj*.

At the entrance to each heaven the scene depicted in the *Miraj* is repeated. The guardian angel is refused entry until the identity of the travellers is disclosed. The soul is then either welcomed or abused according to its conduct during life. In each sphere it undergoes an examination on one of the precepts of Islam, in the following order : Faith, prayer, almsgiving, fasting, pilgrimage, honour of parents, love of fellow-men, religious zeal and purity of heart. From the Lotus-tree of the Boundary the soul ascends through seas of light, darkness, fire and water and finally of snow and ice— all as in Version C of Cycle 2. When the veils that shroud the Divine Throne are drawn aside the catechism of the soul by God Himself begins.[1]

4. In other similar legends,[2] the guardian angels are portrayed as presenting to God each day the good deeds of the believers entrusted to their care.

In each of the seven heavens the angel at the gate denies admission to the good deed whenever its author is found guilty of any sin. Only those good deeds that have been inspired by Divine love may rise through the seven spheres to the presence of God, Who declares them accepted in His sight.

5. In these early adaptations, the ascension is accredited solely to personified metaphysical conceptions or to the souls of the departed. In each case, moreover, Mahomet himself is made to tell the story, in order to lend greater authority to it. The deep religious respect felt for the Prophet forbade any encroachment. Nevertheless, the Sufis or mystics were not long in arrogating to themselves the role of protagonist that had hitherto been reserved for Mahomet.[3] The pretext

---

[1] *Tadhkira*, 18, and IBN MAKHLUF, I, 51–52. The examination to which the soul is subjected in each heaven in this legend may be compared with Dante's catechism on the three theological virtues in the eighth heaven (*Par.* XXIV–XXVI). Noteworthy also is the close relation between each heaven and a corresponding virtue peculiar to the souls that succeed in ascending to it ; this is what characterises the moral structure of Dante's paradise. Cf. ROSSI, I, 147.

[2] *Minhaj* of Algazel, p. 69.

[3] This presumption on the part of the Sufis was regarded as a sin against the faith. Proof of this is furnished (in *Al-Yawaqit*, II, 174) by Ash-Sharani's denunciation of the Murcian Ibn Arabi who claimed to have visited heaven and hell. Such arrogance may be explained by the Sufi doctrine which admits of the possibility of the saint's acquiring the dignity of a prophet. Cf. ASÍN, *Abenmasarra*, 82.

for their audacity was provided by the interpretation of the *Miraj*, that Mahomet had been raised by God to heaven in order that he might experience the supreme delight of the Beatific Vision and his heart be freed from all earthly ties.[1] It was natural, therefore, for the Sufis to generalise this interpretation and apply it to the real or symbolical ascension of the soul, which breaks its worldly bonds and flies towards God, as the essence of spiritual perfection. Indeed, one of the most famous masters of early Moslem mysticism, Abu Yazid al-Bistami, who lived in the ninth century, is credited with an actual ascension to the Divine Throne through the same stages as were traversed by Mahomet in his *Miraj*.[2]

Thus the legend gradually reaches the climax of its evolution. The Sufi, as a type of humanity capable of perfection by gradual purification from passion, rises to such heights of contemplation that he enjoys a foretaste of eternal bliss in the Beatific Vision[3].

6. The more interesting of these later adaptations are the work of the Murcian Muhyi ad-Din ibn Arabi, the prince of Hispano-Moslem mystics, who died twenty-five years before the Florentine poet was born.[4] One of these works is based upon the *Miraj*, in which he seeks to discover a hidden moral. He treats it as an esoteric teaching of the revelations manifested to the soul of the mystic in the course of its ascension to God. This work, which unfortunately has not yet been edited, is entitled " The Book of the Nocturnal Journey towards the Majesty of the Most Magnanimous."[5] The

---

[1] Cf. *Tafsir* of QUMMI, XV, 6. Other Sufi interpreters account for the inclusion of the *Miraj* in the Divine Scheme by the necessity of Mahomet's being able to explain the mysteries of the after-life with the authority of one who had been an eye-witness. Cf. MS 105 Gayangos Coll., fol. 213 ; also AL-HORAYFISH, 104.

[2] Cf. MS 105, fol. 214, line 2 inf.

[3] Avicenna, in his *Risala at-tayr*, pp. 26–32, adapts the *Miraj* to the flight of birds, symbolising the exaltation of the souls of sinners which, having cast off all worldly ties, fly towards God over eight mountains towering one above the other.

[4] Cf. ASÍN, *Abenmasarra*, 110–115, where other works by the author and his master Ribera on the life and system of Ibn Arabi are quoted.

[5] Extant at the Kgl. Bibliothek, Berlin (Nos. 2,901/2) and at Vienna (No. 1,908), according to BROCKELMANN, I, 443, No. 16. Another copy is in the possession of the author, to whom it was presented by his learned friend Hassen Husny Abdul-Wahab, Professor of History at the Khalduniya

poetical fragment, of which a rendering is given hereunder, will suffice to indicate its general outline.

The Sufis or mystics are the heirs of the Prophet whose life and doctrine they follow. By devoting all their days to meditation and the practice of the mysteries of the Koran and maintaining the memories of their Beloved, they are at last led into the presence of God. Boraq, the beast of heaven that conveys them swiftly on their journey, is the symbol of divine love. The holy city of Jerusalem, the emblem of light and truth, forms the first stage of the journey. Here, as did the Prophet, they tarry close to the wall, representing purity of heart, that bars access to the profane. Having partaken of milk, the symbol of the true direction of revealed doctrine, they knock at the gate of heaven, allegorical of bodily mortification. Beyond the gate they see paradise and hell. With the right eye they witness the happiness of the blessed ; with the left, they weep over the terrors of the infernal fires. They reach the Lotus-tree, the symbol of faith and virtue, and eat their fill of the fruit, whereby the most sublime powers of man become perfected. Thus prepared, they arrive at the final stage of their journey. The veils enshrouding the spirit are drawn aside and the hidden secret of the mystery of mysteries is made manifest to them.[1]

The significance of this subtle poem in its interpretation of Dante's allegories is apparent. Upon the author's own showing,[2] three esoteric meanings are conveyed by both the

of Tunis. The *Book of the Nocturnal Journey* comprises 108 folios, of which the greater part is commentary. In the prologue, Ibn Arabi states that the theme is a *Miraj* of the soul written both in verse and prose and in a style combining allegory with literal fact. He begins by saying : " I set out from the land of Alandalus (Spain) in the direction of Jerusalem my steed the faith of Islam, with asceticism as my bed and abnegation as provision for the journey." He meets a youth of spiritual nature, sent from on high to act as his guide ; but in the Ascension from Jerusalem is guided by another, " the envoy of Divine Grace," with whom he ascends through the celestial spheres into the presence of God.

[1] Similar allegorical and mystical adaptations of the *Miraj* recur in several of the lesser works of Ibn Arabi. In the *Futuhat*, III, 447–465, he devotes a whole chapter, No. 367, to this subject of the *Miraj*. It contains a brief mystical commentary on the legend of the Prophet ; an adaptation of the legend to the Ascensions or spiritual raptures of the Sufis and saints ; and a long *Miraj*, in which the author, following the same route as Mahomet, is supposed to have risen to the heavens and to have conversed at length on theological and mystical subjects with all the prophets.

[2] In his *Epistola a Can Grande della Scala* (*Opere minori*, III, epist. XI, No. 7, p. 514).

Divine Comedy and the " Convivio "—the first a personal, and the second a moral, allegory ; whilst the third is anagogical. Seen in this light, the Divine Comedy is a complex allegory of Dante's own life and the redemption of mankind. Dante, representing mankind, has been led from the straight path ; but, guided by reason, faith and grace, he shakes off the fetters of evil ; and the expiation of, and purification from, his sins are symbolised by his journey to hell and ·purgatory. Having attained moral perfection, he ascends by the path of contemplation to the eternal bliss of the Divine Essence. Thus Dante, like the Moslem Sufis in general and the Murcian Ibn Arabi in particular, availed himself of the alleged historical fact of the ascension of a man to the heavens, in order to represent in symbol the mystical drama of the regeneration of souls by faith and theological virtues.[1]

This further surprising coincidence of the allegorical ·intentions of the two legends must, therefore, be added to the many other analogies existing between them. As the symbolical character of the Divine Comedy is, in the eyes of all critics, the most forcible proof of its original inspiration, a closer enquiry into these wonderful coincidences will not be amiss. The affinity between another mystical allegory of the Murcian Ibn Arabi and Dante's poem is obvious.

7. The Ascension in question appears in a voluminous work entitled *Al-Futuhat al-makkiya*, or the *Revelations of Mecca*. It is the main theme of an entire chapter, the heading of which, " The Alchemy of Felicity," in itself implies an esoteric allegory.[2] The narrative is prefaced with a synopsis, of which the following is an abstract.

The aim of the soul, from the day on which the Creator unites it with the body, is to acquire the knowledge of the essence of its principle, God. In their search for the path leading to this end, the souls meet with a messenger sent by God to lead them towards that knowledge of the Creator wherein lies their happiness. Some gratefully accept the

---

[1] Cf. *Monarchia* (*Opere Minori*, II, 404). Likewise FRATICELLI, pp. 28–31 of Preface to his edition of the Divine Comedy. Also ROSSI, I, 152–157.

[2] *Futuhat*, II, Chap. 167, pp. 356–375. The allegory of the Ascension proper begins on p. 360.

heavenly messenger's guidance[1] ; others disdain it on the plea that his powers of cognition can in no way be superior to theirs. The former then follow the direction of the doctrine as revealed by God to His messenger ; whilst the latter are merely guided by the light of their own reason.

Here the mystical allegory begins, the protagonists being two travellers, one of each category. Thus, a theologian and a rationalist philosopher set out simultaneously on the path that is to lead them towards God. The first stages of the journey represent the perfection and happiness enjoyed by the soul through restraint of the passions. In these stages the teachings of philosophy and theology practically coincide, so that both travellers succeed in shaking off the fetters that bind them to earth and free themselves from the baneful influence of passion.

At this point begins the actual Ascension to heaven, the plan of which is modelled upon the *Miraj*. The first seven stages correspond to the astronomical heavens—the Moon, Mercury, Venus, the Sun, Mars, Jupiter, and Saturn. Each is visited in succession by the two travellers, who ascend at the same speed, the philosopher mounted on Boraq, the celestial beast that carried the Prophet and the allegorical figure of reason, and the theologian, by means of the Rafraf or shining wreath, representing the light of Divine Grace, which also conveyed Mahomet to the Divine Throne. But, although both reach the gates of the heavens at the same time, their receptions are different. The theologian is welcomed by the prophets inhabiting each sphere, but the philosopher is obliged to stand apart until he is received by the " Intelligences," who in the neo-Platonic cosmology move the celestial spheres and to whom in this allegory the humble role of servants to the prophets is assigned. The theologian is filled with rejoicing, but his different treatment causes sadness and pain to the philosopher, who from afar witnesses the warm welcome given to his companion and only gleans vague information about the sublime mysteries revealed to the other by the prophets. Not that the philosopher is altogether neglected. The " Intelligence " of each sphere instructs him on problems of physics or cosmology, the solutions of which are dependent upon the natural influence exercised by the planet in question on the phenomena of this

[1] Note the interest this prologue offers for the allegorical interpretation of the prologue to the Divine Comedy.

lower world. He finds, however, that the prophets explain the significance of these problems to the theologian from a loftier point of view and much more clearly than is done by natural science alone.

By this means the author Ibn Arabi ingeniously introduces many points from his own theological system, and the work becomes a veritable encyclopædia of philosophy, theology, and the occult sciences, set forth in the form of debates or speeches made by the prophets.

Thus in the heaven of the Moon, Adam instructs the theologian on the creative influence of Divine names. These are the prototypes of all creatures and are equivalent to the prime causes of philosophy. The phenomena of the sublunar world ; the changes in the material elements ; the growth of all living things ; the generation of the human body—all are shown to the philosopher by the " Intelligence " to be effects of the direct action of this first astronomical sphere. But the theologian learns their primary and transcendental cause, which lies hidden in the mystic influence of the Divine names.

In the second heaven, whilst the philosopher is received by the Intelligence of Mercury, the theologian meets the two prophets Jesus and John, who discuss with him the subject of miracles, more particularly those performed by the cabbalistic virtue of certain words, the creative mystery of the word " Fiat," and of the Divine breath that brings beings into existence. Then Jesus, the Spirit of God, reveals to his disciple the esoteric working of the miracles he performed in Israel. All these phenomena of healing, restoration of life, and so forth are derived from this sphere. When effected *praeter ordinem naturae*, they are miracles due to the supernatural alchemic powers of Jesus ; when produced naturally they are the effect of the virtue possessed by the Intelligence of Mercury. The latter is all that the philosopher learns.

A similar difference between the results obtained by the two travellers holds throughout ; and it will suffice to summarise the knowledge acquired in each sphere.

In Venus, the prophet Joseph interprets the mystery of the order, beauty, and harmony of the Cosmos, and expounds the art of poetry and the interpretation of dreams.

In the sphere of the Sun, the prophet Enoch explains the astronomical cause of day and night and its many mystical applications.

The prophet Aaron, in Mars, talks at length on the government of nations, and commends to the theologian's attention the Revealed Code as a supreme criterion of the Divine policy, based rather on mercy than on wrath.

In the heaven of Jupiter, Moses expounds the pantheism of Ibn Arabi. Starting with the interpretation of the miracle when he transformed the rod into a serpent, he ends with the thesis that all form in the universe is mutable ; but the substance is ever the same, namely God in different relations, which are dependent upon the subjective impression produced in the mind of the contemplator.

Lastly, in Saturn, Abraham, reclining upon the wall of the House of Habitation, explains to the theologian the problem of the life hereafter. Meanwhile, the dejected philosopher awaits him in the dark dwelling of the Intelligence. When, repentant of his conduct, he would be converted to Islam and share in the supernatural illumination of the faith, Abraham, the father of the faithful, rejects him and leads the theologian by the hand into the House of Habitation.

Here begins the second part of the ascension. The theologian leaves the temple and ascends again on high ; while his companion waits below.

The stages of this second part of the ascension are, with the exception of two astronomical spheres, all scenes of mysticism and theology. The theologian first ascends to the Lotus-tree of the Boundary, the fruit of which are emblems of the good deeds done by the faithful. At its foot run four mystic rivers, representing the Pentateuch, the Book of Psalms, the Gospel and the Koran. The last is the greatest and is the source of the others.

Thence the traveller rises to the sphere of the Fixed Stars, where corruption is unknown and myriads of angelic spirits dwell in a thousand mansions. Each one he visits and tastes the supreme delights of God's elect.

In the last sphere—the Zodiac—are revealed to him all the marvels of the celestial paradise, which are derived from the virtue of this sphere. Immediately thereafter he arrives at the stool on which rest the feet of the Almighty—the symbols of His mercy and justice—by whose favour he is instructed in the dread problem of the eternity of reward and punishment in the life hereafter.

The ineffable light radiating from the Throne and the

sweet harmony of the spheres thrill him to the innermost
recesses of his heart. In an ecstasy, he suddenly realises
that he has been raised to the Divine Throne, the symbol of
God's infinite mercy. The Throne appears to him held on
high by five angels and the three prophets, Adam, Abraham,
and Mahomet ; and from them he learns of the mystery of
the Cosmos, which is inscribed within the sphericity of the
body of the universe, which is the Throne of God.

The remaining stages all belong to the spiritual world, or
world of Platonic ideas. The traveller is finally wafted into
the vapour which is the primitive epiphany or manifestation
of God *ad extra* and the type of the *prime matter* common to
Creator and creature in the pseudo-Empedoclean theosophy
of Ibn Arabi.[1] Enraptured, the traveller beholds the
ineffable mysteries of the divine essence and its attributes,
both the absolute and those relative to the creatures. The
sublime vision ending with this apotheosis, the theologian
rejoins the philosopher, who becomes converted to the
Moslem faith so that he too may participate in the glories
of mystical contemplation.[2]

8. The points of contact between this allegorico-mystical
journey and Dante's ascension stand forth plainly. A perusal
of the passages in Dante's *Monarchia* and *Epistola a Can
Grande della Scala*, in which he outlines the esoteric meaning
of his Divine Comedy, will clearly show how his interpretation agrees with that of Ibn Arabi's allegory. Both
thinkers imagine the journey as a symbol of the life of the
soul in this world, into which it has been placed by the
Creator to prepare for the attainment of its final aim, which
is to enjoy the bliss of the Beatific Vision. Both writers
hold this to be unattainable without supernatural intervention or theology ; for, although philosophic reasoning,
alone, can guide man in the first stages of his mystical
journey, that is to say, in the practice of the virtues, only
the light of grace can raise him to paradise, the symbol of
the highest virtues. The main difference between the two
allegories lies in the fact that, whereas in Ibn Arabi's work

---

[1] For the value of these symbols in Ibn Arabi's system, cf. the author's
Abenmasarra, p. III, *et seq.*
[2] The close relation existing between this allegory and that of Ibn Tufayl
in his *Self-taught Philosopher* or *Epistle of Hayy ibn Yaqzan* is noteworthy.

there are two protagonists, in Dante's story there is one, who is led successively by two guides, Virgil and Beatrice, representing philosophy and theology. A further difference is that Virgil does not accompany Dante to the astronomical heavens, to which the philosopher of the Moslem allegory ascends. This is due to the fact that in Ibn Arabi's cosmological system the spheres of the stars, as belonging to the material world, come within the scope of philosophical speculation. On this point Ibn Arabi certainly was more logical than the Florentine poet, who is less interested in Beatrice as a symbol than in her glorification as a real person. The effect of this difference, however, is practically annulled by the fact that when he sets out on his ascension with Beatrice, Dante may be said to be acting in a dual capacity ; firstly, as a philosopher, by the experience gained from Virgil's teaching ; and secondly, as a theologian, now taught by Beatrice. Thus in some of the spheres, Dante is seen reasoning as a philosopher independent of the aid of Beatrice or the blessed, who, on the other hand, enlighten him on supernatural or mystical problems. And this is precisely what happens in Ibn Arabi's story. The philosopher learns in each sphere of the natural phenomena produced in the sublunar world by its physical virtues ; whilst the theologian from the prophets receives the same instruction as the philosopher on matters pertaining to nature, supplemented by illumination of mystical and theological subjects.

A few features of resemblance in episode may help to complete the parallel.

9. In Dante's hell the souls of the damned are seen in the dwellings in which they are destined to remain for all eternity. In paradise, however, the blessed descend from their abode, the Empyrean, and appear to Dante in the various astronomical spheres, welcoming him or making him sensible to the various degrees of bliss. They are, however, supposed to return to the Empyrean, for, in the heaven of the Fixed Stars Dante again sees them assembled in one large body.[1]

[1] Rossi, I, 151.

This same artifice was used by Ibn Arabi in his allegorical adaptation of the *Miraj*. The prophets in the various spheres descend to bid him welcome, but in the heaven of the Fixed Stars he beholds all the spirits of the blessed together, and at the Divine Throne he sees Adam and Abraham, whom he had previously seen, the one in the first, and the other in the seventh heaven.

The criterion, in accordance with which the souls as first seen by Dante are distributed, is twofold—astrological and moral. The blessed either appear in the heaven of the star that influenced their lives or in a higher or lower sphere according to the merit of their life.[1] The same principle is discernible in the allegory of Ibn Arabi. The prophets do not appear in chronological order; for, whilst Adam is in the first heaven, Abraham is in the seventh, Moses and Aaron are in different heavens; and Jesus is in the sphere next to Adam. The guiding principle is thus either greater dignity or moral excellence. Moreover, the celestial spheres unlike the preceding versions where they are numbered, bear the name of their star. Thus a relationship, similar to that between each heaven and the souls in the Paradiso, is here established between the spheres and the prophets appearing in them. It is true that the meaning underlying this relationship is nowhere actually expressed. But it is significant that Joseph, celebrated for beauty and chastity, should be assigned to the sphere of Venus; Moses, as law-giver to Israel and victor over Pharaoh, to the sphere of Jupiter, the vanquisher of the Titans; and Jesus, the Living Word of God, to Mercury, the messenger of the gods and himself the god of eloquence.[2]

Lastly, the desire that obsesses Dante to display his learning often at the expense even of artistic effect has a striking parallel in the Moslem tale. Dante made of the Divine Comedy a veritable scientific treatise by attributing to Beatrice and others, for the instruction of the pilgrim,

---

[1] Rossi, I, 147.

[2] Ibn Arabi adheres to the astrological principle much more closely than Dante, with whom he disagrees on the relationship between each sphere and its inhabitants.

lengthy dissertations on philosophy, theology and the like.
Ibn Arabi resorts to a similar device to present his theo-
sophical problems, when he causes these to be discussed in
lengthy and complicated discourses by the prophets.[1]

Thus the two works agree in subject-matter, action and
allegorical purpose ; in their principal and secondary persons ; in the architecture of the astronomical heavens ;
and in the didactic trend of ideas and the use of literary
devices to produce in abstract a national cyclopædia. To
these features of resemblance must be added the similarity
in style ; both works are so abstruse and involved at times
as to suggest to the reader the mysteriousness of an oracle.
In the face of all these reasons it is not too much to say
that Ibn Arabi's work is of all Moslem types the most akin
to the Paradiso in particular and the whole Divine Comedy
in general, in so far at least as the latter may be regarded
as a moral and didactic allegory.

VII

LITERARY IMITATIONS OF THE LEGEND

1. To adapt the scenes of the ascension of Mahomet to a
story of which the protagonist, though a saint, is a man of
flesh and blood, was permissible perhaps to the Sufis, who
claimed to be able to attain spiritually to the dignity of
prophets and whose aim, in writing such adaptations, was
always a religious one. Presumption, however, would appear
to border on irreverence when the ascension is attributed to
a mere sinner ; when the aim is frankly profane ; and the
style affected is one of literary frivolity or irreligious irony.

---

[1] It is precisely on account of the abstruseness of these discourses that
the analysis of the allegory, which is of extraordinary length, has been
curtailed above. Ideas from all branches of philosophical and theological
lore are developed in them, and allusions are made to the cabbala of
numbers and letters, to magic, astrology, alchemy and other occult sciences.
In short, Ibn Arabi endeavoured to introduce into his allegory, as Dante
did later into his poem, the whole encyclopædia of his age. A precedent
for the literary device of the discourses is provided by versions of the *Miraj*,
in which, as has been seen, theological discussions are attributed to the
prophets and Gabriel.

Evidently there are but few such works. One alone has been handed down to us, and its author, as a writer of audacious satire on Islam, stands unique.

2. This is the blind poet, Abu-l-Ala al-Maarri, famous to the present day in Islam, and even in Europe. A Syrian of the tenth and eleventh centuries of our era, he has been named " the philosopher of poets and the poet of philosophers."[1] The Risalat al-ghufran, or Treatise on Pardon, is one of his less-known works.[2] Written in the form of a literary epistle, it is really a skilful imitation of those simpler versions of the Nocturnal Journey in which Mahomet does not rise to the astronomical heavens.

The author appears to have had a dual aim in view. With a touch of irony so delicate as to be almost imperceptible, he censures the severity of the moralists as contrasted with God's infinite mercy, and protests against the damnation of many men of letters, especially poets, who, though atheists and sinners, were famous both in ancient and Islamic Arabic literature. The epistle is a reply to a literary friend, Ibn al-Qarih, of Aleppo, who, while professing great admiration for Abu-l-Ala, had inveighed against those poets and men of letters who lived in impiety or debauchery.[3]

---

[1] Abu-l-Ala Ahmed, the son of Abd Allah al-Maarri, was born at Maarrat Alnoman, a village in Syria lying between Hama and Aleppo, in 973 A.D. At the age of four he lost his eyesight as the result of an attack of smallpox ; nevertheless his powers were so brilliant that under the sole direction of his father he soon acquired vast learning in the domain of Arabic philology and literature. By intercourse with philosophers he added to his culture and sharpened his critical faculties. After residing only one year at Baghdad, the centre of learning and literature of his time, he returned at the age of thirty-five to his native village, where he died in 1057 A.D. Apart from poetry, he wrote mainly critical works on the Arabic classics. Influenced by Indian philosophical thought, he certainly appears to have been a free-thinker. Cfr. BROCKELMANN, I, 254. Also YAQUT's Dictionary, pp. 162 et seq. ASÍN, Algazel, Dogmática, pp. 110 et seq.

[2] Nicholson described and translated fragments in the JRAS of 1900 to 1902. Cfr. also NICHOLSON, Hist. pp. 313–324. The Risala really consists of two parts ; the first, to p. 118, contains the miraculous journey to the realms beyond the grave ; the second is a piece of literary criticism on the verses and ideas of certain poets who were reputed to be freethinkers or atheists.

[3] Abu-l-Hasan Ali, the son of Mansur, known as Ibn al-Qarih, was born at Aleppo in 962 and died at Mosul sometime after 1030. A professor of literature in Syria and Egypt, he was also a mediocre poet, cf. YAQUT's Dictionary, VI, 5, p. 424. Ibn al-Qarih's epistle, to which the Risala is a reply, has not been preserved.

Without alluding directly to the problem of the extent of Divine mercy, he seeks to show with literary skill that many of the libertine and even pagan poets, who finally repented, were pardoned and received into paradise. The theological thesis, however, is of secondary interest. The main object of the epistle is the interpretation and criticism of the works of the writers in question.

This double purpose he achieves by ingeniously harmonising apologetics and literary criticism in the narration of a journey, like that of Mahomet, to the realms beyond the grave.

3. (a) In the prologue he tells how God has miraculously raised Ibn al-Qarih to the celestial regions, in reward for his writings in defence of the faith.

(b) There he first comes to a garden shaded by trees, of great girth and height, and laden with fruit, beneath which repentant sinners are seen reclining. Rivers of water, milk, wine and honey flow through this garden of delight and pour balm upon the hearts of the poets dwelling therein. Freed from the envy that embittered their lives on earth, the men of letters here live in unwonted peace and harmony. Groups of poets, novelists, grammarians, critics, and philosophers are engaged in friendly conversation. Drawing near, Ibn al-Qarih hears Abu Ubayda tell tales of ancient chivalry and the grammarian, Al-Asmai, recite classical poetry.[1] He joins in the conversation and expresses sorrow that some of the pre-Islamic poets, being pagans, should have been denied admission. Then, mounted on a celestial camel, and chanting apt verses of old-time poetry, he rides on through the garden. To a voice suddenly heard asking by whom these verses were composed, he replies that it was the satirist, Maymun al-Asha, whereupon the poet himself appears on the scene. He tells the traveller how, despite his fondness for the flowing bowl, he had been saved by the Prophet, whose Divine mission he had foretold. Thereafter Ibn al-Qarih meets many of the ancient poets who, though infidels, were saved by Divine mercy. With each he converses at length, discussing their works.

---

[1] For particulars about the writers named in the *Risala* the general reader should consult the histories of Arabic literature by NICHOLSON, BROCKELMANN, or HUART.

(c) The episodes of this miraculous journey are so numerous that it would be impossible either to refer to them all or transcribe the series of animated discussions on learned subjects so ingeniously introduced into the work. The traveller meets the most distinguished writers, generally in select groups which gather and disperse, as in passing he recognises and talks to them, and then proceeds on his way. In the course of conversation an absent poet is often alluded to and, upon the traveller's expressing a desire to converse with him, the poet's abode is pointed out or a guide provided to lead the traveller thither.

(d) These wanderings through paradise, though enlivened by episodes and digressions that enhance the literary value of the work, are individually of little interest for the purpose of comparison with Dante.[1]

(e) The traveller now attends a celestial feast, followed by music and dancing, in which all the Chosen join. Eventually he finds himself in the company of two houris, whose charms he warmly praises. But his amorous advances meet with derision from the two beauties, who mockingly ask him whether he does not recognise them. Upon his replying that surely they are two heavenly houris, they laughingly explain that they are women well-known to him on earth— one, Hamduna, the ugliest creature in Aleppo, who was repudiated by her husband, a ragpicker, for her foul breath ;

---

[1] One of the poets he consults begs to be excused on the plea that he lost all memory of his poetry in the fright he received at the time of Judgment, when he was in imminent danger of falling into hell. The traveller takes this opportunity to relate his adventures prior to entering paradise. The story is told with so fine an irony, that the reader is continually in doubt as to whether it is to be taken seriously or not. For, after depicting in vivid colours the severity of the Judge and the terror of the souls condemned to fire, the traveller proceeds to relate the artful dodges by which he managed to escape his due reward and enter heaven. After a vain endeavour to suborn the angels at the gates, he appealed to Hamza, an uncle of Mahomet, who referred him to Ali ; the latter demands the certificate proving his repentance and this the traveller remembers he must have dropped in the confusion of the judgment scenes when called upon to intercede in favour of a literary master. In vain he offers to provide witnesses in place of the missing document, and he is on the point of being dragged off to hell, when he espies Fatima, the daughter of Mahomet, approaching in a brilliant procession accompanied by Khadija, the Prophet's spouse and his sons, mounted on steeds of light. Fatima allows him to seize her stirrup and he is carried to the bridge leading to the celestial mansions ; this he crosses riding on the back of one of her maidens. A final obstacle remains to be overcome on the other side ; the angel janitor refuses to admit him without a ticket, but one of Mahomet's sons intervenes and drags him inside paradise.

the other, Tawfiq the negress, who handed out the books at the Baghdad library.   An angel who happens to pass by explains to the bewildered traveller that there are two kinds of houris—those created in heaven, and women raised to paradise in reward for their virtues or repentance.

(*f*) The delights experienced in paradise awaken a desire to visit hell, in order that the contrast may render him still more sensible of the bounty of the Lord.   Forthwith he sets out on the second part of his marvellous journey.

(*g*) He first sees strange cities lying scattered in valleys and but dimly lit by the light from paradise.   This region, he is told, is the garden of the genii who believed in the Divine mission of Mahomet.   At the mouth of a cave sits Khaytaur, their patriarch.   The pilgrim hails him, and together they discuss the poems attributed to the Jann and the language spoken by them.   Khaytaur satisfies his curiosity and recites to him the epic poetry of his race.

(*h*) Taking leave of the old genie, the traveller has barely set out again when his path is barred by a lion of ferocious aspect.   At the sight he pauses, when lo ! the beast is moved by the spirit of God to explain that he is the lion whom the Almighty tamed in order that he might protect Utba, the son of Abu Lahab and a relative of the Prophet's, on a journey to Egypt.   In reward for the service, he has been received into paradise.

(*i*) This danger past, the pilgrim proceeds, until of a sudden a wolf rushes out fiercely to meet him.   His fears are soon calmed, however, when he hears the wolf tell how it helped to spread the Faith by converting an Arab infidel.[1]

(*j*) Pursuing his way to the borders of paradise and hell, he meets two other pre-Islamic poets : Al-Hutaiya, who has been saved from hell in recognition of the sincerity of his satires ; and the poetess Al-Khansa, who recites her funereal elegies at the foot of a lofty volcano, from whose crater pennons of flame shoot forth.   This is the entrance to hell.

(*k*) Thither Ibn al-Qarih fearlessly ascends and from the top discerns Iblis, the king of the infernal regions, struggling in vain as he lies bound in iron fetters and held down by fiends armed with long forks.   Heaping curses on helpless Iblis, the traveller accuses him of having consigned countless

---

[1] Some of the many miracles attributed to Mahomet consist in his making animals, such as the ass, goat, gazelle and particularly the wolf, preach his Divine mission to the Arabs.

souls to torture. To an enquiry from Iblis he replies that he
is a man of letters from Aleppo. " A sorry trade, forsooth,"
retorts Iblis, " by which a man can barely earn his daily
bread, let alone support a family—and very risky for the
soul," he adds, " for how many like you has it not ruined ?
You may count yourself lucky to have escaped." He then
begs to be told of the pleasures of paradise.

(*l*) In the course of conversation Baxxar ibn Burd, the
blind but ribald poet happens to be mentioned ; and straightway he rises from the infernal depths, his eyes opened by the
fiends, to add to his torture. Ibn al-Qarih, after lamenting
the poet's fate, seizes the opportunity to consult him on some
obscure passages in his poems ; but the other is in no humour
for talking and makes no reply.

(*m*) The traveller now desires to speak with Imru-l-Qays
the vagabond king, held by Mahomet to be the father of the
ancient poets. Iblis points him out close at hand, and again
a lengthy discourse begins on obscure points in the poet's
qasidas. In the midst of their talk, the traveller catches
sight of Antara, the epic poet who sang of Arabian chivalry.
Wrapt in flame, the bard nevertheless replies to all the
other's questions about his works. Ibn al-Qarih bewails the
sad lot of so excellent a poet, who to his mind had been
worthy of a better fate.

(*n*) Other great pre-Islamic poets appear in succession.
He sees Al-Qama and Tarafa and enquires about their life on
earth and praises their works. But Tarafa rejects all praise,
declaring he would rather have been a simple boor and so
have entered paradise. A similar lament is heard from Aws
ibn Hajar, the poet of the chase and war ; who, maddened
by thirst, turns a deaf ear to all enquiries. Proceeding,
the traveller sees another of the damned, whose features are
unknown to him ; this, he finds, is the minor poet Abu Kabir
al-Hudali, whom he questions but also in vain ; for the poet
suffers such exquisite torture that he can only utter cries of
pain.

(*o*) Writhing in flames and roaring like a wild beast lies
another sufferer, whom he also fails to recognise. The
demons tell him it is Al-Akhtai, the Christian poet at the
court of the Ommeyad Caliphs, whose pungent epigrams on
Islam and anacreontic verses have brought this judgment on
him. Over him the visitor gloats, taunting him with the life
of low debauchery he led with Caliph Yazid, the second of the

Ommeyads.   The poet heaves a sigh of pain as he recalls
the orgies at the Royal Palace of Damascus, whose walls
resounded with his ribald satires upon Islam, echoed in
sacrilegious appreciation by the Caliph, the supreme head of
the Faith.   Carried away by his memories, Al-Akhtal begins
to recite one of those very satires ; but this provokes even
Iblis, who rebukes his fiends for letting their charges indulge
in such impiety.

(*p*) The traveller is on his way back to paradise, when it
occurs to him that he has forgotten other no less famous poets
in hell.   Retracing his steps, he calls aloud for the poet
Muhalhil, whom the demons after some delay point out.   In
the lower storeys of hell, too, he sees the Al-Muraqish poets
Ash-Shanfara and Tabatasharran, but, though he plies them
with questions about their lives and loves and verses, they
barely deign to answer him, pleading that they have lost
their memory.   Realising the futility of further attempts,
the traveller desists and returns to the celestial garden.

(*q*) On the way other incidents, which are related in the
epilogue to the story, occur.   Meeting Adam, he questions
him on some Arabic verses attributed to him.   Adam affably
points out that, although he spoke Arabic in paradise, when
driven out he adopted Syriac and only recovered the use of
the former when he ascended to heaven, a repentant sinner ;
whereas the verses in question, to judge by their meaning,
must have been composed on earth.   After touching upon
other literary subjects, the pilgrim leaves Adam and, passing
through a garden in which wonderful serpents address him by
word of mouth, finally reaches paradise.

(*r*) At the gate he is met by the houri appointed to attend
him.   In reply to her gentle chiding for tarrying so long
below, he pleads the great desire he felt to talk with the
poets in hell.   Now that his wish has been gratified, he can
give himself up entirely to the joys of paradise.   Side by
side they wander through fields and gardens gay with
flowers, the while his fair companion recites sweet verses
composed by Imru-l-Qays for the day when he should meet
his beloved in paradise.

(*s*) Of a sudden he sees another heavenly maiden standing
on the bank of a celestial river and surrounded by a bevy
of beautiful houris ; her loveliness of face and form so far
surpasses the beauty of her companions that the traveller
believes her to be the very beloved of Imru-l-Qays the poet,

(*t*) Awhile he lingers talking with these lovely creatures and then approaches the abode of the poets who wrote in the imperfect metre, known as " rejez," which he discusses with them. Then assisted by the maidens and pages who attend him, he is conveyed on a vehicle of gold and topaz to the heavenly mansion in which he is to live in bliss for all eternity.

4. As will at once be seen from the above summary, this literary imitation of the Mahometan ascension is rich in analogies with the Divine Comedy.

In the first place, the supernatural element which is so striking a feature of the *Isra* and *Miraj*, is almost wholly absent. Like Dante, the protagonist is simply a man. Nor are the secondary persons mainly saints or prophets, but mere sinners, often indeed repentant infidels. Thus the human and realistic touch imparted by Dante to the two first parts of the Divine Comedy is to be found in this earlier Moslem work. The coincidence in the realism of the two stories is, of course, not absolute ; but, if the discrepancies are for the moment set aside, a systematic comparison will show the features of resemblance to be grouped under two headings, viz., general artifices, common to both stories, and actual incidents that are either similar or identical in each.[1]

5. Abu-l-Ala, to achieve his twofold aim of composing a treatise that should be at once theological and literary, avails himself of the ingenious device of making the protagonist of his tale, Ibn al-Qarih, meet a great number of persons in heaven and hell. Thus the author peoples the realms of the beyond with a host of men and women,

---

[1] The main differences may here be briefly stated. Naturalism is so pronounced a feature of this journey that at times the imitation sinks to the level of a mere parody of the Mahometan ascension ; and, in this respect it clearly bears no resemblance to the Divine Comedy, the solemn earnestness of which is only very rarely interrupted by an introduction of the burlesque element. Nor is there any resemblance in the architecture of the realms, for Abu-l-Ala's journey is practically effected on one plane and, though hell is laid at the bottom of a volcano, the traveller does not visit its mansions. Other fundamental differences are that the protagonist is not the author of the story ; the order of the realms is inversed, heaven being described before hell ; and, finally, the story begins *in medias res*, for the incidents of his entrance into heaven are told by the traveller in the course of conversation with the poets he meets in paradise.

Christians, Moslems and pagans, nobles and commoners, rich and poor, young and old. These for the greater part are sinners, and almost all are men of letters or poets ; for, as stated above, the author's main aim was literary criticism, and his secondary idea, to denounce the narrow-minded views of the theologians of his day. Nearly all the persons are historical, and most of them famous writers. Some were his contemporaries, or lived shortly before his time.

According as they appear in heaven or hell, their distribution differs. In heaven, the traveller meets them gathered in small groups, each formed of a certain class of writer, such as philologians, lyrical poets, satirists, writers in the rejez metre, and so forth. In hell, on the other hand, they appear alone.

Often the traveller inquires after a writer whom he would like to see, and they with whom he is conversing point out the other's dwelling or provide him with a guide. At times, the desired person himself appears, when the traveller frequently fails to recognise him and has to ask his name.

The conversation both in heaven and hell turns mainly on literary points connected with the poets' works ; but allusions are not lacking to the virtues or vices that have led to their salvation or damnation.

The liberal principle which guided the author in consigning his characters to heaven or hell was bound to bring him into conflict with the narrow-minded clergy and lay masses, to whom it must have seemed akin to sacrilege to place men in heaven who on earth had been notorious unbelievers or libertines. Apart from this religious tolerance, the author is swayed by literary sympathies or personal feeling. The sight of the damned almost always moves him to pity, for only rarely does he gibe with bitter sarcasm at some unfortunate sufferer ; whilst the good fortune of the blessed calls forth his warmest congratulations.

Dante has recourse to the same devices, though on the far grander scale on which the Divine Comedy is planned. Working on the same lines, he rises above the mere literary aims of the Moslem tale and conceives the story, much richer in detail than the other, of a transcendental journey to the realms of the after-life. This gives him a pretext for displaying his views, not merely on literature, but on the whole field of intellectual endeavour. The Divine Comedy is, in fact, an encyclopædia of mediæval learning. Mankind in general ; Italy in the thirteenth century, and Florence in particular ; the Papacy and the Empire ; religious institutions ; literature and the other arts—the history of all is told in its tercets, not in an impersonal or abstract manner, but as seen through the mind of Dante under the influence of his poetic temperament. Thus, just as Abu-l-Ala aimed almost exclusively at displaying his literary learning and passing judgment on the great Arabic writers ; so did Dante seek to leave in his divine poem a record of his vast erudition and his views on religion, politics and art, as practised in his century. Accordingly, the number of characters in the Divine Comedy is incomparably greater than in Abu-l-Ala's tale. But, though more groups are thus formed, they are of the same variety, the literary categories of the Moslem story being replaced in Dante's poem by classifications according to calling and social position. The personages of the Divine Comedy, again, are either legendary, historical or nearly contemporary with the author ; and all are portrayed with a vivid realism.

In heaven the souls appear to the travellers in groups and not, as in hell, singly. Thus, the literary coteries of Abu-l-Ala are equivalent to the crowns or circles seen by Dante in each heaven and composed of theologians, soldiers, judges and others.

The colloquies between Dante and the souls begin in a like way. Either he inquires for a certain soul, and is directed to the dwelling ; or of a sudden a soul appears, whose features the poet fails to recognise, and he is obliged to ask his name.[1]

It is only natural that the colloquies of Dante should present a greater variety of subjects than the mainly literary discussions of Abu-l-Ala ; but, in both stories, the conversa-

[1] Cf. Rossi, I, 163, 164, 166, 167.

tion repeatedly turns upon incidents in the life of the souls
or the mysteries of the after-world. Moreover, certain of
the discourses of Dante with the poets and artists in hell or
purgatory bear a striking resemblance to the animated
causeries of the Moslem tale. Thus, when Dante meets his
former master, Brunetto Latini, they converse on events
of their life on earth ; Brunetto mentions the grammarian
Priscian and the lawyer Francesco d'Accorso among his
fellow-sufferers ; finally, he recommends to him his *Tesoro*.[1]
In purgatory the poet meets Casella, the Florentine musician,
and begs him to sing " Amor que nella mente mi ragiona,"
a song of Dante's that Casella set to music.[2] Again, Sordello,
a poet of Mantua, recognises Virgil and lauds his verses.[3]
The painter, Oderisi, discusses Italian art with Dante,
praising the two Guidos, Guinicelli, and Cavalcanti.[4] The
Latin poet, Papinius Statius, tells Dante and Virgil the story
of his life, and of the influence on his Thebaid and Achilleid
of the Aeneid of Virgil ; and when the latter discloses his
identity, Statius praises and quotes verses from the master-
poet's works. In answer to his inquiries about the fate of
other poets, such as Terence and Plautus, Virgil acquaints
him with the lot which has befallen these and other classic
authors.[5] Buonagiunta, a mediocre poet of Dante's time,
makes himself known to Dante and discusses the " new
style " of Dante's poems, admitting that they show more
poetic inspiration than those of Jacopo da Lentino or Guittone
da Arezzo.[6] Finally, Dante sees the great poet of Bologna,
Guido Guinicelli, being cleansed in fire from the taint of
lubricity. Dante hails him as the father and master of the
dolce stil nuovo ; but Guinicelli modestly refers him to the
Provençal, Arnauld Daniel, whom he points out close at
hand ; and, as Dante steps forward to converse with the
troubadour, the latter greets him with verses of great beauty
in his mother tongue.[7]

A further coincidence is apparent in the spirit of tolerance
displayed by both authors in excluding from hell famous

[1] *Inf.* XV.   [2] *Purg.* II.   [3] *Purg.* VI–VIII.   [4] *Purg.* XI.
[5] *Purg.* XXI–XXIII.   [6] *Purg.* XXIV.   [7] *Purg.* XXVI.

pagans or infidels. Thus, Aeneas, Cæsar, Saladin, Socrates, Plato, Aristotle, Virgil, Cicero, Seneca, Avicenna, and Averrhoes are placed in the limbo[1] and Cato of Utica in purgatory.[2] St. Thomas Aquinas shares the same heaven as one of his greatest adversaries, Sigier of Brabant, a follower of Averrhoes[3]; and King David is placed with Trajan and Ripheus of Troy.[4] On the other hand, many persons, including popes and princes, Dante condemns to hell out of mere personal or party feeling. Finally, the spectacle of eternal bliss or torment rouses in Dante's heart, as in that of the Moslem pilgrim, the same feelings alternately of admiration and pity, joy and wrath.[5]

6. A comparison of a few of the episodes of the Moslem journey with incidents in the Divine Comedy will disclose a resemblance even more striking than the similarity in general artifice.

One such episode is the encounter of Ibn al-Qarih with Hamduna of Aleppo and the negress Tawfiq, whom he takes to be houris, until they disclose their identity.

This scene, were it not for the semi-jocular tone of its description, closely resembles the passages of Dante's meeting with La Pia of Sienna, in purgatory; with Piccarda Donati of Florence, in the heaven of the Moon; and with Cunizza of Padua, in the sphere of Venus. The two first-mentioned, like Hamduna, bemoan the trials of their married life; and Dante admires the wonderful beauty of Piccarda, as Ibn al-Qarih had marvelled at the fair complexion of the negress Tawfiq. Moreover, just as the two pseudo-houris revealed themselves to Ibn al-Qarih, so do the three Christian beauties, in answer to Dante's inquiries, make themselves known to him.[6]

7. The journey to hell, undertaken by the Moslem immediately after the above episode, presents further similarities, though the sequence is inversed; for Dante visits hell before paradise.

[1] *Inf.* IV. [2] *Purg.* I. [3] *Par.* X.
[4] *Par.* XX. Cf. *Par.* IX, 31–6, where Cunizza, famous rather for her amorous adventures than her penitence, is placed in heaven.
[5] Cf. ROSSI, I, 163. [6] *Purg.* V, 133; *Par.* III, 49; IX, 32.

Dante, at the outset of his journey, finds his path barred by a leopard, a lion, and a she-wolf. Escaping from these dangers, he meets Virgil, the prince of epopee and patriarch of the classic poets, who leads him to the garden of the limbo, where dwell the geniuses of antiquity. Later begins the descent to hell itself.

The Moslem pilgrim before encountering any obstacle meets Khaytaur, the patriarch of the genii. Chanting their deeds in epic verse the aged spirit sits at the entrance to the garden wherein they dwell. This garden, like Dante's limbo, is an intermediate region between paradise and hell, of which latter it forms, as it were, the antechamber.

In vain have Dante students endeavoured to discover the meaning the poet sought to convey by the symbolic figure of the three wild beasts that bar the way to hell.[1] Innumerable as are the hypotheses that have been advanced, nowhere is so perfect a prototype for this passage to be found as in this Moslem tale. For, before he reaches hell, the Moslem pilgrim's path is barred by a wolf and a lion, two of the very beasts that attack Dante. Drawing his inspiration from the Moslem source, the divine poet would appear to have adapted this episode with some slight changes to his allegorical purposes.[2]

8. Another Moslem episode very similar to a scene in Dante is the meeting between Adam and the pilgrim, when, on the latter's return from hell, they discuss the language originally spoken by Adam. Dante also meets Adam (in the eighth heaven), and the burden of their conversation is likewise the language spoken by the father of mankind when he dwelt in the garden of Eden.

9. Lastly, the two scenes described on Ibn al-Qarih's return to heaven recall the two episodes in Dante's purgatory immediately preceding the poet's ascension to the celestial

---

[1] Cf. FRATICELLI, *Della prima e principale allegoria del poema di Dante* (in *La Divina Commedia*), pp. 18–27. For the bibliography on this point see ROSSI, I, 173.

[2] VOSSLER, II, 169, quotes Jeremiah V, 5, in which the lion, wolf, and leopard are mentioned ; but in the story of the Moslem journey the analogy is more complete, for a wolf and a lion are mentioned as *barring the pilgrim's path to hell.*

paradise.   The houri who receives the traveller with gentle words of reproach for his long absence and then converses with him, as they walk through gardens of flowers, appears as the prototype of Matilda, who with bright eyes and laughing lips awaits the poet at the entrance to the wood in earthly paradise, and with winning grace answers his questions as they walk through meadows strewn with flowers. Of a sudden, Dante beholds on the bank of a river of paradise the marvellous pageant of old men and maidens in whose midst is Beatrice, his beloved.   So, too, the Moslem traveller is amazed by the sight of a throng of houris, who, gathered upon the bank of a celestial river, form a court of beauty around a heavenly maiden, the fair beloved of Imru-l-Qays, the poet.

10. A general observation, applying equally to both works, may serve as a conclusion.   Abu-l-Ala, in his literary adaptation of the legend of the *Miraj*, pursued an aim that was mainly artistic ;   and this is a quality that also characterises Dante's immortal poem.   For, whatever else the Divine Comedy may be—an encyclopædia of theological learning, a moral allegory, and what not—it is above all a sublime work of literary art, in which the poet tells the story of a legend of the after-life, cast in the mould of his inspired tercets. Abu-l-Ala likewise displays supreme skill in the difficult technique of Arabic metre ;   and, though it is not actually written in verse, the *Risala* is enriched with all the splendour of that poetic style known in Arabic literature as rhymed prose.

VIII

SUMMARY OF COMPARISONS

1. In the preceding chapters an attempt has been made to outline the story of the origin and evolution, within the world of Islam, of the religious legend describing the Nocturnal Journey and ascension of Mahomet to the realms of the after-life.   The different versions of the legend have been minutely examined and compared with Dante's poem ;   and the

features of resemblance between the two tales have been demonstrated. It would, then, be as well here to sum up the points that have thus been established.

Around a verselet in the Koran alluding to a miraculous journey of Mahomet to the realms beyond the grave, popular fancy wove a multiplicity of versions of one and the same legend. The myth found expression in the tales of the traditionists, who with a wealth of detail describe the two main parts of the journey—the visit to hell and the ascension to paradise. All these versions had become popular throughout Islam as early as the ninth century of our era ; and even in some of the earlier versions the two parts of the legend are fused to form, as in the Divine Comedy, a single dramatic action.

2. In almost all these versions Mahomet, like Dante, as the supposed author, is made to tell the story. Further, both journeys are begun at night when the protagonists awaken from profound sleep. In an imitation of the Moslem journey a lion and a wolf bar the road to hell, as do a leopard, lion and she-wolf in Dante's poem. Khaytaur, the patriarch of the genii, whom the Moslem traveller meets, is clearly a counterpart of Virgil, the patriarch of the classics who leads Dante to the garden of the limbo. Virgil appears before Dante exactly as Gabriel before Mahomet ; and throughout their journey each guide does his best to satisfy the pilgrim's curiosity. The warning of the approach to hell in both legends is identical, viz., a confused noise and violent bursts of flame. In both stories again, the wrathful guardians of the abode of pain exclude the traveller, till their anger is appeased by an order invoked by the guide from on high. The fierce demon who pursues Mahomet with a burning brand at the outset of his Nocturnal Journey has his duplicate in the devil who pursues Dante in the fifth pit of the eighth circle ; Virgil, by a brief word of command, disarms the fiend, just as Gabriel, by a prayer taught to the Prophet, quenched the fire of the glowing brand.

The general architecture of the Inferno is but a faithful copy of the Moslem hell. Both are in the shape of a vast funnel or inverted cone and consist of a series of storeys, each the abode of one class of sinner. In each, moreover, there are various subdivisions corresponding to as many subcategories of sinners. The greater the depth, the greater is the degree of sin and the pain inflicted. The ethical system in the two hells is also much alike, the atonement is either analogous to, or the reverse of, the sin committed. Finally, both hells are situate beneath the city of Jerusalem.

Nor are instances of close resemblance between the torments in the hells lacking. For instance, the adulterers, who in Dante's poem are swept hither and thither by a hellish storm, are in the Moslem legend hurled upwards and downwards by a hurricane of flame. The description of the first circle of the Moslem hell exactly tallies with the picture of the city of Dis—a sea of flame on whose shores stand countless tombs aglow with fire. The usurers, like the souls in Dante who have been guilty of crimes of violence, swim in a lake of blood ; guarded by fiends who hurl fiery stones at them. Gluttons and thieves are seen by Dante, tortured by serpents, as are the tyrants, the faithless guardians and the usurers in the Moslem hell. The maddening thirst of the forgers in the Divine Comedy is also suffered by the Moslem drunkards ; whilst the forgers with the swollen bellies have their counterpart in the usurers of another Moslem version. Again, Griffolino of Arezzo and Capocchio of Sienna scratch the scab off their leprous sores, as do the slanderers in the hell of Islam. The *barattieri*, held down in a lake of boiling pitch by the forks of fiends, suffer like the undutiful children in the Moslem legend, who, submerged in flame, are at each cry for mercy prodded by demons armed with forks. Finally, the awful punishment, dealt out in Dante's poem to the authors of schisms, of being knifed by demons and brought to life again, only for the torture to be repeated without end, is the grim torment appointed in the Moslem hell to. murderers.

3. The Moslem traveller, heartened by his guide, toils up a steep mountain, even as Dante, encouraged by Virgil, ascends the mount of purgatory. Allegorical visions abound

in both legends and, at times, they agree in symbol and
signification. Thus, for example, the woman who, despite
her loathsome ugliness, endeavours in the fourth circle of
purgatory to lure Dante from his path is almost a counterpart of the hag who tempts Mahomet at the beginning of his
journey. Moreover, Gabriel and Virgil agree that the vision
is a symbol of the false attractions of the world. A river
separates purgatory from paradise in both stories, and each
traveller drinks of its waters. Nor is this all ; after his visit
to hell, Dante thrice has to submit to lustral ablution. Virgil,
upon the advice of Cato, with his own hands washes Dante's
face, and, upon leaving purgatory, the pilgrim is immersed
by Matilda and Statius in the rivers of Lethe and Eunoe,
the waters of which efface all memory of sin. In the Moslem
legend, the souls are likewise purified three times in rivers
that flow through the garden of Abraham and whose waters
render their faces white and cleanse their souls from sin.
At the gates of paradise the Moslem traveller is met by a
comely maid, who receives him kindly, and together they
walk through the gardens of paradise, until in amazement
he beholds the houris on the bank of a stream forming a court
of beauty around the beloved of the poet Imru-l-Qays.
Dante, when he enters the earthly paradise, also meets a fair
maiden, Matilda, and is walking by her side through fields
rich with flowers, when on the banks of a stream he sees
the marvellous procession of old men and maidens who
accompany Beatrice, his beloved, as she descends from
heaven to meet him.

4. The architecture of both the Christian and the Moslem
heavens is identical, inasmuch as it is based upon the
Ptolemaic system. As they pass through the nine heavens,
the travellers meet the spirits of the blessed whose real
home, however, is the last sphere or Empyrean, where they
are ultimately found all together. The denomination also
of the nine spheres is in some cases the same, namely, that
of their respective planets. Occasionally, too, the ethical
systems are alike ; the souls are grouped in the spheres
according to their different virtues. At times, again, their

distribution in both legends is based upon astrology, or upon a combination of astrology and ethics.

In some versions of the Moslem legend, the description of heaven may be said to be as spiritual as the picture that has immortalised the Paradiso. The phenomena of light and sound are alone used by both travellers to convey their impression of the ethereal spheres. Both are dazzled by a light which grows in brilliance at every stage. In fear of blindness, they raise their hands to their eyes ; but their guides calm their fears, and God empowers them to gaze upon the new light. Both travellers frequently confess their inability to describe the majesty of the sights they see. Both again, led by their guides, ascend through the air in flight, with a speed that is compared to the wind and the arrow. The duties of both guides are manifold ; not only do they lead the pilgrims and comfort them, but they pray to God on their behalf and call upon them to thank the Lord for the signal favour He has shown them.

And, just as Beatrice leaves Dante at the last stages of his ascension, so Gabriel leaves Mahomet when the Prophet is wafted to the Divine Presence by the aid of a luminous wreath.

In each of the planetary heavens and in the different mansions the Moslem traveller meets many of the Biblical prophets, surrounded by the souls of their followers on earth. He also meets many personages famous in the Bible or Moslem lore. Into the literary imitation of the Islamic legend there is introduced a host of men and women who, although of all ranks and faiths, are nearly all writers of note in the history of Islam ; many are contemporaries and even acquaintances of the traveller, and all are grouped in circles according to their school of literature. Thus it is that both the heaven and hell of this imitation are peopled by the same multitude of minor personages that forms so striking a feature of the Divine Comedy. Both authors, too, have resort to the same device for introducing new actors into their scenes : either the traveller inquires where a certain soul is to be found ; or of a sudden the latter appears and remains

7

unrecognised until the guide, or a soul at hand, makes his identity known to the traveller. In both legends the pilgrims converse with the souls in heaven and hell on theological and literary subjects, or on events in the lives on earth of the departed.

Lastly, in allotting the souls to the various regions of the world to come, the two writers—although at times influenced by personal feeling are in the main guided by the same spirit of tolerance. Both, as they behold the souls in bliss or in pain, give vent to feelings of joy or pity, although occasionally they gloat over the sufferings of the damned.

But it is not merely in general outline that the two ascensions coincide ; even the episodes in the visions of paradise are at times alike, if not identical.

Dante, for example, in the heaven of Jupiter sees a mighty eagle formed of myriads of resplendent spirits all wings and faces, which, chanting exhortations to man to cleave to righteousness, flaps its wings and then comes to rest. Mahomet sees in heaven a gigantic angel in the form of a cock, which moves its wings whilst chanting hymns calling mankind to prayer, and then rests. He sees other angels, each an agglomeration of countless faces and wings, who resplendent with light sing songs of praise with tongues innumerable. These two visions merged in one, at once suggest Dante's heavenly eagle.

In the heaven of Saturn Dante beholds a golden ladder that leads upwards to the last sphere. He sees the spirits of the blessed descending by this ladder and, at the instance of Beatrice, he and his guide ascend by it in less time than " it takes to withdraw the hand from fire." Mahomet, in his ascension, sees a ladder rising from Jerusalem to the highest heaven ; angels stand on either side, and by its rungs of silver, gold, and emerald the souls ascend ; led by Gabriel, the Prophet rises by it " in less than the twinkling of an eye."

Dante meets in heaven Piccarda of his native city and Cunizza of Padua, women well known to him ; and in like manner the Moslem traveller (in the literary imitation of the Mahometan ascension) meets two women, acquaintances of his, to wit, Hamduna of his own town of Aleppo and the negress Tawfiq, of Baghdad. In both legends the women make themselves known to the pilgrim, tell him of the troubles of their married life or leave him struck with admiration at their matchless beauty.

Like Dante, the same Moslem traveller meets Adam in heaven and converses with him on the subject of the primitive language he spoke in' the Garden of Eden.

The examination of the theological virtues which Dante undergoes in the eighth sphere of heaven, is similar to that to which the soul of the departed is subjected in some allegorical adaptations of the *Miraj*.

The angels flying over the mystic rose of Dante's paradise, with faces of flame and bodies whiter than snow, have their counterpart in the angel, half fire and half snow, seen by Mahomet.

As they stand on high above the planetary heavens, both pilgrims are urged by their guides to cast their eyes downwards, and they see with amazement how small the created world is in comparison with the heavenly universe.

The apotheoses in both ascensions are exactly alike. In each legend the traveller, exalted to the Divine Presence, describes the Beatific Vision as follows : God is the focus of an intense light, surrounded by nine concentric circles of myriads of angelic spirits, who shed a wonderful radiance around. In a row near the centre are the Cherubim. Twice does the traveller behold the majestic sight of those nine circles ceaselessly revolving around the Divine Light ; once from afar, before he reaches the end of his journey, and again as he stands before the Throne of God. The effects of the Beatific Vision on the minds of the two pilgrims are again identical. At first they are so dazzled by the brilliance of the light that they believe they have been blinded, but gradually their sight is strengthened until finally they can gaze steadfastly upon it. Both are incapable of describing the Vision and only remember that they fell into an ecstasy that was preceded by a wondrous feeling of supreme delight.

5. Nor does the similarity between the two journeys end

here. A common spirit may also be seen to pervade the two legends.

The moral meaning that Dante sought to convey in his Divine Comedy had previously been imparted by the Sufis, and particularly by the Murcian Ibn Arabi. The Moslem mystics, like Dante, made use of a dramatic story—which was alleged to be true—of the journey of a man, Mahomet, to the nether regions and his ascension to the heavens, in order to symbolise the regeneration of the soul by faith and the practice of the theological virtues. In Dante's conception, as in Ibn Arabi's, the journey is symbolic of the moral life of man, whom God has placed in the world to work out his destiny and attain to supreme bliss, as represented by the Beatific Vision. This he cannot do without the guidance of theology; for natural reason can only lead him through the first stages of the journey, which symbolise the moral and intellectual virtues. Those sublime mansions of paradise, which stand for the theological virtues, can only be reached by the aid of illuminative grace. Accordingly, the pilgrim in the imitations of the Mahometan ascension of Ibn Arabi and others, is no longer Mahomet, or even a saint, but merely a man and a sinner, like Dante; often, like Dante, he is a philosopher, a theologian or a poet. The minor characters too, even those appearing in heaven, are real men and sinners and often repentant infidels. Thus, like the Divine Comedy, the Moslem ascension combines in one story the antithetical elements of realism and allegorical idealism.

6. The same involved and enigmatical style characterises Dante's poem and the ascension of Ibn Arabi. Moreover, both authors seek to display their vast erudition by attributing to their characters lengthy and abstruse discourses on philosophy, theology and astronomy. If, in addition, it is borne in mind that the Moslem ascension, like that of Dante, had a host of commentators, who endeavoured to discover the many meanings conveyed by the slightest detail; that the poet Abu-l-Ala's work was written with the definite purpose of handing down to posterity a masterpiece of

literary art and that its rhymed prose presented technical difficulties as great as, or perhaps greater than, those of Dante's tercets, in view of the accumulation of evidence, the following facts must be accepted as undeniable :—

7. Six hundred years at least before Dante Alighieri conceived his marvellous poem, there existed in Islam a religious legend narrating the journey of Mahomet to the abodes of the after-life. In the course of time from the eighth to the thirteenth centuries of our era—Moslem traditionists, theologians, interpreters of the Scriptures, mystics, philosophers and poets—all united in weaving around the original legend a fabric of religious narrative ; at times their stories were amplifications, at others, allegorical adaptations or literary imitations. A comparison with the Divine Comedy of all these versions combined bewrays many points of resemblance, and even of absolute coincidence, in the general architecture and ethical structure of hell and paradise ; in the description of the tortures and rewards ; in the general lines of the dramatic action ; in the episodes and incidents of the journey ; in the allegorical signification ; in the roles assigned to the protagonist and to the minor personages ; and, finally, in intrinsic literary value.

8. The interesting problems to which these coincidences give rise will be considered at a later stage ; but to forestall any objections that might be made, a few words may be added on the origin of the Moslem legend.

The story of the Nocturnal Journey and the ascension of Mahomet is not autochthonous in Islam. Its real source is in the religious literatures of other and older civilisations. But the question of the origin of the *Miraj* is of secondary interest. Let it suffice to say that its genesis may have been influenced by many similar tales, Hebrew, Persian, and Christian. It is not difficult to find features common to the Moslem legend and the Judæo-Christian ascensions of Moses, Enoch, Baruch and Isaiah ; or the fabulous journey of Ardâ Virâf to the Persian paradise ; or finally, the descent of Our Lord Jesus Christ to the bosom of Abraham blended into one story with His glorious ascension and the uplifting of St. Paul to the third heaven.[1] None of these journeys and ascensions, however, was so fully developed or expanded in the literature to which it belonged as the Islamic legend. Appearing, as it did, after the others, the Moslem tale was able to draw upon them and mould into the form of one story both the diverse incident they offered and much new matter that was the spontaneous outcome of Arabian fancy. In Islam, moreover, the legend was the wider spread among both learned and illiterate, seeing that it was accepted as an article of faith. To the present day it is the occasion of a religious festival celebrated throughout Islam and of a national holiday in Turkey, Egypt and Morocco,[2] which proves how deep-rooted and widely disseminated is the belief of the Moslem people in the fabulous ascension of their Prophet.

[1] Cf. FRANÇOIS MARTIN, Le Livre d'Henoch; EUGÈNE TISSERANT, Ascension d'Isaie; R. CHARLES, The Assumption of Moses; R. CHARLES, The Apocalypse of Baruch. For the Judaeo-Christian origin of these legends Cf. BATIFFOL, Anciennes Littératures chrétiennes; La Littérature grecque, p. 56. HIRSCHFELD, in his Researches into ... the Quran, p. 67, note 64, quotes a rabbinical legend of a journey through hell and paradise and points out certain analogies to a hadith of Bukhari. For the influence of the Persian ascension of Ardâ Virâf, see BLOCHET, L'Ascension au ciel du prophète Mohammed, and prior to BLOCHET, CLAIR-TISDALL in The sources of Islam, 76–81. Cf. MODI, Dante papers; Virâf, Adaaman and Dante, a work I have not been able to consult.

[2] The festivity of the Miraj is celebrated on the 27th day of the month of Recheb, the seventh of the Moslem calendar. At Constantinople the Sultan attended with his court at the services held at night in the mosque of the Seraglio. LANE, on p. 430 of his book, An account of the manners and customs of the modern Egyptians, describes the processions and festivals held in honour of the Miraj at Cairo. Throughout Morocco, the Miraj is celebrated in the same manner; it is a day of fast and alms-giving for the stricter Moslems, and the Government offices are closed.

PART II

THE DIVINE COMEDY COMPARED WITH OTHER MOSLEM LEGENDS ON THE AFTER-LIFE

THE DIVINE COMEDY COMPARED WITH OTHER MOSLEM LEGENDS ON THE AFTER-LIFE

I

INTRODUCTION

1. THE close resemblance that the Divine Comedy has been shown to bear to the legend of the *Miraj* gives rise to a multiplicity of problems in the history of literature, all relevant to the originality of Dante's poem. These problems are so important that a more minute examination of the poem in its several parts—limbo, hell, purgatory and the earthly and celestial paradises—is required in order to resolve whether or not many of the descriptive features and even whole scenes and episodes, although successfully standing the test of comparison with the *Miraj*, are, nevertheless, traceable to other Moslem legends and beliefs.

2. As a preliminary, it may be well briefly to set forth the doctrine of Islam on the future life ; for it will be possible to admit or reject *a priori* the likelihood of any resemblance between the conceptions of Dante and the Arabs according as the Islamic doctrine agrees or disagrees with the teaching of Christianity on the same point.

3. Now, on no question are the two religions in closer agreement than on that of the future life, in which, according to both, the souls exist in four different states. By the eleventh century at the latest definite expression had been given to this doctrine by the orthodox clergy of Islam, and notably by the great moralist and theologian, Algazel.[1]

The state of everlasting damnation, reserved for the souls of those who denying God gave themselves up to worldly

[1] *Ihia,* IV, 17–23. Cf. *Ithaf,* VIII, 548 *et seq,*

pleasures is equivalent to the Christian hell; and, just as in the latter the pain inflicted is both physical and moral, so in the Moslem state the soul, in addition to being subjected to the torture of everlasting fire, is made to suffer anguish through its separation from God.

Everlasting salvation, corresponding to the Christian heaven, is the state of those souls that lived in the true faith and died either innocent or repentant, free from all taint of sin. Their reward is double, for over and above the sensual pleasures promised by Moslem revelation, they experience the infinitely greater bliss of the contemplation of the Divine essence.

The two states intermediate between heaven and hell approximate to our purgatory and limbo. According to Algazel, the punishment in purgatory differs from that in hell only in that it is not eternal, but temporary. True, the Christian purgatory is the place where venial sins are expiated, or deadly sins whose guilt has been washed away; whereas the Moslem purgatory is assigned to those souls who, although guilty of deadly sin, have until the moment of death kept the root of faith alive within their hearts and been deprived by death alone of the possibility of repentance. As, according to Algazel, the faith that saves is not the dead but the living faith expressed in religious feeling and good deeds, this act of living faith in God and in the intercession of the Prophet is then practically the same as the spirit of contrition required to save the Christian.

The fourth state, which represents the Christian limbo, is that of the souls who, having neither served nor offended God, are exempt from punishment, although denied eternal bliss. This is the condition of lunatics, idiots, the children of infidels, and those adults who, never having heard the call of Islam, may be said to have died in ignorance of their infidelity.

The brief outlines sketched above will suffice to show how similar are the moral foundations upon which the Christian and Moslem conceptions of the after-life are based. Nor is this a matter for wonder, seeing that so great an authority as St. John of Damascus held Islam to be but an heretical form of Christianity, heretical inasmuch as it denied both the Trinity and the Divinity of Christ,[1] and that Algazel himself confessed the whole of the teaching of the Christian faith, apart from these two points of doctrine, to be infallible truth.[2]

II

THE MOSLEM LIMBO IN THE DIVINE COMEDY

1. The first of the nether regions visited by Dante is that set apart for such souls as have done neither good nor evil, To this place Dante gives the name of " limbo."[3]

The Latin noun " limbus," the origin of which is obscure. is used by classical writers, such as Virgil, Ovid, and Statius, with the meaning of " fringe or border adorning the lower part of a garment." In the sixth century it is used with the meaning of " coast." In the Bible and ecclesiastical writings the abode of indifferent souls is named the " Bosom of Abraham," but never the " limbo " ; and it is not known who introduced the term into Christian literature. It appears suddenly in the works of the commentators of Peter the Lombard, contemporaries of Dante, who designate by it both the abode of unbaptised children (*limbus puerorum*) and the dwelling of the patriarchs of the Old Testament (*limbus patrum*).[4]

---

[1] Cf. *De Haeresibus* (Opera Omnia), Paris, vol. I, 110–115, No. 100.

[2] Cf. *Qistas*, p. 60 : " Should someone say to thee, ' Say that there is but one God and that Jesus is His Prophet,' thy mind would instinctively reject the statement as being proper to a Christian only. But that would but be because thou hast not sufficient understanding to grasp that the statement in itself is true and that *no reproach can be made to the Christian, for this article of his faith, nor for any of the other articles,* save only those two—that God is the third of three, and that Mahomet is not a prophet of God. *Apart from these two all the other articles (of the Christian faith) are true.*" For the influence of Christianity on Islam, and particularly on Algazel, cf. Asín, *La mystique d'Al-Gazzali*, pp. 67–104, and *Abenmasarra*, pp. 12–16.

[3] *Inf.* IV, 45.

[4] Cf. PETAVIUS, *Dogm. Theolog.* IV (Pars sec.) lib. 3, cap. 18, §5. The texts DUCANGE refers to in his *Glossarium* (s. v) are later than the twelfth century. St. Thomas in the *Summa theologica* (pars 3, q. 52) calls the limbo of the Patriarchs *infernus* and *sinus Abrahae*, but in the *Supplementum tertiae partis* (q. 69) he already adopts the name *limbus*.

Dante places this abode immediately above hell, as if it were an antechamber of the latter, and divides it into two parts—the ante-inferno, a wide plain inhabited by the indifferent souls,[1] and the angels that remained neutral in Lucifer's rebellion against God,[2] and the limbo proper, a deep and shaded valley, in the midst of which stands a fortress surrounded by seven walls with seven gates leading to a pleasant meadow.[3]

The limbo is inhabited by children that died innocent, but unbaptised, and, in addition, by a host of men and women who, though righteous, were either pre-Christian pagans or true followers of Mahomet and who, moreover, are famous as poets, moralists, philosophers, or heroes.[4]

The suffering of these spirits is purely moral, and arises from their insatiable longing to behold God. Debarred from the joys of paradise, and exempt from the physical punishment of hell, they may be said to be in suspense (*sospesi*) between heaven and hell.[5] This intermediate state would appear to give them special opportunities of knowing and dealing with both the blessed and the damned. Thus Virgil is in direct communication, from the limbo, with Beatrice[6] ; and, as he guides Dante through hell and purgatory, he names and describes to him the sinners and fiends, whose features are evidently well known to him.

2. The absence of almost all Biblical or theological precedents for Dante's picture need hardly be insisted upon. The name, the picturesque description of the place, the exact classification of the dwellers, who are pagans and at times even Moslems, the many details of their life and condition —none of these can find full justification in Catholic dogma, which is as discreet on these as on most other points of eschatology.[7]

---

[1] *Inf.* III, 34.   [2] *Inf.* III, 38.   [3] *Inf.* IV, 106, 110, 116.
[4] *Inf.* IV, 28, *et seq.*   [5] *Inf.* IV, 28, 42, 45. Cf. *Inf.* II, 52.
[6] *Inf.* II, 53, 75.
[7] Cf. St. Thomas, *Summa Theol.* pars 3, q. 52, and *Supplementum*, q. 69. PERRONE, in his *Praelectiones theol.*, II, 157, says of the limbo : " Reliqua autem, quae spectant sive ad hunc inferni locum, sive ad poenarum disparitatem .... fidem nullo modo attingunt, cum nullum de his Ecclesiae decretum existat."

In Islam it is otherwise. The absence of any one and unquestionable authority to distinguish between matters of faith and of free thought enabled a large number of myths and legends to be introduced from other Oriental religions—especially Judaism, Mazdaism, and Eastern Christianity—and, being attributed to the Prophet and his companions, to acquire a weight almost equal with the text of the Koran.

A search in this direction may perhaps provide a clue to the reading of the riddle of Dante's limbo, which Christian theology leaves unsolved.

3. The Koran (VII, 44, 46) speaks of a mansion " Al Aaraf " that separates the blessed from the wicked. The word " Aaraf " by derivation means " the upper part of a curtain or veil " ; it is also used to denote " the mane of a horse, the crest of a cock and, in general, the highest or most prominent part of anything " ; in its wider sense it is applied to " any limit or boundary between things."[1] Thus, it is similar to the classical *limbus* ; but, whereas *limbus* did not acquire the meaning of a region beyond the grave until the thirteenth century, the Arabic word had this meaning, in addition to its ordinary meaning, as early as the time of Mahomet.[2]

The Moslem limbo is variously described in the legends—as a pleasant vale studded with fruit trees ; as a valley lying behind a lofty mountain ; as a circular wall of great height, with battlements and a gate, rising between heaven and hell ; or simply as an eminence or mount. These conceptions, grouped together, present a picture not unlike that of Dante's limbo ; especially, if the picture is completed with the description, recurrent in the *Miraj*, of the Garden of Abraham and the entrance to the Moslem hell, which, like the castle that forms the antechamber of Dante's hell, also has seven gates. Again, this castle, surrounded as it is by seven

---

[1] *Tacholarus*, VI, 194, s.v. *Ithaf*, VIII, 564. KHAZIN, *Tafsir*, II, 90. Cf. FREYTAG, *Lexicon*, and LANE, *Lexicon*, s.v.

[2] The theological meaning of the word Al Aaraf may be derived from the eschatology of St. Ephrem (*id*.373), who divided the celestial paradise into the summit, slopes and *border* ; in the latter penitent sinners who have been pardoned dwell until the Day of Judgment, when they will ascend to the summit. Cf. TIXERONT, *Hist. des dogmes*, II, 220.

walls with seven gates, is an almost exact reproduction of the Islamic castle of the garden of paradise, which is surrounded by eight walls with eight gates[1] ; as if Dante, in blending the Moslem designs of heaven and hell, had sought to symbolise the neutral nature of the souls dwelling in the limbo.

The Moslem limbo has, on the authority of Algazel himself, been shown to be the abode of those that lived neither in virtue nor in vice. In keeping with this doctrine, Moslem tradition specifies the following groups : Martyrs of holy warfare who are denied the reward of paradise through having disobeyed their parents ; men of learning whose merit was nullified by their vanity ; infant children of Moslems and infidels ; and, finally, angels of the male sex or genii that believed in the Prophet. These groups correspond very fairly to the groups in Dante's limbo of the unbaptised children and the heroes, poets and philosophers whose virtues and talents were neutralised by their lack of faith. As regards the angels of male sex, they are indeed as enigmatical as Dante's neutral angels.

The only suffering that, according to the Koran and the theologians, is inflicted on the inhabitants of the Moslem limbo is a vain longing to enter paradise : " They cannot enter for all their longing."[2] As the good they have done is balanced by their sins, they neither sink into hell nor rise to heaven, but remain in suspense between the two.[3] Thus placed, they are acquainted and converse with both the blessed and the damned.[4]

[1] Cf. *Futuhat*, I, 416 ; III, 567, 577. *Tadhkira*, 88.
[2] *Koran*, VII, 44. Cf. *Ithaf*, VIII, 565 ; *Kanz*, VII, 213, No. 2,312. The Koran here refers to the dwellers in the limbo and not, as Kasimirski has it on p. 122 of his French translation, to *les réprouvés*. Cf. KHAZIN, *Tafsir*, II, 91 ; also *Tafsir* of AL-NASAFI and FIRUZABADI in *Tafsir* of Ibn Abbas, I, 102.
[3] Compare the passages quoted above of the *Ithaf* and the *Tafsir* of KHAZIN with *Inf.* II, 52, and IV, 45.
[4] Other less striking features of resemblance might be quoted. Thus the crowd running behind the flag in the Ante-inferno (*Inf.* III, 52) is reminiscent of many Moslem tales of the Day of Judgment, which depict groups led by standard-bearers.
Thus, Moslems will be led by Mahomet bearing the banner of the Glory of God. The prophet Xoaib with a white banner will lead the blessed that are blind ; Job, with a green banner, the patient lepers ; Joseph, likewise with a green banner, the chaste youths ; Aaron, with a yellow banner,

THE MOSLEM HELL IN THE DIVINE COMEDY

1. Dante lovers of all ages have dwelt admiringly upon the originality shown by the poet in his conception of the architecture of hell. His compatriot Christoforo Landino wrote as follows in the fifteenth century[1] : " Benche questo poeta in ogni cosa sia maraviglioso, nientedimeno non posso sanza sommo stupore considerare la sua nuova, ne mai da alcuno altro escogitata inventione." And in modern times, Rossi, after showing how feeble were the stereotyped descriptions of hell prior to Dante's and how poor in this respect were the Biblical and classical sources available to him, concludes by saying : " L'ingegno poderoso e l'alta fantasia del poeta svolsero e rimutarono con piena libertà questo abbozzo, fecondarono quegli elementi e ne trassero un tutto nuovo, originale, grandioso, definito in ogni parte con esatteza quasi matematica."[2]

The admiration of the critic is justified. But, before the originality of Dante's conception can be regarded as established beyond all doubt, it must be shown that no similar description existed in the literature of other religions. This demonstration has often been attempted. Vossler, for instance, has given a complete summary of the researches made by Dantists in their endeavour to find religious, philosophical and artistic precedents for the Divine Comedy.[3] With wonderful scholarship he has reconstructed what he calls the *prehistory* of the sublime poem. The myths contained in religions prior to Christianity, as well as the

the true friends who loved each other in God ; Noah, with a many-coloured banner, the god-fearing ; John, with a yellow banner, the martyrs ; Jesus will be the standard-bearer of the poor in spirit ; Solomon, of the rich ; the pre-Islamic poet Imru-l-Qays will be the ensign of the poets in hell ; and the traitor will bear a banner of shame. Cf. IBN MAKHLUF, I, 154, and II, 8 and 14.

As to the swarms of wasps and flies that plague the inhabitants of the Ante-inferno, the Moslem hell is depicted as " swarming with insects of all kinds, except bees." Cf. *Al-Laali*, II, 245.

[1] Cf. LANDINO, on the 14th page of the preliminary study.

[2] ROSSI, I, 139–140. Cf. D'ANCONA, *Precursori*, 28–31, 36, and *passim*.

[3] VOSSLER, I, 21.

teaching of the Old and New Testaments, are drawn upon as sources. One religion alone is excluded from his survey—the Mahometan.[1] Yet of all religions Islam is the richest in legends on the after-life.[2] Islam, the spurious offspring of Judaism and Christianity, blended the doctrine of the Old and New Testaments with elements drawn from other Oriental faiths ; and the fact that it appeared at a later date and spread rapidly through countries inhabited by the most religious peoples of the ancient world aided the process of assimilation. Accordingly, in no other religious lore do we find so minute and graphic descriptions of the abodes and life of the blessed and the wicked souls as in the Koran and the traditions built up around it ; and a comparison of the Moslem hell with Dante's Inferno may well throw new light upon the question of the originality of the great poet's conception.

2. Beginning with the general outlines of the two conceptions, we find no precise topography of hell in the Koran.[3] But Moslem tradition agrees with Dante in placing hell beneath the earth's crust ; the tales represent it as a dark chasm, or concave opening in the earth, so deep that a stone or ball of lead dropped into it would take seventy years to reach the bottom.[4] As in the Divine Comedy, its mouth is laid at Jerusalem, near or behind the Eastern wall of the temple of Solomon.[5] Dante maintains the unity of his architectural design by placing the celestial Jerusalem in a

---

[1] It is difficult to account for his silence on this point, for evidently any influence the Egyptians, Assyrians, Babylonians and Phœnicians may have exercised over the Divine Comedy must have been more remote ; yet he devotes a separate paragraph to each of these peoples and not a single line to Islam.

[2] Cf. CHANTEPIE, *Hist. des rel.* Reference to the quotations in the index, s.v. *Enfer*, will show that the Moslem hell is superior to all others in wealth of descriptive detail.

[3] Cf. KASIMIRSKI's translation of the Koran, p. 122, footnote and refer to the index, s.v. *Enfer*.

[4] Cf. *Kanz*, VII, 244, Nos. 2,756 to 2,791.

[5] Cf. ROSSI, I, 140, and see the general plan *Figura universale della D.C.* in FRATICELLI, p. 402. For the Moslem traditions cf. *Kanz*, VI, 102, Nos. 1, 538 ; 1,546 and 1,601 ; and VII, 277, Nos. 3,076/7. The belief that the mouth of hell is situated beneath Jerusalem is still held in Islam, for the Moslems believe that below the subterranean chamber underneath the present Mosque or dome of the rock (*Qubbat al-sakhra*) standing in the precincts of the Temple, lies the pit of the souls (*Bir al-arwah*).

vertical line with the city on earth ; and the same vertical projection applies, as will be shown later, to the Moslem paradise.

But there are further coincidences. In Version B of Cycle 2 of the *Miraj* the Moslem hell was seen to be formed, like that of Dante, of a series of concentric circular strata gradually descending from the mouth to the bottom. This conception of the structure of hell was invented by the Moslem traditionists in their endeavour to interpret the Koranic text (XV, 44), which says : " (Hell) has seven gates ; to each gate, a separate group." The commentators could furnish no explanation of this verse, if the current meaning of " door " or " gate " were to be given to the Arabic word *bab*. Accordingly, a metaphorical interpretation was soon applied to the word in the sense of " step " or " circular stratum," which allowed hell to be conceived as a place of imprisonment consisting of seven pits, each reserved for one class of sinners.[1] To give this interpretation greater authority, it was attributed to Ali, the son-in-law of Mahomet.[2]

" Know ye of what manner are the gates of hell ? " he asked his hearers, and they answered, " as are the gates we know " ; but he said, " not so, for they are thus," and, as he spake, he laid one hand flat upon the other.

The idea of parallel planes thus suggested is carried further in other tales, attributed either to Ali or to Ibn Abbas, Mahomet's uncle. In these the words " step " or " circular stratum " are used in place of " gate " ; the seven divisions are expressly stated to lie one above the other ; and the distance between each is measured in terms of hyperbole.[3]

---

[1] This metaphorical interpretation is not justified on philological grounds, for the Arabic lexicons only give the following indirect meanings :— chapter ; sum of a calculation ; mode, category or condition, etc. LANE in his *Lexicon* (I, 272), however, suggests that in Egypt the word was applied to a sepulchral chamber, or cave in a mountain, and was derived from the Coptic " bib." [2] *Kanz*, VIII, 278, No. 3,079.

[3] Cf. *Kanz, ibid.* No. 3,078. Also TABARI, *Tafsir*, XIV, 25, and KHAZIN, *Tafsir*, III, 96. Cf. also MS 234, Gayangos Coll., fol. 100 v°.

" Ibn Abbas says that hell is formed of seven floors, separated one from another by a distance of five hundred years."

In other *hadiths* the words *gate, floor,* and *step* are replaced by the word *pit.* Cf. *Kanz*, III, 263, No. 4,235.

8

The division into seven is characteristic of Moslem cosmography.   The Koran itself says (LXV, 12) : " Seven are the astronomical heavens and seven the earths, as are seven the seas, the gates of hell and the mansions of paradise." [1] Dante, in dividing each of the realms of hell, purgatory and paradise into ten regions, betrays a similar obsession for symmetry, coupled with a belief in the esoteric virtue of a given number.[2] Although the coincidence does not extend to the numbers themselves, the principle underlying both cosmographies is the same.

Like the different circles of the Inferno, each of the stages of the Moslem hell has a name of its own and certain physical features peculiar to it, and is reserved for one class of sinners condemned to one particular torture.   It would be difficult, if not impossible, to reduce to one scheme the heterogeneous descriptions furnished in the tales.   Nor is it claimed that they agree in detail with Dante's description of hell.   But a brief review of some of these tales will, notwithstanding the simplicity of the setting, reveal the general features of resemblance mentioned above.   Thus a tradition dating from the second century of the Hegira gives the divisions of hell, reckoned downwards, as the following [3]:—

1. *Jahannam*, or Gehenna, for Moslems guilty of deadly sins.   2. *Lazi*, or glowing fire, for Christians.   3. *Al-Hatma*, or greedy fire, for Jews.   4. *As-Sair*, or flaming fire, for Sabians.   5. *Saqar*, or burning fire, for Zoroastrians.   6. *Al-Jahim*, or intense fire, for polytheists.   7. *Al-Hawiya*, or abysm, for hypocrites.

Other traditions classify the seven earths into which God divided our planet and which correspond to the seven stages of hell, as follows [4]:—

1. *Adim*, or surface, inhabited by mankind.   2. *Basit*, or

---

[1] A collection of *hadiths* dealing with this division into seven may be found in *Qisas*, 4–11 ; on p. 7 is a *hadith* by Wahb ibn Munabbih, which says :—
" Of almost all things there are seven—seven are the heavens, the earths, the mountains, the seas . . . the days of the week, the planets . . . the gates and floors of hell . . ."
[2] Cf. Rossi, I, 141.   [3] *Hadith* of Ibn Jurayj in Khazin, *Tafsir*, III, 96–97.   Cf. MS 64 Gayangos Coll., fol. 22.   [4] Thaalabi, *Qisas*, 4.   Cf. *Kanz*, III, 218, No. 3,407.   Also *Badai az-Zohur*, 8–9.

plain, the prison of the winds, inhabited by men that eat their own flesh and drink their own blood. 3. *Thaqil*, or region of distress, the antechamber of hell in which dwell men with the mouth of a dog, the ears of a goat, the cloven hoof of an ox and the wool of a sheep. 4. *Batih*, or place of torrents, a valley through which flows a stream of boiling sulphur to torment the wicked ; the dwellers in this valley have no eyes and in place of feet, have wings. 5. *Hayn*, or region of adversity, in which serpents of enormous size devour the infidels. 6. *Masika*, or store and *Sijin*, or dungeon, the office where sins are recorded and where the souls are tormented by scorpions of the size of mules. 7. *As-Saqar*, or place of burning, and *Athara*, place of damp and great cold ; this is the home of Iblis, who is chained in the midst of the rebel angels, his hands fastened one in front of and the other behind him, except when set free by God to chastise his fiends.

It need hardly be pointed out how great the distance is that separates this scheme, childish in its simplicity, from the complex moral structure of Dante's hell. It should be borne in mind, however, that here we are not dealing with the systematic works of accomplished writers—they will be discussed at a later stage—but with popular tales that lived, and still live, in the mouth of the illiterate people ; and they are quoted, not as counterparts of the Inferno, but as rough sketches, in which analogies, even of detail, with the poem are to be found.[1] Thus, the second stage is, like Dante's second circle, a place of winds ; and in the fifth region enormous serpents devour the sinners, as in the eighth circle of Dante they do the thieves. Again, the glacial region of the last surface is an exact counterpart of Dante's lowest circle, with Lucifer corresponding to Iblis the Moslem king of evil ; Iblis, moreover, appears chained

---

[1] How popular these descriptions of hell were is shown by the fact that they passed into the Arabian Nights Tales. Thus, Tamim Dari and Boluqiya each visit hell, where the latter finds seven floors of fire, containing: (1) impenitent Moslems ; (2) polytheists ; (3) Gog and Magog; (4) demons ; (5) Moslems forgetful of prayer ; (6) Jews and Christians ; and (7) hypocrites. The severity of torture increases with the depth ; the floors are separated by a distance of a thousand years, and in the first there are hills, valleys, houses, castles and cities to the number of seventy thousand. Cf. CHAUVIN, *Bibliographie*, VII, 48 and 56.

with one hand in front and one behind, just as does the giant Ephialtes.[1]

As more and more traditions come to be consulted, each adding fresh picturesque details, the description will be found to lose its original baldness and acquire a relief as marked as that of Dante's picture. These tales were collected by the ascetics of Islam, who have handed the collections down to us in their writings.[2] A comparison of the picture of the Moslem hell with the Inferno shows a remarkable resemblance. Like the latter, the former is depicted with a wealth of orographic, hydrographic and architectural features—rocks, hills and mountains, chasms and valleys; rivers, lakes and seas; sepulchres, dungeons, castles and bridges. As in the Inferno, many of these topographical features bear special names; and, again, in the naming the same principles are followed as in Dante. The latter either names the regions after the sinners suffering in them, such as the abodes of the traitors[3]; or, like the eighth circle, Malebolge, from the physical and moral conditions of the place itself. Apart from the names of the principal stages that are quoted above, the hell of Islam has many names for special topographical features.

Thus, a mountain formed of the smoke of hell is named *Zal Yahmum*; a rock on which libertines are tortured is called *Sijin*, or dungeon; *Khandaq as-sokran* is the name of a pit from the bottom of which spring water and blood wherewith drunkards seek to quench their thirst; *Maubiq*, or perdition, is a valley through which runs a river of fire; *Atham*, or place of crimes, is the name of another valley; *Al-Wayl*, or misery, is the deepest of the valleys, in which the pus from the sores of the sinners gathers and is drunk by the polytheists; *Al-Khabal*, or ruin, and *Al-Hazan*, or sorrow, are the names of two other valleys; *Lamlam* is the name of a round valley, the intense heat of which strikes terror into the hearts of all the dwellers in hell; *Al-Gassaq*, or infection, is a

---

[1] *Inf.* XXXI, 86.

[2] The *Tadhkira* of the Cordovan, or Memorial of the Future Life, is one of the richest of such collections and was popular in the East and West. It is the one mainly drawn upon for the present purpose.

[3] See the list of such names quoted in the index to Fraticelli's edition of the Divine Comedy.

spring from which flows sweat exuded by serpents, in the poisonous waters of which the flesh of the damned rots away from the bone.[1] Some regions take their names from famous sinners, such as the abode of tyrants, from Pharaoh ; that of the polytheists, from Abu Jahl ; and so forth.[2]

From this brief summary it will be seen that the hell of primitive Islam agrees with Dante's hell in being an abyss of great depth, formed of stages, steps or circular strata, each lying at a depth proportionate to the torture meted out therein ; each main stage is subdivided into a number of secondary storeys ; and in both schemes the stages or steps bear special names and are set apart for certain categories of sinners.

The agreement in outline between the two conceptions cannot be explained on the ground that both were derived from a common early Christian model ; for the eschatology of early Christianity, both Occidental and Oriental, is of marked sobriety.[3] Nor is it in Islam that the origin of this complex architectural scheme must be sought, but farther East, particularly in Buddhism.[4]

3. The outlines of hell, traced by the early Moslem tradi-

---

[1] *Tadhkira*, 19, 39, 74. Cf. *Kanz*, III, 76, No. 1,436 ; V, 217, Nos. 4,479 and 4,484 ; VII, 245, Nos. 2,777 and 2,784. *Corra*, 12. *Al-Laali*, II, 245. TABARI, *Tafsir*, XXIII, 114. Many of the proper names of the mansions of hell are appellative names taken from the Koran.

[2] *Corra*, 12 and 31. *Al-Laali*, II, 196.

[3] St. Thomas finds no precise topography of hell in Christian tradition and can only record the probable opinion of the theologians that " ignis inferni est sub terra," though formerly he had accepted the statement of St. Augustine : " In qua parte mundi infernus sit, scire neminem arbitror " and of St. Gregory, " Hac de re temere definire nihil audeo " (cf. *Summa Theol.* Supplementum tertiae partis, q. 97, art. 7). St. Isidore of Seville supposed hell to be " in superficie terrae, ex parte opposita terrae nostrae habitabili," but in the thirteenth century this opinion was no longer common. Thus in a Mapa mundi extant in MS in the Biblioteca Nacional of Madrid and the Biblioteca Escurialense (cf. Boletin de la Real Sociedad Geográfica, vol. L, p. 207) and attributed to St. Isidore though it really belongs to the thirteenth century, hell is described as lying in the middle of the earth " at the lowest and bottommost spot." Curiously enough, unlike Dante's and the Islamic picture, hell is here conceived as being narrow at the top and wide at the bottom ; this probably is due to the faulty interpretation of Moslem documents.

[4] Not in the Vedas. Cf. CHANTEPIE, *Hist. des rel.* 346 and 382. Also ROESKÉ, *L'enfer cambodgien* (in *Journal Asiatique*, Nov.–Dec. 1914, 587–606). For the rabbinical hell cf. BUXTORF, *Lexicon chaldaicum* (Basle, 1639), p. 231 a.

tionists, were filled in with a wealth of detail by the theologians of later centuries ; the mystics, especially, enhanced the tales with fantastic comment and even endeavoured graphically to represent by means of designs the picture thus formed.

Prominent among the mystics living before Dante's time was Ibn Arabi of Murcia, whose allegorical ascensions have been shown to be curiously similar to the work of Dante.[1] Entire chapters of his monumental work, *Futuhat*, are devoted to the description of hell, which is represented in the traditional manner as a pit or abyss of fabulous depth, formed of seven steps or circular strata.[2] The innovations introduced by the Sufi are, however, of great interest. Above all, the sinners are distributed among the seven circles according to the nature of their sins and the organ, or part of the body, with which they committed them, viz., the eyes, ears, tongue, hands, belly, pudenda, and feet. Thus, the principle governing the distribution is no longer dogmatic, but, as in the Divine Comedy, ethical. Ibn Arabi, indeed, combines both principles, inasmuch as he subdivides each circle into quadrants, reserved for unbelievers, polytheists, atheists, and hypocrites respectively. In addition, and on a different principle, each circle is divided into semi-circles— the one for sinners guilty of *external* sin, or sin actually committed ; the other for those who committed the same sin *internally*, or in thought. Finally, each circle is composed of a hundred secondary circles or steps, subdivided into abodes or cells, the total number of which equals the

---

[1] Cf. *supra*, pp. 45–51.

[2] *Futuhat*, I, 387–396 ; II, 809 ; III, 8, 557, 575–577. Other picturesque features might be added to those mentioned above ; thus, in hell there is both heat and cold ; the heads of sects suffer special torture, and Iblis, the Lucifer of Islam, undergoes the severest torture of all ; suffering in hell is of two kinds, physical and moral. As in Dante (cf. ROSSI, I, 151), the sufferers may not leave the pit to which they are condemned, but move freely within its limits (*Futuhat*, III, 227). Finally, Ibn Arabi imparts a strong flavour of realism to his pictures by painting them as if he had actually seen the originals in visions. Thus, on p. 389 of vol. I, he says :—

" In this vision I saw of the circles of the damned . . . such as God was pleased to show me. And I saw an abode, called the Abode of Darkness, and descended some five of its several steps and I beheld the tortures in each one . . ."

number of mansions in heaven.[1] But Ibn Arabi goes further than this. Accustomed to the use of geometrical design for the illustration of the most abstruse metaphysical thought, he has recourse to this means for interpreting his conception of hell.[2] As a follower of the school of Ibn Masarra, he, like other Spanish Sufis, conceived hell to have the external aspect of a serpent.[3] And indeed, as the Moslem hell, like that of Dante, consists of a structure of circular layers or strata, the diameter of which decreases with their depth, the whole seen from above in ground plan would provide a figure formed of concentric circles not unlike the spiral formed by the coils of a serpent. This is, in fact, the plan that Ibn Arabi has given us in his *Futuhat*[4] and which is here reproduced in Fig. 1.

The Dantists also, in graphic illustration of the poet's descriptions, have drawn designs of the architectural plan of hell and the other regions beyond the grave. Thus, Manfredi Porena in his " Commento grafico alla Divina Commedia per use delle scuole " (Milan, 1902) gives a ground plan of Dante's hell (see upper part of Fig. 2) that is almost identical with Ibn Arabi's design, the main difference lying in the number of circles, of which there are ten in Dante and seven in Ibn Arabi.

Porena also gives the elevation of the inferno (see lower part of Fig. 2), which resembles the section of an amphitheatre having ten steps or tiers. The same elevation appears in Fraticelli's edition of the Divine Comedy. Ibn Arabi does not give us this figure, but the elevation of the Islamic hell was drawn by the Sufis and their design appears in the Turkish encyclopædia, " Ma' rifet Nameh," by Ibrahim Hakki.[5] A glance at the reproduction of this design in Fig. 3 will show it to be identical with the elevation of Dante's hell.

---

[1] The theme of the symmetry between the hell and heaven of Islam will be developed further in the discussion of the latter.

[2] Cf. Asín, *Abenmasarra*, pp. 111 and 161.

[3] *Futuhat*, I, 388. Cf. *Abenmasarra*, 109. The figure of the serpent he no doubt derived from Ibn Qasi, a disciple of the Masarri school and head of the Muridin, who ruled as sovereign in Southern Portugal until 1151 A.D.

[4] *Futuhat*, III, 557.

[5] It is here reproduced from the Turkish author's two general plans of the Cosmos given by CARRA DE VAUX in *Fragments d'Eschatologie musulmane* pp. 27 and 33.

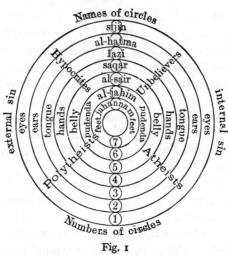

Fig. 1

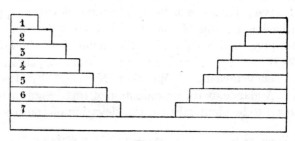

Fig. 3

Fig. 2

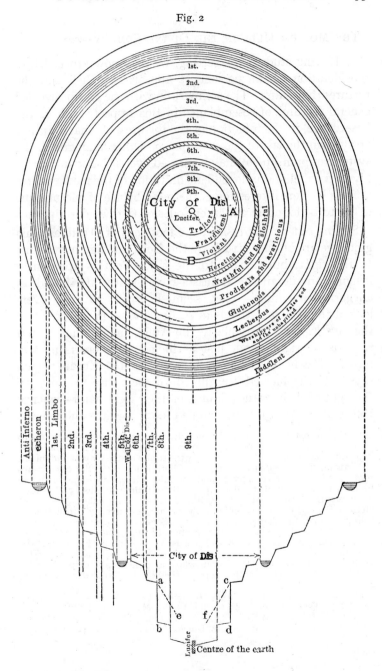

IV

The Moslem Hell in the Divine Comedy—*continued*

1. Having studied the setting, we may now proceed to a consideration of the personages appearing in hell and the tortures they suffer. The comparison with the *Miraj* revealed general features of resemblance in this respect, such as the observance, in the infliction of the tortures, of what Dantists aptly term the law of the *contrapasso*. Other analogies in the systems of punishment may be passed over as being due possibly to parallel and independent imitation of the mediæval *lex talionis.*[1] More interesting is the resemblance of picturesque detail to be found in actual episodes of the two descriptions.

Setting out on our task in the footsteps of Dante and his guide we are at once struck by the fact that they never turn to the right, but always to the left. To this apparently insignificant detail the Dantists have rightly attributed an allegorical meaning. They seem, however, to have overlooked the fact that this is in reality a Moslem feature ; for the mystics, and particularly Ibn Arabi, taught that in hell there is no right hand, just as in heaven there is no left hand. The belief is based on a text of the Koran, which says that the blessed are guided on their way to glory by the light of their virtues shining on their right hand—whence Ibn Arabi infers that the damned move towards the left.[2]

[1] Infernal tortures based on this principle were found in several versions of the *Miraj*, but they recur in far greater number in other traditions depicting the torments of the sinners or the scenes on the Day of Judgment.

In them, thieves suffer amputation of both hands ; the liar has his lips torn asunder ; the nagging wife and the false witness are shown hanging by their tongues ; unjust judges appear blind ; the vain, deaf and dumb ; hired mourners go about barking like dogs ; suicides suffer throughout eternity the torture of their death ; the proud are converted into ants and trampled upon by all the other sinners. Some categories of sinners are obliged to bear the *corpus delicti* as a stigma ; thus, the drunkard carries a bottle slung round his neck and a glass or a guitar in his hand ; the tradesman who gave short weight carries scales of fire hanging from his neck ; and the reader of the Koran who was puffed up with pride at his accomplishment appears with a copy of the holy book nailed to his neck ; and so forth.

Cf. *Corra*, 12–25, 31, 37, 43. *Al-Laali*, II, 195. *Kanz*, VII, 2,086, No. 3,173. Gayangos Coll. MS 64, fol. 15 v° ; MS 172, fol. 33 v°.

[2] Inf. XVIII, 21 ; XXIX, 53 ; XXXI, 82. The Koranic texts are LVII, 12, and LXVI, 8, glossed by Ibn Arabi in *Futuhat*, I, 412, line 14.

2. In the second circle Dante sees the adulterers swept hither and thither in the darkness of a hellish storm. An outline of this scene appeared in Version B of Cycle I of the *Miraj* ; and, as has just been seen, in the legends describing the division of the Moslem hell into seven stages or tiers the second is also referred to as the region of winds. In addition, there is a tale attributed to Mahomet that says : " In hell there blows a dark storm of wind, with which God torments such of the wicked as He chooses."[1] This wind is the same dread gale that God sent to punish the city of Ad for its wickedness, a scene that is repeatedly described in terms similar to those used by Dante, in the commentaries on the Koran and the collections of legends of the Prophet.[2]

A black cloud or storm, a hurricane wraps all in gloom except for the sinister light from what appears to be a flame in its midst ; a dry and desolating wind roars as it whirls around ; the ground trembles under the perpetual blast, which sweeps all before it ; with each violent gust men and women are swept along, thrown up into the air and dashed to the ground ; this hurricane is the dread instrument of Divine vengeance, the merciless torture of sinners who gave themselves up to the delights of the senses, to gluttony and lust ; tossed hither and thither by the gale and smitten by the wind, they cry out in bitter anguish.

Compare this scene with that described by Dante : A hellish storm, a wind of utter darkness but for streaks of purple light[3] blows furiously without ceasing ; roaring like the sea in tempest, it sweeps the lustful along in its whirl, turning them around, vexing and bruising them ; it carries them now in this, then in that direction, it throws them up and casts them down ; and, as it wounds them, it wrings cries of pain and anguish from the sufferers.

[1] Cf. *Kharida*, 182.

[2] See index of KASIMIRSKI's translation, s.v. *Ad*. Cf. KHAZIN, *Tafsir*, II, 104, and *Qisas*, 40.

[3] *Inf.* V, 89 : " l'aer perso." In *Convivio*, IV, 20, Dante himself gives a definition : " Perso è un colore misto di purpureo e di nero, ma vince il nero e da lui si denomina."

As may be seen, the similarity of the descriptions extends to the very wording of the texts.[1]

3. Let us now descend to the sixth circle of the inferno. Version B of Cycle 2 of the legend of the *Miraj* told how Mahomet beheld a sea of fire, on the shores of which stood cities formed of countless fiery sepulchres, in which the wicked lie tortured. The literal resemblance of this scene to the city of Dis in the sixth circle, described in Cantos IX, X and XI of the Inferno, was remarked upon above.[2] It may be added here that the punishment of sinners in coffins of fire is mentioned in several other Moslem legends describing the tortures of hell.[3]

4. The torture of the Sodomites in the third ring of the seventh circle also has its parallel in the Moslem hell. Dante depicts them as unceasingly treading the circle they inhabit, under a rain of fire that sears their naked bodies.[4] One of the sinners is his former master, Brunetto Latini, and, as he walks awhile with him, he expresses his astonishment and grief at finding him there, for he remembers the wise teaching he received from him on earth.

A double series of Moslem traditions may be quoted as prototypes of this episode. In the first place, the Moslem hell contains a torture very similar to that of the rain of fire :

A rain of boiling water or molten brass will fall unceasingly upon their heads and, penetrating their skin, will eat away their entrails and emanate from between their feet, when the body will return to its former state.[5]

More specifically, though indeed referring to the fate of the wicked at the final judgment, it is stated in the Koran (LV, 35) : " Upon you shall God send down flames of fire and molten brass."

The second group of tales refers to the punishment of the wise men whose conduct was at variance with their teaching.

---

[1] Compare *Qisas*, 40, lines 18 and 21 ; 24 ; 22 ; 27 and **33 ; 32, 34 and 37** with *Inf.* V, 31, 49 and 51 ; 89 ; 51 ; 86 ; 32, 33, 43 and **49** respectively.
[2] Cf. *supra*, p. 16.   [3] *Corra*, 3 and 20. *Kanz*, VIII, :88, No. 3,288.
[4] *Inf.* XIV, XV and XVI.
[5] *Kanz*, VII, [246, No. 2,800. IBN MAKHLUF, II, 41. Cf. KHAZIN, *Tafsir*, IV, 348–9.

" Cast into hell, they will be made to go round and round
without rest, even as a donkey in turning the wheel of a well
or a mill. Some of their disciples, on beholding them from
heaven, will descend and accompany them in their ceaseless
rotation, asking, ' What has brought you hither, seeing
that it was but from you we learnt ? ' In other versions
the disciple exclaims : ' Master ! What has befallen thee ?
Didst not thou haply teach us what to do and what not
to do ? ' In other versions again they ask, ' How came
ye to enter hell seeing that we gained heaven but by your
teaching ? ' To which the sages make reply : ' We bade
you do what was right, but we ourselves did otherwise.' "[1]

As will be seen, the similarity between the two texts, the
Moslem and the Christian, extends down to the very form
of expression.

5. The first valley of Malebolge, Dante's eighth circle,
contains the panders, who, as they hurry naked through
the valley, are scourged by fiends.[2] This is the very punishment allotted by Moslem tradition to those that neglected
the rite of prayer or falsely accused people of adultery—
angels or fiends, the tradition runs, shall whip both classes
of sinners, smiting them cruelly on the face, ribs and
shoulders.[3]

As for the flatterers, whom immersed in filth Dante
places in the second chasm,[4] their punishment is equivalent
to that of the drunkards in the Moslem hell, whose thirst

---

[1] *Kanz*, V, 213, No. 4,383 ; 214, No. 4,415 ; 217, Nos. 4,479 and 4,484.
IBN MAKHLUF, II, 37. *Tadhkira*, 74.

[2] Before leaving the circle in which Dante finds Brunetto, Virgil explains
to him the hydrography of hell, the four rivers of which have their common
source in the island of Crete. On Mt. Ida stands a monument, in the form
of a statue of a Great Old Man, composed of gold, silver, brass, iron and
clay ; in every part, except the gold, there is a fissure from which drop
tears, which flowing downhill form the rivers (*Inf.* XIV,94 *et seq.*). Whatever
be the esoteric meaning of Dante's allegory and however evident the
analogy with the statue of Daniel is, it is of interest to note that tales
dealing with the common source of the four rivers of paradise were very
popular in Islam. According to these tales, the Nile, Euphrates, Jihun
and Sihun spring from a monument in the form of a dome, made of gold
or emerald, standing on a mountain and having four mouths or fissures.
The obscure origin of the sources of the Nile gave rise to similar legends,
which describe its waters as flowing from the mouths of eighty-five statues
of bronze, or else from a mountain on which stands the figure of an old
man, the mythical Khidr. Cf. *Badai az-Zohur*, 21–23.

[3] *Corra*, 8 ; *Al-Laali*, II, 195. Cf. *Inf.* XVIII, 35.   [4] *Inf.* XVIII, 113.

is quenched with the loathsome lees of hell, the sweat, the pus and the blood flowing from the wounds of the other sinners.[1]

The third fosse of Malebolge is set with pits of fire, in which the Simonists are roasted head downwards. A parallel to this scene" is the Moslem torture of murderers, who are likewise held in pits of fire.[2]

6. On reaching the fourth pit, Dante meets with a procession of sinners whose necks he describes as being strangely twisted, for their faces are turned towards their backs. More than once he seeks to describe the strange sight, by saying that the tears of these souls fell down their backs, that their shoulders were turned into their breasts, that they walked backwards, and so forth.[3]

This curious torture, the originality of which has often been commented on, would seem to be but an adaptation of a passage in the Koran, which reads :—

" Ye that have received the Scriptures, beware of disbelieving in what God has sent down from heaven in witness of your holy books, *lest We should wipe out your features and turn your faces in the opposite direction.*" [4]

The warning that God is thus supposed to address to the Jews who denied the truth of the Koran, was variously interpreted both in a literal and figurative sense. The ninth century commentator Tabari has recorded the different meanings.[5] But the literal interpretation prevailed, supported as it was by a belief in Islam, based on Talmudic legend, according to which some of the demons appear to man in the same distorted shape.[6] Moslem tales of the Day of Judgment also depict certain sinners as brought to life again in this condition—with their faces turned towards their backs they read their sentence, which is fixed to their shoulders.[7] The very vividness of the picture stamped it on the Moslem

---

[1] *Al-Laali*, II, 195. *Tadhkira*, 77. *Corra*, 17. IBN MAKHLUF, II, 83. Cf. *Koran*, XXXVIII, 57 ; LXXVIII, 25.
[2] *Inf.* XIX. *Corra*, 72. Their peculiar posture is also mentioned in some descriptions of hell attributed to Ibn Abbas. Cf. MS 234, Gayangos Coll., fol. 105. [3] *Inf.* XX, 11, 23, 37, 39. [4] *Koran*, IV, 50.
[5] *Tafsir*, V, 77. [6] Cf. *Qazwini*, I, 373. [7] *Tadhkira*, 47, line 10.

mind with the result that it was used both in the popular sermons addressed to the Moriscoes and in the works of thinkers such as Algazel.[1]

7. The torture of hypocrites in the sixth pit of Malebolge also appears to be an adaptation from two scenes, common in Moslem tradition, blended into one. Dante depicts them as walking slowly along, groaning under the weight of leaden mantles, the external gilt of which dazzles the eye.[2] In the Arabian tales of the Day of Judgment misers are punished by being obliged to walk on and on without rest under the weight of the hoards they had gathered on earth [3]; and both the Koran and the traditions of Islam represent sinners, particularly carnal sinners, as being clothed in tunics or mantles of metal glowing with heat.[4]

While conversing with two of the hypocrites the poet is horror-stricken at the sight of the awful suffering of Caiaphas, who lies impaled upon the ground and writhes in agony as he is trampled under foot by the other hypocrites.[5]

This is another instance of the artistic blending of scenes characteristic of the Moslem legends on the after-life. A *hadith*, attributed to Ibn Abbas, describing in pathetic language the tortures of the final judgment and hell, contains the following passage :—

" How many youths of tender age and fresh in features will be crying out in hell : ' Alas, my unhappy childhood, my luckless youth ! Woe is me that my strength should have failed me and my young body been so wretched in its weakness ! ' For they will lie in bitter affliction fixed to the ground with stakes." [6]

The complementary scene is related in the following apocryphal tradition :—

" He who in this life treats his neighbour with contempt will be brought to life again on the Day of Judgment in the figure of an ant and all mankind will trample him under foot. Thereafter he shall enter hell." [7]

---

[1] *Colección de textos aljamiados* by Gil, Ribera and Sánchez (Saragossa, 1888), pp. 69 and 71. ALGAZEL, *Ihia*, IV, 21–22 ; *Ithaf*, VIII, 561.
[2] *Inf.* XXIII, 58–72. [3] *Kanz*, III, 251, No. 4, 013. [4] *Koran*, XIV, 51. Cf. TABARI, *Tafsir*, XIII, 167–8 ; *Corra*, 26. [5] *Inf.* XXIII, 110–126.
[6] MS 234 Gayangos Coll., fol. 100. [7] *Al-Laali*, II, 195.

8. The seventh pit of Malebolge is the place where thieves expiate their crimes. Dante sees them rushing hither and thither in a vain attempt to escape the hydras that, after seizing and twining themselves around their victims, sting them in the neck, face and navel with fangs so poisonous that their flesh is consumed and reduced to ashes, only to reappear for the torture to be renewed.[1] Dante enhances his description with features borrowed from the classical poets, more particularly Ovid. If these are eliminated, the picture will be found to agree very fairly with several scenes of torture that abound in Moslem tales of the final judgment and hell, especially the tales of the *Corra*, the collection that has so often been drawn upon for the purposes of this work.[2] If allowance is made for Oriental hyperbole, a comparison with the following will at once suggest a likeness between the two :—

" On the Day of Judgment the miser who had refused to give the ritual alms will find himself face to face with a serpent of great size, with eyes of fire and teeth of iron, which will pursue him saying, ' Give me thy miserly right hand that I may tear it from thee.' The miser will attempt to flee, whereupon the serpent will say, ' Where dost thou hope to find refuge from thy sins ? ' and, coiling itself around him, will bite off his right hand and devour it, when the hand will at once grow again. Thereupon the serpent will devour his left hand, which likewise will reappear. At each bite of the serpent, the miser will utter such a shriek of pain that all around him will be stricken with horror."—" In the valley of hell called Lamlam there are snakes, as thick as a camel's neck and as long as a month's journey, that sting all who neglected the rite of prayer ; the poison they inject burns the flesh throughout seventy years."—" There is another valley in hell called the Sad Valley, in which are scorpions like black mules, each provided with seventy fangs swollen with poison to sting the sinners who were remiss in prayer ; the virus they deposit burns in the wounds a thousand years, when the flesh of their victims rots away."—" The drunkard will be taken to a den full of scorpions as large as camels, which will seize hold of him by the feet."—

[1] *Inf.* XXIV–XXV.
[2] *Corra*, II, 25, 37, 65. *Kanz*, VII, 280, No. 3,087.

" Usurers will lie in hell with their bellies open and swarming with snakes and scorpions."—" Adulterers will be stung by serpents in the very parts of their bodies on which they bestowed their kisses."—" The infidel will be seized by the hydra of the naked head, which will devour his flesh from head to foot, but the flesh will grow again over his bones so that the hydra may again devour it from foot to head."

9. As Dante sets foot in the ninth pit of Malebolge he meets with a sight so awful that he is at a loss for words to describe it.[1] A crowd of sinners guilty of having sown discord among men are being driven round the valley by demons who with sharp swords cut them in twain ; but as the victim moves on the wounds heal, only to be opened afresh on his return. Three scenes of torture particularly attract the poet's attention. Mahomet, with his entrails trailing at his feet, is seen following his cousin Ali, who appears cut open from chin to belly. Mosca degli Uberti, whose hands have been cut off, raises his bleeding stumps as he makes himself known to Dante. Finally, Bertrand de Born appears decapitated, holding his head by the hair in his hand like a lantern.

The outlines of this scene in general and of the three episodes already existed in Moslem legend.

" He who takes his own life "—says a tradition[2]—" shall with the same knife be done to death throughout eternity by the angels in the valleys of hell. . . . At each stab a jet of blood blacker than pitch will spout from the wound, which will heal again at once for the torture to be repeated without end."

The picture that Dante draws of Mahomet and Ali occurs in many Moslem tales of hell; one of which depicts two groups of sinners as follows :—

" Cursing and wailing they tread the space between two circles of hell ; the ones drag their entrails behind them as they go ; the others are spewing blood and matter."

Variants of these legends depict the sinners treading, like an ass that turns the wheel of a grindstone, round and round

---

[1] *Inf.* XXVIII.   [2] *Corra*, 71.

the valley in hell, with their entrails, torn out by the fiends, trailing behind them. The very same torture, moreover, was allotted to two men notorious throughout Islam for their cruelty, the fifth Ommeyad Caliph Abd al-Malik Ibn Marwan and his bloodthirsty general Al-Hajjaj, whom tradition. represented either as walking in hell with their bowels dangling between their legs, or as being assassinated seventy times for each murder they had committed on earth.[1]

The bloody fate of Mosca degli Uberti also has its Moslem counterpart in the torture of thieves and the avaricious :—

" He who bereaves another of a part of his wealth shall on the Day of Judgment appear before God bereft of both hands."[2]

Lastly, the horrifying apparition of Bertrand de Born would seem to be but an artistic adaptation of a scene in a Moslem description of the final judgment :—

" On that day the victim of murder will appear before God carrying in one hand his head hanging by the hair, with the blood pouring from the veins of his neck and, dragging his murderer with him, will cry out ' Oh, Lord ! Ask Thou of this man why he killed me.' "[3]

10. In the last chasm of Malebolge deceivers and falsifiers of all kinds are seen undergoing various forms of torture ; some lie piled one upon the other or drag themselves along on all fours ; itching all over, they scratch the scab from off their sores or tear one another with their teeth ; others lie with swollen bellies, suffering unquenchable thirst.[4]

In Version B of Cycle 2 of the *Miraj* three similar scenes were described, showing the tortures suffered by slanderers, usurers and drunkards. Many other tales in Islam also depict the torture of sinners in terms greatly resembling those of Dante. Thus it is said, " The itch will seize upon the sinners, who will scratch themselves to the bone ; " or, " They will suffer such pangs of hunger that they will devour their own bodies " ; or, again, " A maddening thirst will consume

---

[1] *Kanz*, VIII, 188, No. 3,288 ; V, 214, No. 4,415 ; SUYUTI, *Sudur*, 30 and 121. [2] *Kanz*, V, 327, No. 5,717. *Corra*, 65. [3] *Kanz*, VII, 287, No. 3,201. Cf. also Nos. 3,218, 3,220, 3,221, 3,223, 3,224.
[4] *Inf.* XXIX–XXX.

them and they will cry out, ' Oh, but for a sip of water to slake my thirst ! ' "[1]

V

THE MOSLEM HELL IN THE DIVINE COMEDY
(CONCLUSION)

1. To reach the place allotted to the traitors, Dante and his guide are obliged to cross a deep chasm inhabited by sinners of giant stature who have been guilty of rebellion against God. The chief of these are Nimrod and the giants of classical mythology, Ephialtes, Briareus, and Antaeus. The last-named takes the poets in his hand and gently deposits them in the abyss of the lowest circle.[2] Dante delights in describing the giants in terms of hyperbole. The head of Nimrod appears to him as large as the Cone of St. Peter's, or rather more than five fathoms in height and width ; his other members are in proportion, so that his total stature, according to the commentators, would be forty-three fathoms.

The Christian works prior to the Divine Comedy provide no satisfactory explanation of this scene. True, the personality of the giants is well defined in the Bible and in mythology, but none of these sources warrants their being placed in hell. The Moslem sources, however, at once furnish a key to the riddle. The eschatological books of Islam devote whole chapters to the tales of the Prophet describing the enormous stature of the infidels who, like Dante's giants, occupy the lowest circle of hell and whose proportions are measured, hyperbolically indeed, but with a mathematical exactitude similar to that displayed by Dante.[3]

---

[1] *Kanz*, VII, 247, No. 2,826.   MS 172 Gayangos Coll., fol. 34.   *Corra*, 12.
[2] *Inf.* XXXI.
[3] *Tadhkira*, 75.   Cf. *Kanz*, VII, 212, No. 2,301 ; 237, Nos. 2,668, 2,671 and 2,801–2,808.   Moreover, the existence of giants in hell was traditional in Islam, for the dwellers in Ad, who were condemned to hell by the Koran, were of gigantic stature.   In *Qisas*, 39, the head of one of these giants is compared to the dome of a great building.   The coincidence in stature of the giants of Dante and those of Islam is also curious.   According to the *Tadhkira* (p. 75, line 4 inf.) the latter measure 42 fathoms ; and Landino, basing his calculations on Dante's text, says of Nimrod : " Adunque questo gigante sarebbe braccia quarantatre o più " (p. 30 of his prologue to the Divine Comedy).

" On the Day of Judgment the infidels will appear with black faces, their stature increased to a height of sixty fathoms and their heads crowned with a diadem of fire. . . ."
" The bodies of the sinners are of the size of mountains. . . . Each of their teeth is as large as a man and the rest of their body is in proportion. Their thighs are as big as Mount Albaida (three miles distant from Mecca). The space they fill when seated is as the distance from .Mecca to Medina. Their bodies are so massive that a roaring noise, as of wild beasts, is heard between the skin and the flesh. Their total stature is forty-two fathoms."

The object of giving the victim this monstrous size is simply to provide more material for torture. Finally, the hypothesis of the Moslem origin of Dante's picture is supported by two facts—the one, that Iblis lies in the lowest circle chained in the same curious manner as the giant Ephialtes, with one hand in front and the other behind[1] ; the other, that Islam relegates Nimrod and Pharaoh, as the prototypes of Satanic pride, to the same region in which Iblis suffers punishment for his rebellion.[2] Dante accuses Nimrod of the same sin of rebellion and places him at the entrance to the lowest circle, that of Lucifer.

2. One and the same torture, that of cold, is suffered by all sinners in this lowest circle. The lake Cocytus, which fills the entire space, is kept frozen by the icy blast from the wings of Lucifer ; and in its congealed waters traitors of four different classes are shown in diverse attitudes.[3]

It need hardly be remarked that Biblical eschatology makes no mention of any torture of cold in hell. The Moslem doctrine, however, places this torture on the same footing as torture by fire.[4] True, the Koran alludes to it but vaguely in saying that the blessed shall suffer neither from the heat of the sun nor the cold of *zamharir*.[5] But, as comment on this passage, there arose a number of traditions, attributed to Mahomet, in which intense cold is acknowledged as a torture of hell and, indeed, a torture more painful

[1] Cf. *supra*, pp. 89–90. [2] *Ihia*, III, 240, and *Futuhat*, I, 393. Cf. *Al-Laali*, II, 196. [3] *Inf.* XXXII–XXXIV. [4] *Futuhat*, I, 387. [5] *Koran*, LXXVI, 13.

even than that of heat.[1] Its introduction into the Moslem
scheme of hell was due, not merely to a desire for symmetry
and antithesis in torture, but rather to the assimilation by
Islam of a Zoroastrian belief. The theologian Jahiz, writing
in the ninth century, says that this torture is peculiar to
the Persian hell of Zoroaster, by whose religion fire is held
sacred.[2] If, therefore, it is accepted unhesitatingly by Tabari
a century later, it is probable that it had in the meantime
been introduced by Zoroastrians converted to Islam. More
interesting, however, than the question of the remote origin,
is the fact that some of the traditions interpret the Koranic
zamharir as a frozen lake.[3] " What is the *zamharir* of hell ? "
they asked Mahomet, and he replied, " It is a pit into which
the unbeliever is cast, in which his members are rent asunder
by intense cold." If it is borne in mind that the word had
the scientific meaning of " glacial wind " or " air of the
atmospheric region intermediate between the earth and the
sphere of the moon "[4] it will be seen that, as in Dante's hell,
the sinners of Islam suffered the double torment of exposure
to an icy blast of wind and contact with frozen water.

The picturesque description of the various attitudes in
which Dante depicts the different groups of traitors is a
feature that constantly recurs in the pictures of the Moslem
hell, though not indeed in connection with the torture of
cold. Thus, a tradition attributed to Ibn Abbas says that
" some are punished standing, some lying on their sides ;
others lie stretched out on their backs, or stand leaning on
their elbows ; while many are to be seen hanging head
downwards."[5] A very popular legend of hell adds :

" The fire will be well aware of the guilt of the sinners
and the suffering they deserve. . . . Thus, in some it will

---

[1] Cf. Gayangos Coll. MS 172, fol. 34, and MS 234, fol. 105.
[2] JAHIZ, *Hayawan* (*Book of Animals*), V, 24. A summary of the life
and writings of Jahiz is given in the author's *Abenmasarra*, Appendix I,
133–137. According to OSCAR COMETTANT, *Civilisations inconnues* (quoted
in LAROUSSE, *Dict. Univ.* s.v. *Purgatoire*), torture by cold also occurs in
the Buddhist hell.
[3] *Tadhkira*, 69.   [4] Cf. *Qazwini*, I, 93.
[5] MS 234 Gayangos Coll., fol. 105. Cf. *Inf.* XXXII, 37 ; XXXIII, 92 ;
XXXIV, 13.

reach the ankles ; in others, the knees, the waist, the chest, and even the neck."[1]

One Moslem scene of torture is even identical with the most violent of the postures in which Dante places the sinners in the frozen lake of Cocytus :

" The fiends will seize the sinner from behind, will break his ribs in twain and, bending back his belly, with his hair will tie his feet."[2]

3. At the bottom of the lowest pit of hell, that is to say, at the centre of the earth, Dante places Lucifer, the king of the realm of pain, set in the ice from the lower part of his chest downwards. Of gigantic stature and monstrously misshapen, he bears on the trunk three faces, underneath which are enormous wings shaped like the wings of a bat ; the flapping of these wings produces the icy wind that blows in this region. With his three mouths he devours three traitors. Dante in terror manages to slip between the hairy shoulders of Lucifer and the ice and reach the southern hemisphere through a long subterranean passage. As he escapes, he beholds the enormous legs of Lucifer hanging unsupported in the air ; and Virgil explains how the fallen angel, on being cast out of heaven, with his head had struck the surface of the southern hemisphere and, penetrating to the centre of the earth, had remained fixed there to that day.[3]

The originality of this picture has always been greatly admired. Graf, bringing all his erudition and insight to bear on the subject, detects three elements in the demonology of Dante—theological elements, based on Thomistic doctrine ; popular elements, in harmony with opinion current at his time ; and elements peculiar to Dante, such as he may have acquired in exile, particularly at the University of Bologna.[4] Among the last-named he includes this description, saying, " Questa mirabile immaginazione è, per quanto io so, tutta propria di Dante."

---

[1] *Tadhkira*, 82 ; and *Kanz*, VII, 246, No. 2,810. Cf. *Inf.* XXXII, 34 ; XXXIV, 11. [2] MS 172 Gayangos Coll., fol. 34. Cf. *Inf.* XXXIV, 15
[3] *Inf.* XXXIV, 28–139.
[4] GRAF, *Demonologia di Dante*, in *Miti*, II, 79–112.

4. However much the power and beauty of Dante's description are to be admired, prototypes of it are not lacking in the theological literature of Islam.

The position of Lucifer, fixed in the lowest pit of hell, has been shown to be common to many Moslem descriptions. Nor, given the principle of the division of sinners, could he be conceived in any other place ; for the Iblis of Islam being, like Lucifer, the father of all rebellion against God, must necessarily suffer the severest torture.

But the similarity of the two conceptions extends even to the very nature of the torture. Ibn Arabi definitely states that Iblis is exposed to the torture of ice, and this assertion he bases on the fact that Iblis, like all demons, is a genie and thus was created from fire ; his punishment, he infers, must therefore by contrast consist in exposure to the severest cold, or *zamharir*.[1] Contemporaries of Ibn Arabi had on similar grounds accounted for the immunity of the fiends from the effect of the fire of hell. Thus, Abu-l-Hasan al-Ashari argues that the demons, being fallen angels, were created from light and, accordingly, are insensible to torture by fire.[2]

As to Lucifer's monstrous appearance, the multiplicity of faces is the very stigma that for their double-dealing is imposed upon traitors in the Moslem hell ; and Lucifer, it must be remembered, as a rebel against God, is the arch-traitor and, as such, is confined by Dante in the traitors' pit. An early apocryphal tradition says : " He who in this world has a double face and a double tongue, to him shall God give two faces and two tongues in hell." [3] Other early legends depict the fiends also as two-headed monsters.[4] Even hell itself, considered not as the place, but as the embodiment of tortures, is vividly represented as a hydra-headed monster in Moslem legends of the Day of Judgment ; with its many mouths this monster devours sinners of different categories,

---

[1] *Futuhat*, I, 391.   [2] MS 64 Gayangos Coll., fols. 1–27.   [3] *Al-Laali*, II, 196.
[4] *Qazwini*, I, 373, gives a *hadith*, telling of the dealings of Solomon with genii and demons, that is of interest for the study of the demonology of Islam, which shows marked resemblance to that of Dante, particularly in the matter of the names. On this point cf. DAMIRI, I, 237 ; KHAZIN, *Tafsir*, III, 201 ; and DHARIR, 188.

and some versions even fix the number at three.[1] Finally, the many popular tales of fantastic voyages frequently describe similar monsters—such as the beast named Malikan, which has two wings and numerous heads and faces and devours the animals of the sea that land upon its island ; or Dahlan, which is depicted as a fiend that rides upon a bird like an ostrich and seizes on all men that set foot upon its isle in the Indian Ocean.[2]

There remains to be considered Dante's description of the fall of Lucifer from heaven. The only allusion in pre-Dante Christian literature to the fall of Lucifer is the brief passage in the Gospel according to St. Luke (X, 18) : " And he said unto them, I beheld Satan as lightning fall from heaven." The Koran, on the other hand, describes the rebellion and expulsion from heaven of Iblis in more than seven passages [3]; and, though no details of his descent are given, these were filled in by the traditions depicting the punishment God inflicted on Adam and Eve, the serpent and Iblis.[4] In addition, there exists a cycle of cosmogonical legends, which serve to complete the myth of the fall of Iblis.

Mention has been made in a former chapter of tales describing the division of the earth into seven floors or stages, which were identified with the seven mansions of hell.[5] These tales were intended to explain the cosmogonical legends above referred to ; and all are in the end but comment on a passage of the Koran to the effect that heaven and earth were created as one sole mass and only later were separated and each divided into several strata.[6]

" Immediately after their division," the legend says, " God sent an angel from His throne, who, falling upon the earth, penetrated the seven strata thereof and there remained, sustaining them upon his shoulders, with one hand stretched

[1] *Kanz*, II, 109, No. 2,652 ; *Tadhkira*, 70 ; Gayangos Coll., MS 64, fol. 24, and MS 234, fol. 94. [2] *Kharida*, 87 and 95.
[3] Cf. Kasimirski's translation, *Table des matières*, s.v. *Eblis*.
[4] *Qisas*, 26, ch. 7. [5] *Supra*, p. 88. [6] *Koran*, XXI, 31.

towards the East and the other towards the West, his feet lacking all support." [1]

The legend does not indeed identify Iblis with this angel, but the fact that he was sent from the very throne of God and *fell* to earth would seem to favour the suggestion.

The two myths, blended together, may well have served as a model for Dante's picture. That there exist grounds for this hypothesis may be shown by a review of the different features of resemblance furnished by the Moslem descriptions Iblis is an angel cast out of heaven for rebellion against God, who, in falling to the earth, penetrates its several strata and is embedded in the ice, with his feet unsupported ; although of gigantic stature—he supports the different strata—he is yet an angel and thus provided with wings ; but sin has changed his beauty into hideousness and thus he appears as a many-headed beast that devours men, as a monster that is half man, half ostrich. [2]

VI

THE MOSLEM PURGATORY IN THE DIVINE COMEDY

1. Through the dark and winding passage leading from the centre of the earth to the surface of the southern hemisphere Dante and his guide pass to reach the shores of

---

[1] *Qisas*, 3, line 10 inf. The immediate purpose of this legend was indeed to explain the stability of the earth in the midst of space, but the adaptation to other purposes of a picturesque description is a common feature in literary imitation.

[2] So great is the wealth of picturesque detail in the descriptions of the Moslem hell that minor features of resemblance to Dante have been omitted as being open to doubt. Thus the Koran repeatedly mentions a tree in hell, called *Az-Zaqum* (cf. KASIMIRSKI, s.v.), the fruit of which is bitter and repugnant like the heads of demons (cf. KHAZIN, *Tafsir*, IV, 18 and 116 ; *Tacholarus*, VIII, 326 ; *Ihia*, IV, 381 ; *Ithaf*, X, 515). In itself this tree bears little resemblance to the human trees into which Dante converts the suicides (*Inf.* XIII), which cry out when their branches are torn and which Dante admits he copied from Virgil's episode of Polydorus (Aeneid, III). In Arabian tales of miraculous journeys to hell, however, there are frequent descriptions of trees the branches of which resemble human heads and cry out on being torn (cf. CHAUVIN, *Bibliographie*, VII, 33 and 56 ; *Qisas*, 222 ; also René Basset's " Histoire du Roi Sabour et de son fils Abou'n Nazhar " in *Rev. des trad. popul.*, XI, 273, 278, and 280).

purgatory, which the poet conceives as a lofty mountain shaped like a truncated cone and set in the midst of a boundless ocean. Seven terraces divide this mountain into as many mansions of expiation, one for each capital sin ; and at the foot two mansions form the antechamber of purgatory, where the disobedient and negligent spirits await admittance. On the table-land at the top of the mountain and bordering on the sphere of the ether is the earthly paradise. The mount of purgatory may thus be variously considered as consisting of seven, nine or ten mansions, which are connected by a steep and arduous path. The spirits in purgatory are those guilty merely of venial sin, or of deadly sins for which full penitence has not been done ; these they expiate in the successive mansions under the guard of angels who guide them in their ascent—a task that is rendered easier by the prayers of their friends on earth. Dante, too, though only in a mystical sense, is subjected to this progressive purification, the guardian angel marking his brow seven times with the letter P, the symbol of sin, which is washed away in each of the seven terraces. As they rise, the ascent becomes easier and, finally, the poets reach the summit, or earthly paradise, where, by bathing in the waters of two rivers, Dante cleanses his soul and is prepared for his entry into heaven.

2. Nothing in Christian eschatology seems to warrant so detailed and precise a description of the site of purgatory. Not until a century after the appearance of the Divine Comedy did the existence of purgatory as a special condition of the soul, engaged in temporary expiation of sin, become a dogma of the Christian faith.[1] The site was never mentioned, either at the Council of Florence held in that century, or at the Council of Trent, or on any other occasion, for, as a matter of fact, the Church has always endeavoured to avoid fantastic descriptions of the realms beyond the grave, and particularly of purgatory.[2] Not that purgatory was an

---

[1] Cf. TIXERONT, II, 200, 220, 350, 433 and III, 270, 428.
[2] Cf. PERRONE, II, 122 : " Omnia igitur quae spectant ad locum, durationem, poenarum qualitatem, ad catholican fidem minime pertinent, seu definita ab Ecclesia non sunt."

innovation of the fifteenth century; indeed, the belief in it was deeply rooted in scholastic and patristic tradition, as well as in revealed doctrine. But the dogma never went beyond the admission of its existence as a state of the soul, and ecclesiastical tradition, especially of Western Christianity, was ever discreetly silent upon its site and descriptive detail. Prior to Dante, only a few writers, such as Hugh of St. Victor, St. Thomas and Ricardo de Media Villa, had made timid attempts to portray purgatory, and their conceptions differed greatly from Dante's picture. Landino, accordingly, concludes his review of all possible models, classical or Christian, with the remark : " Ma Dante, huomo di mirabile ingegno e di mirabile inventione, trovo nuovo sito, il quale niente e contra sustantialmente all opinione christiana." [1]

3. As has been seen, Islam, the successor of Eastern Christianity, admitted purgatory as a state of temporary penitence to be undergone by all sinners that die in the true faith. [2] To determine its locality and the nature of the trials to which the souls are subjected, it is necessary to have recourse to the plethora of Islamic legends on the after-life. The dogmas of the resurrection of the body and the final judgment caused a certain confusion in the minds of the theologians who were called upon to decide the question of the penalties and rewards awaiting the soul during the time between death and the end of the world. Are the souls alone, or the bodies also, subject to sanction ? Can the dead body feel physical pain and pleasure if it is not resuscitated in the tomb ? Again, what useful purpose can be served by final judgment, if sentence and sanction are to begin at death ? As it is impossible to make a critical selection of the legends or to distinguish between tales dealing with expiation immediately after death and those describing purgation following upon final judgment, a few descriptive features taken indiscriminately from the whole group of legends will be compared with the corresponding scenes in Dante.

[1] LANDINO, prologue to *Purg.*, fol. 194 v°; also to *Inf.* III, fols. 25 v° and 26. [2] Cf. *supra*, p. 80.

To begin with, the purgatory of Islam is represented as being near to, but separate from hell; and, whereas the latter is placed in the interior of the earth, the former is described as lying outside and above the earth. This is clearly borne out by a tradition which, in addition to this topographical feature, gives an outline of the expiation of sin[1]:

" There are two hells, or gehennas; the one the *internal*, the other the *external* fire. The former none shall ever leave, but the latter is the place in which God chastises the faithful for their sins. Then, when at His will the angels, prophets and saints intercede on their behalf, the blackened bodies of the sinners will be withdrawn from the fire and cast upon the banks of a river in paradise, called the River of Life. When sprinkled with the waters of the river they will come to life again like seeds sprouting in dung. Their bodies made whole, they will be bidden to enter the river and to wash themselves and drink of its waters, so that later they may be called upon to enter heaven. In heaven they will be known as the ' Men of Hell ' until such time as God shall consent to remove this stigma, when the brow of each will bear the legend ' Freedman of God.' "

Thus, the final episode of Dante's purgatory, in which, when the poet enters the garden of the terrestrial paradise, the allegorical mark of sin is wiped from off his brow and he is washed in the rivers of Lethe and Eunoe, is given in this Moslem legend with typical details similar in their turn to those already noted in versions of the *Miraj*.[2]

A tale of another cycle describes purgatory essentially as Dante conceived it, as " a mount rising between hell and heaven on which the sinners are imprisoned."[3] True, purgatory here is either confused or blended with the limbo, for the region is named *Al Aaraf*, and is said to be inhabited by Moslem sinners whose sins are counterbalanced by their virtues. But, inasmuch as these sinners, after being purified of their sins in the River of Life, are capable of entering

---

[1] *Kanz*, VII, 242, Nos. 2,725 and 2,730; VII, 218, No. 2,376.
[2] Cf. *supra*, p. 9.
[3] *Ithaf*, VIII, 566. The *hadith*, attributed to Ibn Abbas, cannot date later than the tenth century.

heaven, the characteristics of purgatory may be said to prevail.

So far, then, the purgatory of Islam stands revealed as a hill or mount definitely situated outside and above hell and rising between it and heaven. The description is carried further in the legends, adopted by Islam from Persian eschatology, that deal with the bridge or path that has to be traversed by the souls before they can enter heaven.[1] The Persian Chinvat, or luminous bridge, which stretches over the abyss of hell between heaven and a mountain rising from the centre of the earth, assumed in Islam the various forms of a path or road ; a lofty structure, vaulted bridge or viaduct ; a natural bridge or slippery passage ; or, again, a slope or ramp difficult of ascent. With the exception of the image of the bridge, these features reappear in the Purgatorio ; and even Dante's mount is in reality but an enormous bridge, providing as it does the only means of passing from earth to heaven and rising above hell, or, rather, like the *sirat* or path described in the Moslem books of eschatology, above the back of the abyss of hell.[2]

4. Ibn Arabi, commenting in his *Futuhat* upon the words attributed to Mahomet on this point says, " the souls that are not cast into hell shall be detained in the *sirat*, where strict account shall be taken of their sins, for which they will be punished." He adds that " the *sirat* will be over the back of hell and form the sole means of entering paradise."[3] In another passage he completes the picture saying, as if indeed he were speaking of Dante's conception, " the *sirat* will rise in a straight line from the earth to the surface of the stellar sphere and end in a meadow lying outside the walls of the heavenly paradise ; the souls will first enter this meadow, called the paradise of delight."[4]

---

[1] For a collection of these legends cf. *Tadhkira*, 58 *et seq.* ; IBN MAKHLUF, II, 25 ; *Ithaf*, X, 481 *et seq.*

[2] It should be borne in mind that Dante's mount of purgatory rises above the southern hemisphere, which is entirely covered with water, and reaches to the ether, the last sphere of the sublunar world, bordering on heaven ;' its base stands on the back of hell, the entrance to which is in the northern hemisphere, near Jerusalem.

[3] *Futuhat*, I, 411. Cf. *Ithaf*, X, 482. [4] *Futuhat*, III, 573.

In other legends two *sirats* appear, and the souls that have succeeded in passing the first without falling into hell are subjected to the trial of the second. The latter is often represented as a high structure (*cantara*) between hell and heaven, which serves as a place of temporary expiation of sin : " in it the souls will be detained until they mutually restore the debts that' by their guilt they contracted on earth, and they are purified " ; whereupon angels will receive them with loving words of welcome and guide them on the path that leads to eternal bliss.[1]

The resemblance of the purgatory of Islam to that of Dante is most striking, however, in the form given to it by the mystics, who multiply the primitive *cantara*, or place of expiation, into a number of chambers, enclosures or abodes. As usual, it is Ibn Arabi who paints the picture with the greatest detail.[2] In the legend of the Prophet that he has handed down to us, there are fifty stations, distributed into four main groups. Of these the last is the most interesting to us, since, like Dante's purgatory, it consists of seven enclosures. called bridges or slippery passages, beset with obstacles which the souls have to surmount by ascending seven steep slopes of a height hyperbolically couched in terms of thousands of years. The principle on which these different abodes of trial and expiation are distinguished is, as in Dante, ethical ; it is based on the seven capital sins of Islam, which consist in the breaking of the rules of faith, prayer, fasting, almsgiving, pilgrimage, ablution, and just dealing with one's neighbour.

Once started in this direction, the imagination of the faithful soon overstepped the narrow limits of the scheme outlined above, and the topography was amplified by the addition of other partial purgatories of ten, twelve, or fifteen sections. Here, again, the principle is ethical ; although it must be confessed that the distribution is neither logical nor based on any philosophical or theological system, but is rather the outcome of a desire on the part of the casuist

---

[1] IBN MAKHLUF, II. 33. Cf. *Kanz*, VII, 237, No. 2,677.
[2] *Futuhat*, I, 403-406.

to leave no wrongdoing unpunished. The result is thus a heterogeneity of vices and failings.[1]

Judging by the wealth of detail with which the place of expiation is described in the eschatology of Islam, it is evident, then, that in the matter of topography Dante's conception can hardly be claimed to be original.

5. As for his description of the punishments of purgatory, no such claim has ever been made. Indeed, having exhausted the whole gamut of suffering in his picture of hell, he would no doubt find it difficult to conceive new torments, so that a very brief comparison of Dante's with the Moslem scenes will be sufficient for our argument.

The disobedient and neglectful souls are punished merely by being withheld indefinitely from the place of expiation. At the foot of the mount they lie, awaiting the help of friends and relations, the prayers of whom will shorten the term of Divine wrath. It is in this antechamber of purgatory that Manfred of Sicily and Belacqua make themselves known to Dante and implore him to give news of their sad fate to their friends on earth.   Under the shade of a rock Belacqua with his head between his knees sits in an attitude of utter dejection.[2]

In the religious literature of Islam similar scenes abound in the form of visions of souls in purgatory, who appear to their relations in their sleep and beseech them to pray for their eternal rest.[3] One scene in particular bears a striking resemblance to Dante's description ; Abu Dolaf al-Ijli, a soldier of the time of Caliph Al-Mamun, appears to his son Dolaf, who thus describes the vision :—

" In a dream I saw my father lying in a place of horror,

---

[1] Thus, the ten purgatorial mansions serve for the expiation successively of : (1) acts forbidden by canonical law ; (2) the holding of advanced opinions on questions of faith ; (3) disobedience to parents ; (4) failure to comply with one's duties towards children and subordinates in the matter of religious education ; (5) harsh treatment of servants and slaves ; (6) and (7) non-compliance with duties towards kinsfolk and blood relations, respectively ; (8) the vice of envy ; (9) deceitfulness ; and (10) treachery.

[2] *Purg*. IV, 100–135.

[3] Special books were written on this theme, such as the oft-quoted *Sudur* by SUYUTI, the *Tadhkira* of the Cordovan, and the work by IBN MAKHLUF.

with dark walls around it and its floor covered with ashes. Naked and sitting with his head resting upon his knees, he called out to me, ' Dolaf,' and I replied, ' May God have thee in His keeping." Then did he recite the following verses : ' Tell our family of the fate awaiting them in this dread purgatory and how account is taken of all our deeds. Hide nothing from them, but thou, have pity on my awful loneliness and terrible fate. If in death we were but left alone, it would at least be a comfort to us ! But, alas ! We are brought to life again and must answer for all our deeds.' And with these words he vanished, and I awoke."[1]

6. The torments of Dante's Purgatorio, like those of the Inferno, are based on the principle of correlation between punishment and sin. Thus, in the first circle the souls that are being purified of the sin of pride are seen wending their way bowed down under a heavy load of stones. This is the very suffering assigned by Islam to the avaricious and such as grew rich by evil means. Tales attributed to Mahomet say[2]:—

" Men of my persuasion will come to me on the Day of Judgment, their shoulders burdened with the goods of this world, and they will implore my aid. . . . But I shall turn my back upon them, saying, ' the faith ye profess is known to me, but your deeds I know not.' For he who stole but a palm of land shall be obliged by God to bear it upon his neck, down to the bottommost part of the earth."

Other legends depict the avaricious as vainly endeavouring to cross the *sirat* under the burden of their riches, or as wandering hither and thither, borne down by the weight of their wealth.

In the second circle Dante portrays the envious with their eyelids sewn together and weeping bitterly as they pray for pardon.

Blindness, though in a milder form, is also one of the punishments reserved in Islam for those that failed to practise the virtues they preached.[3] An apocryphal tradition of Mahomet runs :—

[1] *Sudur*, 121.
[2] *Kanz*, III, 252, No. 4,013 ; VIII, 175, Nos. 3,054, 3,017, 5,736.
[3] *Al-Laali*, II, 196. Blindness, both physical and moral, is a common punishment of infidels. Cf. *Koran*, LXXXII, 6, and *Tadhkira*, 73.

" He who reads the Koran but ignores its teaching shall appear blind on the Day of Judgment. To his cry ' Oh, Lord ! Why hast Thou brought me to life again, deprived of my sight, whereas aforetime I could see ' ? God will give answer, ' Even as my words reached thine eyes and thou didst heed them not, so shall I pay no heed to thee to-day.' "

The wrathful, in Dante's third circle, are enveloped in a cloud of smoke so dense that although their voices can be heard, they themselves cannot be seen.

This is the very torment, referred to in the Koran as a plague of smoke that God will send on the Day of Judgment to punish them that mocked His prophets.[1] The traditionists, in their comment on this passage, filled in the details of the picture, which thus comes to bear a striking resemblance to Dante's scene.[2]

" The smoke will be so dense that the whole earth will resemble a house that is on fire ; the plague will last forty days and forty nights, until the earth from East to West is full of smoke, which will enter the eyes, ears and nostrils of the infidels, suffocating and blinding them, and even the true believers will suffer from faintness ; men will call out one to another, but though their voices will be heard, they themselves will not be seen, so thick will be the fog."

The punishment meted out in the fourth circle of the Purgatorio to the slothful, who are made to run without ceasing, may be passed over as of slight interest. More striking is the torture of the avaricious, in the fifth circle, who as they lie face downwards on the ground, bound hand and foot, bewail their fate with bitter tears.

Sadness and moral pain are among the typical features of the purgatory of Islam that recur in the descriptions of the different abodes or stations.[3]

" Should the soul have been guilty of any of these failings, it will remain in its allotted abode a thousand years downcast and ashamed, naked, hungered and athirst, until such time as it shall have made restitution unto God."

---

[1] *Koran*, XLIV, 9–10 [2] KHAZIN, *Tafsir*, IV, 112–113, and *Tadhkira*, 131. Cf. *Purg.* XV, 142–145 ; XVI, 5–7, 35–36.
[3] *Futuhat*, I, 404–406.

10

The peculiar posture, moreover, in which Dante depicts the avaricious, is that in which, according to Islam, sinners in general, and inebriates in particular, are found on the Day of Judgment and in purgatory itself. A tradition of the Prophet runs: "He, who on earth made you walk upright, may on the Day of Judgment cause you to walk upon your faces." [1] And the author of the *Corra* describes the punishment of the drunkard as follows: "He shall come to life again with his hands and feet fettered and be obliged to drag himself along the ground." [2] Of the passage of the *sirat* a tradition attributed to Mahomet says:

"Some will pass with the swiftness of a race-horse, of the wind, or of lightning; others will merely run or walk; while others, again, will crawl on all fours, like an infant, or drag themselves along on their bellies." [3]

In Dante's sixth circle, where the vice of gluttony is punished, the souls, famished and parched with thirst, are tantalised by the sight and odour of the fruit of two trees, offshoots of the tree growing on high in the earthly paradise.

As has just been seen, the cravings of hunger and thirst are characteristic torments of the purgatory of Islam. It is a further curious coincidence that in a Moslem legend narrating the passage of the soul along the *sirat*, or path of expiation, this incident of the tree should be thrice repeated. [4] Three trees grow by the side of the path at different stages, the last one standing at the gate of paradise. The soul, in its painful progress, begs to be allowed to rest in their shade and eat of their luscious fruit, and God finally grants the prayer. Though the ending is different, the general outline of the incident is very similar in both stories.

The last circle of the Purgatorio is the place of expiation of the sin of lust. Tormented with thirst and scorched by the flames, the souls cry aloud to God for forgiveness. Dante speaks to several who are known to him, and they entreat him to intercede on their behalf.

---

[1] *Kanz*, VII, 246, No. 2,809.
[2] *Corra*, 19. Cf. *Purg.* XIX, 71-72, 94, 97, 120, 123.
[3] *Ihia*, IV, 376.   [4] *Tadhkira*, 80.

Fire is the most common of all the torments, occurring as it does in almost every eschatological system ; in some, indeed, it constitutes the only form of punishment. It would, therefore, be superfluous to point out parallel scenes in Islamic descriptions of the after-life.[1] The Moslem traditionists, however, are careful to distinguish between the expiatory flames of purgatory and the eternal fire of hell. The former, being temporary and merely serving to purify, are limited both as to duration and extent, proportionately to the nature of the sin for which atonement is being made. Numerous are the legends describing the different degrees of this torture and telling of the laments and prayers, addressed by the sufferers to the angels, Mahomet, and the saints, begging them to intercede with God on their behalf.[2]

VII

The Earthly Paradise of Islam in the Divine Comedy.

1. The summit of the Mount of Purgatory is a broad table-land, which Dante describes as a garden of great beauty. This is the earthly paradise, or Garden of Eden, in which our first ancestors dwelt while yet in a state of innocence. As he treads the ground, which is fragrant with flowers, a gentle breeze, laden with the perfumes of paradise, fans his tear-

---

[1] The natural consequences of this torture, viz. the violent thirst and bitter weeping of the tortured, are described with true Oriental hyperbole. Cf. *Corra*, 15. " God will give them such thirst as will burn their entrails." Cf. also *Kanz*, VII, 246, No. 2,811 : " The wicked will weep, as they are burnt, until their tears are spent ; they will then weep tears of blood, which will wear furrows in their cheeks."

[2] Cf. *Tadhkira*, 81, for a description of the purgatorial fire : The souls raise their voices to Mahomet in lament and pray for his intercession. God orders his angelic ministers to apportion the torture to the measure of the sin by preserving from the fire such members of the sinner's body as he had used in His service. " And the fire, which is cognisant of the degree of their guilt, reaches in some to the ankles, in others to the knees, and in others again, to the breast." When God has wreaked his vengeance He lends ear to the intercession of Mahomet and the prayers addressed ' Him directly by the sinners. Finally Gabriel is ordered to withdraw t sinners from the fire, and, as he does so, he immerses their blacken bodies in the River of Life, which flows by the gate of paradise, and t completes their purification.

In other tales the intercessor is an ordinary human being

stained cheeks. In the shade of verdant trees, the rustling of whose leaves murmurs a soft accompaniment to the song of a thousand birds, he comes to a limpid stream, whose course he follows ; here he walks, accompanied by a fair maiden, Matilda, who, gathering flowers as she trips along the further bank, explains to him the nature of the garden. Virgil's mission is now ended, and he is soon to leave Dante ; for, of a sudden, they behold advancing from beyond the stream a marvellous procession of maidens and elders, who, richly attired, lead in triumph a car in which, surrounded by angelic spirits and greeted with songs of welcome, appears Beatrice, the poet's beloved. Calling him by name, she sternly rebukes Dante for his disregard of the holy counsel she gave him in his dreams, for his faithlessness in following other less worthy loves, and for his sins. Dante, confused and repentant, confesses his unworthiness. He is then immersed by Matilda and the maidens that serve Beatrice in the stream of Lethe, on whose banks they are gathered, and upon drinking of its waters loses all memory of sin. Thereafter he succumbs to sleep in the shade of the tree of paradise, and finally, is bathed in the waters of Eunoe, from which he emerges " born again, even as trees renewed with fresh foliage, pure and ready to mount to the stars." [1]

Graf, after minute study of the mediæval legends bearing on the earthly paradise, has shown that there existed precedents for the site chosen by Dante, inasmuch as others before him had laid this garden in the southern hemisphere and on the peak of a high mountain.[2] But he asserts that no one before Dante had thought of placing it precisely on the summit of purgatory. An examination of Islamic literature will therefore be of interest, as it may furnish the key to this riddle of topography by revealing analogies both in outline and in detail with this closing scene of the Purgatorio.

2. From the earliest centuries in Islam the question of the site of the garden in which God had placed Adam and Eve had given rise to animated controversy. The passages

---

[1] *Purg.* XXVIII–XXXIII. Cf. Rossi, I, 150.   [2] Graf, *Miti*, I, 5.

in which the Koran tells the Biblical story in a slightly
altered form, led to a confusion between this paradise and
the abode of glory, thus causing it to be laid in heaven.[1]
According to another interpretation, however, it was supposed
to be situated on earth, more precisely, in the East and on
the highest of all mountains. This explanation, whilst
more in keeping with the Biblical narrative, had the advantage
of being reconcilable with the words used in the Koran ; for
the expulsion of Adam and Eve to the earth would merely
mean that God drove them from the summit to the foot
of the mountain [2]; it would also account for the delights of
the Garden of Eden and its difference from other places on
the surface of the earth. This view, though indeed held
from early times, was mainly propounded by the *Mutazili*
heretics, the philosophers and the mystics. A Spanish
Mutazili ascetic of the ninth century, Mondir 'ibn Said
al-Belloti, who was chief cadi of Cordova, was its most
ardent champion ; and in the tenth century it became
popular throughout Islam through the *Rasail* or encyclopædia compiled by the *Ikhwan as-safa*, or Brethren of Purity,
a heretical sect established in Basra.

" Lying on the summit of the Mountain of the Hyacinth,
which no human being may ascend, paradise was a garden
of the East ; a soft breeze blew day and night, winter and
summer, over its perfumed ground. The garden was well
watered by streams and shaded by lofty trees ; it was full
of luscious fruit, of sweet-smelling plants, of flowers of
different kinds ; harmless animals lived there and birds
of song. . . ." [3]

The earthly paradise that is here depicted in terms similar
to those used by Dante was situated, therefore, on the
summit of the highest mountain of the earth. Exactly which
mountain was referred to is not easy to determine, for on
this point opinion differed. Some authors placed it in Syria
or in Persia ; others in Chaldea or in India.[4] Eventually the

---

[1] Ibn Qaim al-Jawziya, of the fourteenth century, in his *Miftah* (I,
11–34), has left us a record of the various opinions and their chief exponents
both in Eastern and Western Islam.
[2] *Koran*, II, 33, 34.   [3] *Rasail*, II, 151.   Cf. BROCKELMANN, I, 213.
[4] Cf. D'HERBELOT, *Bibliothèque Orientale*, s.v. *gennat*, pp. 378, 773, 816.

belief that it lay in the last-named country was the most generally accepted.[1] The Brethren of Purity refer to the mountain as the " Mount of the Hyacinth," which, according to Arab geographers, is the mountain rising in Ceylon, now known as " Adam's Peak."[2] Rising out of the Indian Ocean to a height of seven thousand feet, it is visible from afar at sea, and this fact would no doubt account for the exaggerated height attributed to it, for its summit was supposed to reach to the sky.

The very name the mountain still bears is a perpetuation of the Islamic legend. Ibn Batutah, of Tangier, the famous fourteenth century traveller, who journeyed to the ends of the world, as it was then known, has left us a picturesque description of its difficult ascent, which Moslem pilgrims were wont to undertake in the belief that a rock on the summit bore the footprint of our father Adam.[3]

A high mount, rising in the middle of an island in the ocean covering the southern hemisphere is, in Dante's conception, the site of the earthly paradise. According to Islam, it is a high mountain rising in the middle of an island in the Indian Ocean.[4] Dante's, it is true, is but a small isle lying in the antipodes of Jerusalem, whereas the island of Ceylon is larger and is situated on the equator ; but the difference in topography is slight.[5]

[1] Cf. DIYARBAKRI, *Tarikh al-Khamis*, I, 61.
[2] The Moslem belief was in its turn based upon a Buddhist myth. Cf. RECLUS, *Géogr. Univ.* VIII, 581 ; and especially GRAF, *Miti*, I, 59–61. GUBERNATIS, in his work *Dante e l'India*, which I have not been able to obtain, identifies Dante's Mount of Purgatory with the island of Ceylon.
[3] IBN BATUTAH, IV, 170 *et seq.*
[4] The belief that the earthly paradise was situated on Adam's Peak endured in Islam until the sixteenth century. It was in that century that the Oriental mystic Ash-Sharani wrote in his *Mizan* (II, 193) :—
" The paradise in which Adam dwelt is not the supreme paradise . . ., but merely the *intermediate* paradise, which lies on the summit of the Mount of the Hyacinth. This is the garden in which Adam ate of the fruit of the tree. From this paradise he was driven to the earth . . . All children of Adam that die at peace with God return in spirit to that paradise. But the sinners first pass through the intermediate fire."
In his *Al-Yawaqn*, II, 172, Ash-Sharani repeats this passage almost literally and attributes it to a writer, who I infer is the tenth century mathematician Moslema, of Madrid.
[5] The ancients, however, held that Ceylon lay in the antipodes of the northern hemisphere. Cf. RECLUS, *Géogr. Univ.*, loc. cit.

3. As Graf has pointed out, however, Dante's conception of the site of the earthly paradise was no novelty in mediæval Christian literature, so that coincidence with Islam on this point alone would not suffice as proof of Moslem influence. But, as mentioned above, there is an element in Dante's topography that Graf does not hesitate to ascribe to the poet's inventive genius, to wit, the position of the earthly paradise on the summit of the mount of expiation, and its conception as the goal of the sinner in his arduous ascent and the last stage of purgation, in which the soul is cleansed of sin and made fit to cross the threshold of eternal bliss.[1]

Among the many Moslem legends dealing with the entry of the souls into the theological heaven there is a whole cycle describing their adventures from the time they finally emerge from the *sirat* or path of purgatory. Close to the *sirat*, and forming as it were the last stage of purgatory, lies the marvellous garden of paradise, which, although not indeed stated to be the earthly paradise, is depicted with all the features proper to it. Its pleasant pastures, gay with flowers, are watered by two rivers, and two only, in which the souls are immersed and cleansed from sin, and of whose waters they drink ; upon emerging, the souls rest, as does Dante, in the shade of trees and are then led by a choir of angels to the abode of glory. But a still more remarkable coincidence is, that on the threshold of the celestial mansion the soul is welcomed by a maiden of surpassing beauty, his promised bride, who for long has awaited his coming, yearning to be united with him in a love at once spiritual and chaste.

4. The resemblance to Dante's picture borne by this brief sketch is such as to call for a more detailed examination of these legends and a comparison of this episode with Dante's story. Originating in the form of gloss on a verselet of the Koran, the myth in its earliest and crudest version reads as follows :[2]

[1] Cf. GRAF, *Miti*, I, 5 : " Che Dante, ponendo il Paradiso terrestre sulla cima del monte del Purgatorio, fece cosa non caduta in mente a nessuno dei Padri e Dottori dell Chiesa, fu notato già da parecchi."
[2] *Koran*, VII, 41 and XV, 47 : " We shall efface all rancour from their breasts."

" The souls that are about to enter paradise first come to two springs ; they drink of the waters of the one, and God blots all rancour and hatred from their hearts ; they bathe in the waters of the other, and their complexions become brilliant, and the purity and splendour of bliss is seen shining on their faces."[1]

These bare outlines were soon filled in by the traditionists, who in the course of time built up the story that has been handed down to us in its most complete and classical form by Shakir ibn Muslim, of Orihuela. Composed in rhymed verse, it is of such extraordinary length that only the most interesting passages can be given here.[2]

" When the souls have left hell behind them and have traversed the *sirat*, or path of purgatory, they issue upon the plain that leads to paradise.[3] Accompanying them are the angels of Divine mercy, who cheer and guide them on their way to glory and wish them joy of their victory and salvation.[4] As they approach the entrance to paradise a gentle breeze, laden with perfume, brings balm to their souls and wipes away the memory of the suffering they endured in the course of their judgment and in the various mansions. . . . At the gate of paradise stand two mighty trees, lovelier than any ever seen on earth. Their fragrance, the richness of their foliage, the beauty of their blossom, the perfume of their fruit, the lustre of their leaves—nothing could ever surpass. The birds on their branches sing in sweet harmony with the rustling of the leaves. . . .[5] At the foot of either tree there springs a fountain of the purest water, clearer than beryl, cooler and whiter than freshly melted snow ; these springs are the source of two limpid streams, whose beds are

---

[1] *Tadhkira*, 99. Cf. IBN MAKHLUF, II, 60, for different versions of this legend.

[2] IBN MAKHLUF, II, 61. A biography of Shakir ibn Muslim, who lived about 1136 A.D., is given in *Tecmila* (Appendix to Codera's edition, biogr., No. 2,686).

[3] Thus, as in Dante, the earthly paradise is the final stage of purgatory. The same position is assigned to it by Ibn Arabi in his *Futuhat*, III, 573. Cf. *supra*, 115.

[4] Observe that angels also guide Dante and Virgil, as they leave purgatory.

[5] The resemblance between the garden described here and that of Dante is noteworthy. Cf. the following passages :—

IBN MAKHLUF, II.	*Purg.* XXVIII.
P. 61, line 8 inf.	Line 7.
P. 62, lines 1, 2, and 12.	Lines 120, 14.

seen to be of pearls and rubies. . . .[1] Along their banks
spread gardens and groves of trees in blossom, laden with
fruit and harbouring birds of sweet song. . . . The souls
bathe in the two rivers ; from the one they emerge whole in
body and cleansed from the marks of fire, with the lustre
of health and joy upon their faces ; they drink of the waters
of the river and, as all memory of past affliction leaves them,
so is all trace of envy, rancour and hatred blotted from their
hearts ; they then bathe in the other stream, and later find
peaceful repose in the shade of the two trees. . . .[2] And,
even as they rest, the angels of the Lord call upon them,
saying, ' Oh, beloved of God, these trees are not your
dwelling ; nigh unto God is your appointed place. Rise,
therefore, and march onward, till ye reach the mansion of
rest and everlasting bliss."[3] And they rise and proceed
through the paths of paradise, following the voice of the
angel herald, who leads them on from garden to garden until
they meet with a brilliant procession of youths and maidens,
dressed in rich attire and mounted on coursers . . . who greet
each one with shouts of joy and congratulation upon his
triumph. . . . ' Be thou welcome, beloved son of God !
Enter thy mansion, covered with glory and honour.' As he
enters, behold ! a damsel of surpassing beauty, arrayed in
robes of brilliant hue, awaits him seated in a tabernacle . . .
the splendour of her countenance dazzles him and his heart
is enraptured with the perfection, grace, and brilliant beauty
with which God has endowed her. Indeed, were it not that
God had granted him extraordinary powers of vision, he
would be bereft of both sight and sense by the intensity of
the light shining in her and the splendour radiating from her
presence.[4] The voice of an angel announces to him, ' Oh,
beloved one of God ! This is thy precious bride, thy dearly

[1] Compare the descriptions of the two rivers in IBN MAKHLUF, II, 62,
line 8, and *Purg.* XXVIII, 28, 133, and 144.

[2] It should be noted that, as in Dante's poem, there are two ablutions in
two rivers, whereas in the Biblical story the earthly paradise is watered
by four rivers. The effects of the double ablution in the Islamic legend
are also similar to those experienced by Dante. Cp. the following
descriptions : IBN MAKHLUF, II, 62, line 13, and *Purg.* I, 95, 128 ;
XXVIII, 128 ; XXXIII, 129, 138, and 142.

[3] Cp. this detail of the Arabic text (p. 62, line 20) with the words of
Dante (*Purg.* XXXIII, 72) " . . . ed un chiamar : Sorgi ; che fai ? " and
(*Purg.* XXXIII, 19). " . . . Ven più tosto."

[4] Cp. the descriptions of Beatrice and the bride of the Moslem tale in
IBN MAKHLUF, II, 63, line 8, and *Purg.* XXX, 31 ; XXXI, 83, 110 and
136 ; and XXXII, 1, 3 and 10.

beloved partner in the life of heaven ; this is the mistress of the damsels, the coy maiden hidden from the gaze of man.' But hardly has she caught sight of him when, unable to restrain the impulse of her love, she hastens towards him with fond words of welcome, ' Oh, beloved of God ! How I have yearned to see thee ! ' "

Of the many points of resemblance shown by this legend to Dante's story of the earthly paradise, some are so evident as to be hardly worthy of mention. The scenic features, for example, are clearly identical, recourse being had to the same rhetorical figures to depict the beauty of the gardens— such as the wealth of flowers, the perfumed air, the soft climate, and the gentle breeze on which is wafted the sweet song of birds. The rivers in which the souls are washed are two in number in Dante's poem and in the Moslem story, as against four in the Biblical paradise. Lastly, both gardens adjoin the path of purgatory, of which in fact they constitute the last division, for in them the soul undergoes final purification from the stain of sin and is prepared for entry into the realm of glory. The resemblance even extends to the manner of purification : the soul is bathed in both rivers and, in addition, drinks of their waters. The effects of the double ablution are also similar ; all physical and moral trace of sin is blotted out and new life imparted to the soul. After ablution, the pilgrim seeks rest in the shade of a tree. Finally comes the procession of youths and maidens leading in the heavenly bride ; the meeting of bride and bridegroom and their mutual recognition.

5. In spite of long and minute research, no literary precedent has so far been found for this latter scene.[1] Yet, as the Dantists justly claim, it is of supreme moment for the whole of Dante's poem, for it not only sheds light on the riddles that precede it, but also foreshadows the significance of what is to come ; and, indeed, but for this scene of the

[1] Neither Labitte nor D'Ancona found any trace of such a scene in Christian or classical legend. Ozanam (p. 457) merely quotes the *Vision of the Shepherd of Hermes*, which tells how a maiden, whom the shepherd had once wished to marry, appears to him in a dream as descending from heaven and calling upon him to serve God. According to Batiffol (p. 62), however, this tale was unknown in Europe before the sixteenth century.

meeting of Dante and Beatrice, neither the descent to hell nor the ascension to paradise would be susceptible of a satisfactory interpretation. At the same time, it must be admitted that the scene bears but little trace of the Christian spirit and is in strange contrast to the asceticism and the horror of sexual love that are characteristic of ecclesiastic literature in general, and that of the Middle Ages in particular.[1] To arrange, as the climax of a journey to the regions beyond the grave, the meeting of the pilgrim with his lost Beloved is a poetic conceit that will in vain be sought for in any of the Christian precursors of the Divine Comedy. Dante was well aware of how singular the note he struck was. So novel did the glorification of Beatrice, which is the avowed object of his poem, appear to him, that many years before, when the plan of the Divine Comedy was shaping in his mind, he remarked about his future poem, " Spero di dire di lei quello que mai non fu detto d'alcuna."[2] No doubt this glorification of Beatrice has its immediate roots in the spirit of chivalry that inspired the troubadours of Provence and the Italian poets of the " dolce stil nuovo " ; in the spiritual and romantic love of woman underlying that literary movement ; and in the mixture of mysticism and sensuality revealed in the temperament of Dante, the man and poet. These explanations may, indeed, lay bare the inner workings of the poet's mind, but they leave unsolved the riddle of the outer literary form in which his mentality manifested itself in this episode of the earthly paradise. In a later chapter of this work it will be shown that the origin of the " dolce stil nuovo " movement itself is most probably to be sought outside Christianity and that long before the appearance of the troubadours in Europe romantic love had inspired the poets of Arabia, and provided food for the speculative minds of Moslem mystics.[3] Here it will suffice to point to the outstanding fact that an episode so typical of the Divine Comedy as the meeting of Beatrice and Dante, and, being foreign to the very spirit of Christianity, unprecedented in Christian

[1] Cf. VOSSLER, I, 199, *et seq.*   [2] *La Vita Nuova*, XLIII.
[3] Cf. *infra.* Part IV, ch. V, §§ 6, 7, and 8.

legend, has a striking parallel in Moslem tradition. Nor is the tale translated above unique ; rather is it the final stage in the evolution of a series of legends that tell the fantastic story of the entry of the blessed soul into paradise. The Moslem heaven, as will be seen later on, is not exclusively the paradise of coarse delight, as depicted in the Koran and many of the traditions, that has become stamped on the mind of educated Europe. By the side of that picture there is another, painted by the ascetics and mystics, that reveals a heaven of purer love, in which, in addition to the large-eyed houris and the wives the blessed knew on earth, a spiritual bride also awaits him. This is his Heavenly Betrothed, who from on high has been waiting and watching for the advent of her lover, guiding him on the path of virtue, inspiring him with lofty aims and ever encouraging him to persevere to the triumphant end, when they will be united in eternal bliss. When death at last leads the blessed soul to paradise, it is she who sallies forth to welcome him, radiant indeed with beauty, yet not as an instrument of carnal delight, but rather as a spiritual companion and moral redemptress who wishes the soul joy of his victory and reproves him for having on occasions forsaken her for other, earthly loves. The picture of this Heavenly Bride is so strikingly like that of Beatrice that it will not be amiss to quote some of the legends on this subject.

6. A very interesting description of the entry of the blessed soul into paradise is contained in the tenth century work *Corrat Aloyun*.[1]

The angel Ridwan leads him to the tabernacle where his bride awaits him. She greets him with the words, " Oh, friend of God, how I have longed to meet thee ! Blessed be the Lord, who has united us ! God created me for thee and engraved thy name upon my heart. While thou on earth wast serving God in prayer and fasting, day and night, God bade his angel Ridwan carry me on his wings so that I might behold thy good deeds from heaven. The love I felt for thee caused me to watch over thy progress unbeknown to thee. When in the dark of night thy prayer went up, my

---

[1] *Corra*, 121. Some phrases are also taken from *Dorar*, 40.

heart was glad within me, and I said to thee, ' Serve and
thou shalt be served, sow and thou shalt reap! God has
advanced thee in glory, for thy virtues have found favour in
His sight, and He will bring us together in heaven. . . .
But, when I found thee neglectful and half-hearted, I felt
sad.' "

Another legend of the same cycle, attributed to the eighth
century traditionist Ibn Wahab, introduces the reproaches
of the bride for her bridegroom's earthly loves.[1]

" They will say to a woman in paradise, ' Would'st thou
see thy spouse who is yet on earth ? ' and, as she assents,
they will draw aside the veils that separate her from him,
so that she may look upon his face and long for the moment
of his coming, even as on earth a woman longs for her absent
man. It may be that between him and his spouse on earth
there have been grounds for resentment such as are common
among wives and husbands, and she will reproach him
saying, ' Oh, wretched man! Why dost thou not forswear
(such loves) that, compared with mine, shall last thee but a
night or two ? ' "[2]

The similarity between these two descriptions and the
two scenes in which Beatrice comes to the moral aid of
Dante is surely evident. Beatrice, when from on high she
sees that her beloved poet is in danger of forfeiting salvation
and, therewith, her companionship in paradise, descends
from heaven to implore Virgil's assistance in setting the
pilgrim on the right path. The scene forms, as it were, the
prologue to the poem.[3] When Dante reaches the earthly
paradise, she again descends and to her greeting adds reproof
for his backsliding, his indulgence in earthly loves, and his
neglect of the holy counsel she gave him in his dreams.[4]

Tales of visions, based on the legends of the same cycle,
are common in Islamic literature. They all tell of a beautiful
and angelic maiden who appears to the devout in their

---

[1] IBN MAKHLUF, II, 129.
[2] From the Arabic text it is not clear whether the heavenly bride is
reproving her lover or his wife on earth. At all events, the analogy in
subject remains very striking. Cf. the words in *Purg.* XXXI, 59 :
" . . . o pargoletta, od altra vanità con sì breve uso."
[3] *Inf.* II, 52 *et seq.*   [4] *Purg.* XXX, 73-145 ; XXXI, 1-63.

dreams, to inspire them with holy thoughts and urge them to serve God with the promise that she will be theirs in the life to come.

A tale attributed to Ali al-Talhi, who lived prior to the tenth century, reads as follows [1]:—

" In a dream I beheld a woman fairer than any of this world. ' Who art thou ? ' I asked, and she replied, ' I am a houri.' I said to her, ' Pray let me be thy husband,' to which she replied, ' Ask me in marriage of my Lord and name my dowry.' I asked, ' What is thy dowry ? ' and she answered, ' That thou shouldst keep thy soul unspotted from the world.' "

Another story, attributed to the ninth century ascetic Ahmed ibn Abu-l-Hawari, runs :—

" In a dream I saw a maiden of the most perfect beauty, whose countenance shone with celestial splendour. To my asking, ' Whence comes that brilliance on thy face ? ' she replied, ' Dost thou remember that night spent by thee in weeping (and devotion) ? ' ' I remember,' I answered, and she said, ' I took those tears of thine and with them anointed my face, since when it has shone in brilliance.' "

A tale, attributed to Utba al-Ghulam, certainly dates before the eleventh century :—

" In a dream I saw a houri of beautiful features, who said to me, ' I love thee passionately and trust thou wilt do no deed that might keep us apart.' I replied, ' Thrice have I abandoned the things of this world and hope never to regain them, so that I may be able to meet thee (in heaven).' "

Sulayman ad-Darani, a great ascetic of the ninth century of our era, is the protagonist of a similar tale [2]:—

" I saw in a dream a maiden of a beauty ' as splendid as the moon,' clad in a mantle that ' seemed as if made of light.' [3] Said the maiden to me, ' Thou sleepest, oh ! delight of my soul. Perchance thou knowest not that I am thy bride ? Rise, for thy prayer is light and thy Lord deserveth thy thanks . . . ! ' and, with a cry, she flew off through the air."

---

[1] For this and the two following tales cf. *Ihia,* IV, 364 ; also *Ithaf,* X, 434.
[2] IBN MAKHLUF, I, 120.   [3] Cf. *Purg.* XXX, 33.

Other legends tell of the visions seen by martyrs of holy warfare, the soldier ascetics of Islam, who later had their counterpart in the knights of the Christian military orders. In those quoted below, the meeting with the heavenly bride, who appears either alone or accompanied by her hand-maidens, is described in terms similar to those used by Dante, and the subject of the earthly loves of the protagonist is also alluded to.

A tale told by Abd ar-Rahman ibn Zayd, of the eighth century, runs as follows [1]:—

" A youth, moved to devotion by spiritual reading, distributes all his patrimony among the poor, keeping only enough to buy a mount and arms, with which he sets off to the holy war. Whilst on service, he fasts during the day-time and spends the nights in prayer and vigil as he guards the horses of his sleeping comrades. One day he cries out in a loud voice : ' Oh, how I long to be with the large-eyed maiden ! ' and to his companions he explains how in a dream his soul found itself in a lovely garden watered by a river ; on the bank of the river stood a group of fair maidens in rich attire, who welcomed him saying, ' This is the bride-groom of the large-eyed maiden whom we serve.' Proceeding on his way, he comes to a second river, where other maidens again welcome him.[2] A few steps further, and he meets the heavenly maiden herself enthroned on a seat of gold within a tabernacle of pearl. When she beholds her betrothed, she wishes him joy of having come to her, but warns him that his present coming is not final. ' The spirit of life yet breathes within thee, but to-night thou shalt break thy fast in my company.' " [3]

The following legend was told by Abd Allah ibn al-Mubarak in the eighth century [4]:—

A soldier in the holy war tells of a vision he had when faint from wounds received on the field of battle. " I seemed

---

[1] Ibn Makhluf, I, 113 and 121–2.
[2] Beatrice's maidens also tell Dante how God has destined them to serve her. Cf. *Purg.* XXXI, 106.
[3] Just as Dante asks of Matilda (*Purg.* XXXII, 85) " Ov'è Beatrice ? " ; so the Moslem bridegroom asks of the handmaidens, " Where is the large-eyed maiden ? " Compare also the promise by the bride, that they will shortly meet in heaven, with the words of Beatrice to Dante (*Purg.*, XXXII, 100).
[4] For this and the following legend see Ibn Makhluf, I, 112.

to be led to a mansion built of rubies, wherein I saw a woman whose beauty enraptured me. She bade me welcome, saying she was not like my wife on earth, whose behaviour she then related to me. I laughed and would fain have clasped her in my arms, but she held me at a distance saying, ' To-morrow in the evening thou shalt come to me,' and I wept because she would not let me draw nigh to her." The legend ends by saying that on the morrow that same soldier died in battle.

A legend, related by Ismail ibn Hayyan, of the ninth century, also tells of a vision seen by a martyr of holy warfare as he fainted away :—

He finds himself led by a man to the mansion of the heavenly maiden, through palaces of paradise inhabited by youths whose beauty is painted in hyperbolic terms. Finally there comes to greet him the beautiful woman who tells him she is his bride and who reminds him of the women of this world with such detail that she appears to be speaking from a record made in a book.

7. The features of resemblance found in this comparison of Dante's story of the earthly paradise with Islamic legend may be summarised as follows : On either hand, this paradise is represented as a garden of delight, situated on the summit of a high mountain rising on an island in the ocean ; other Islamic legends tell of a garden lying at the gate of paradise and forming both the antechamber to glory and the last stage of purgatory, where the souls undergo final purification by being washed in the waters of two streams ; in this garden also the soul is met and welcomed by the heavenly bride, a figure who in appearance and attitude bears a striking resemblance to the Beatrice of Dante.

Versions of the *Miraj* described a similar garden as being watered by rivers in which the souls are purified before they enter heaven. That garden was called the Garden of Abraham. Thus, in Islam, there was a threefold garden beyond the grave—the Garden of Abraham, or Limbo ; the Garden of Eden, or earthly paradise ; and the garden of paradise, lying between purgatory and the theological heaven. Features of all three gardens appear blended in the Divine Comedy in a form foreign to Christian legend, as it existed prior to Dante. The *Risala* of Abu-l-Ala al-Maarri, the literary imitation of the *Miraj* that was quoted in a former chapter, depicted a similar scene. In a garden lying at the gate of the celestial paradise the traveller, on the banks of a river, meets a maiden who has been sent by God to welcome and guide him ; she leads him to the presence of the beloved of the poet Imru-l-Qays, who appears in the wake of a procession of beautiful maidens.[1]

It would thus seem that there was nothing to prevent the legend of the ascension from being extended to include the legends quoted in this chapter, dealing, as they also do, with the after-life. The idea might indeed prove tempting to so consummate an artist as Dante, who, saturated with classical and Christian learning, might well know how to weave into the outline of the story of Mahomet the scenes provided in these legends and the features available in mythology and ecclesiastical tradition, in order to paint his picture of the earthly paradise, in which elements from the Garden of Eden, the Parnassus of the Ancients, and the Paradise of Islam are blended into one.

VIII

THE CELESTIAL PARADISE OF ISLAM IN THE DIVINE COMEDY

1. As we have now reached a point in our argument when it might appear that we were treading on dangerous ground, a few words by way of preface to this chapter may not be amiss. The very suggestion of a comparison between Dante's

---

[1] Beyond the general fact that both Beatrice and the Moslem bride are ushered in by processions, there is no great resemblance. To describe the procession, Dante availed himself of features in Ezekiel and Revelations, to which he gave an allegorical meaning that is not always clear. Vossler (II, 171), however, remarks upon the Oriental colour of the description. Indeed, the maidens and elders that lead in Beatrice are conspicuous rather by their colouring than by their outline, which is barely traced (*Purg.* XXIX, 121–154).

paradise and the paradise of Islam will most likely occasion surprise even in the minds of people of moderate culture. Surely, it will be thought, any such comparison can only serve to show up the utter antagonism between the two conceptions. Indeed, the spiritualism of Dante's paradise seems so far removed from the coarse and sensual materialism of the paradise depicted in the Koran that, if the question were to be decided on that issue alone, there could be but one answer. The Koran, however, as has already been pointed out, does not stand for all Islam, nor does it constitute the main source of its dogma. The traditions early attributed to Mahomet, the explanations of the commentators, and the speculations of theologians and mystics, played at least as great a part as the letter of the Koran in determining the essential points of the creed of the Moslem paradise. Of outstanding interest in this connection is the tradition of the ascension of Mahomet. This legend in its various forms, and particularly in Version C of Cycle 2, showed very clearly that paradise was by no means generally conceived on the gross and sensual lines described in the Koran ; on the contrary, the picture drawn there was almost exclusively one of light, colour and music, which are the very elements that Dante used to express his conception.

The spiritual interpretation of the delights of paradise must have begun in the first centuries of Islam. The famous traditionist and kinsman of Mahomet, Ibn Abbas, was of old credited with a saying which is significant of its early origin : " In paradise there is none of the things of this world ; only their names are there." The earliest traditionists even place in the mouth of the very Prophet who had described in such glowing terms the sensual joys awaiting the blessed, the same sublime words by which Isaiah and St. Paul had represented the glory of heaven ; for a *hadith* attributed to Mahomet says, " I have prepared for my holy servants such things as the eye hath not seen, nor the ear heard, nor the mind of man imagined."[1] To this Divine

---

[1] *Hadith* by Muslim in *Tadhkira*, 85. Cf. *Isaiah*, LXIV, 4, and *First Epistle to Corinthians*, II, 9.

promise the Prophet added the verse of the Koran (XXXII, 17) : " The soul knows not of the delights awaiting it in reward for its good deeds." The Moslem books on eschatology record many similar *hadiths* attributed to Mahomet, in which the Beatific Vision is represented as the supreme bliss reserved for the souls in paradise.[1] It will thus be seen that from the very first centuries Islam had begun to conceive, apart from the sensual paradise of the Koran, a spiritual and essentially Christian heaven, in which beatitude consists in the contemplation of the splendour of the Divine essence.

2. To trace back each of the many controversies that arose in the centuries following would be to exceed the limits of our task. In the end the idealistic conception of paradise emerged triumphant alike over the exegesis of the Koran and the arguments against the anthropomorphism of God of the Mutazili and Kharijite heretics.[2] By the time that the dogma of Islam was given definite shape by its greatest theologians, the Beatific Vision was considered to be the principal, if not the only prize of heaven, and the sensual delights extolled in the text of revelation were discreetly ignored.

The mystics and the philosophers, imbued as they were with Christian theology and neo-Platonic metaphysics contributed to the gradual elimination of the sensual conception of paradise by giving its material delights a mystical or allegorical meaning. And this line of thought was followed by the two great thinkers of the twelfth century, the theologian and mystic, Algazel, and the theologian and philosopher, Averrhoes.[3] Algazel states that, with the exception of the materialists, who denied the immortality of the soul, all cultured minds in Islam more or less openly scouted the idea of any sensuality in connection with the delights of paradise[4] ; the philosophers averred that these

[1] *Tadhkira*, 97. These *hadiths* were based on two passages in the Koran (II, 274 and XIII, 22), in which the vision of the face of God by the blessed is vaguely referred to.

[2] Cf. KHAZIN, *Tafsir*, IV, 335, for a summary of this polemic ; also *Fasl*, III, 2-4.

[3] Cf. ASÍN, *Algazel, Dogmática*, 680, and *Averroismo*, 287.   [4] In *Mizan al-Amal*, p. 5 *et seq.*

delights were purely imaginary ; the mystics went further and denied their existence ; and both philosophers and mystics for the joys depicted in the Koran substituted the sole and sovereign delight of the intellectual vision or contemplation of the essence of God, the enjoyment of which they made equivalent to all the physical and ideal pleasures that man is capable of feeling.[1] This denial, more or less complete in substance, was, however, attenuated in form, to avoid disappointing the masses, who were incapable of so lofty a conception. To save appearances, the philosophers and Sufis affected acceptance of the material descriptions of the Koran on the grounds that they were symbols, the spiritual meaning of which was the patrimony of the enlightened. Algazel and Averrhoes, the champions alike of faith and reason, found means to reconcile the points of view of both the learned and the vulgar by declaring that heaven, as the supreme aim and ultimate bliss of all men, would be a state in which each would attain his particular desire. Those who in this life were tied down to things material, would in heaven be capable of deriving joy only from sensual delights, though they could not say of what these were to consist ; whilst those whose conceptions and desires were free from all material taint, would find delight in the enjoyment of the Beatific Vision alone.

Thus, Algazel and Averrhoes in their picture of the mediæval beliefs of Islam provide us with two heavens—the one, material, and the other, ideal. A few years later, Ibn Arabi of Murcia expressed his views on the question in the same concise terms.[2]

" There are two heavens—the one, sensible ; and the other, ideal. In the one, both the animal spirits and the rational souls enjoy bliss ; in the other, the rational souls alone. The latter paradise is the heaven of knowledge and intuition."

Not content with this formula, he proceeds to explain the psychological motives that led Divine Providence to lay greater stress upon the sensible than upon the ideal paradise

[1] *Ihia*, IV, 219.   [2] *Futuhat*, II, 809.

in the Koran, in contrast to the teaching of Christian revelation. And Ibn Arabi's explanation, arguing as it does the Christian origin of the spiritual conception of paradise in Islam, is so significant that it is worthy of literal transcription.[1]

"God has depicted paradise in accordance with the different degrees of man's understanding. The Messiah defined the delights of paradise as purely spiritual, when, in concluding the instructions given to his disciples in his testament, he said, 'Should ye do as I have bidden you, ye will sit with me to-morrow in the Kingdom of Heaven by the side of my Lord and your Lord and behold around His throne the angels singing His praise and glorifying His holiness. And there ye will enjoy all manner of delights and yet will partake not of either food or drink.'[2] But, if the Messiah was so explicit on this point and had recourse to none of the allegories found in our Book, it was simply because his words were spoken to a people conversant with the Torah and the books of the prophets, whose mind was thus prepared for his words. Not so with our Prophet Mahomet. His Divine mission fell among a rude people, who dwelt in deserts and on mountains; who lacked the discipline of learning and believed neither in the resurrection nor in the future life; who were ignorant even of the pleasures of the princes of this world, let alone those of the kings in heaven! Accordingly, most of the descriptions of paradise in his book are based on the body, in order that they might be understood by the people and serve as an incentive to their minds."

3. The evidence furnished by the Moslem thinkers, Algazel, Averrhoes and Ibn Arabi, is fully confirmed by the writings of the two Christian scholastics who were most versed in Islam—the Spaniards, Raymond Lull and Raymond Martin. Far from falling into the common error of attributing to all Moslems the belief in a voluptuous paradise, they repeat almost literally what those thinkers had affirmed; and Raymond Martin even quotes passages from Algazel, full of the loftiest metaphysical thought, in which this prince

---

[1] *Futuhat* in ASH-S'IARANI, *Al-Yawaqit*, II, 195, and *Al-Kibrit*, II, 194.
[2] This apocryphal passage from the Gospel can only refer to St. Luke, **XXIII, 43.**

of Moslem mystics pictures the sublime delights of the Beatific Vision.[1]

If, therefore, at the very time at which Dante was composing the Divine Comedy two Christian theologians knew of a Moslem paradise just as adaptable as Dante's to the purest and most spiritual Christian doctrine, the idea of comparing the two conceptions, based as they are on dogmas that are so much alike, can no longer be considered as out of place. That a connection between the two artistic conceptions does exist will appear the less unlikely if it is borne in mind that Dante's paradise has no precedent in Christian mediæval literature. Dantists have shown that in none of

[1] Lull, in *Liber de Gentili* (*Op. Omn*, Mayence Edit., vol. II, 89) is clear on this point :—

" Dixit Sarracenus : Verum est quod inter nos diversi diversimode credant gloriam Paradisi ; nam quidam credunt habere gloriam (secundum quod ego tibi retuli) et hoc intelligunt secundum litteralem expositionem, quam ab Alcora accipiunt, in qua nostra lex continetur, et a proverbiis Mahometi, et etiam a proverbiis et a glosis et expositionibus Sapientum exponentium nostram legem. Aliae tamen gentes sunt inter nos quae intelligunt gloriam moraliter, et spiritualiter exponunt eam, dicentes quod Mahometus metaphorice gentibus absque rationali intellectu et insipientibus loquebatur ; et ut eos ad divinum amorem posset trahere, refferebat eis supradictam gloriam ; et idcirco hi tales, qui credunt hujusmodi gloriam, dicunt quod homo in Paradiso non habebit gloriam comedendi et jacendi cum mulieribus et habendi alias supradictas res ; et hujusmodi sunt naturales philosophi et magni clerici . . ."

The following are passages from Martin's *Explanatio Simboli* (Edit. of March, in *Anuari del Institut d'estudis catalans*, Barcelona, 1910, p. 52) :—

" Quoniam vero aliqui sapientes sarracenorum . . . ponentes beatitudinem hominis tantum in anima . . ." *Ibid*. 53 : " Quod autem in errorem induxit sapientes sarracenorum . . . videtur processisse ex Alcorano ; quum ibi contineatur quod post resurrectionem habebunt delectationes corporales, ut delectatio cibi, potus et coitus ; que, in veritate, si in alia vita essent, intellectum a cogitatione et dilectione summi boni impedirent. Unde, quia visum est eis hoc esse inconveniens, sicut est in veritate, negaverunt . . ., ponentes tamen beatitudinem hominis in anima." *Ibid*. 53 (in his explanation of the last article of the symbol, " vitam eternam ") : Preeminentiam autem delectationum spiritualium et divinarum, ad corporales delectationes, necnon et earum comparationem ad invicem, ponit Avicenna in libro *de scientia divina*, tractatu IX, capite VII de promissione divina, loquens de felicitate animae . . ." *Ibid*. 54 : " Item, Algazel firmat idem in libro *Intentionum physicarum* (this should be *philosophicarum*) . . ." *Ibid*. 54 : " Eandem etiam sententiam confirmat in libro qui dicitur *Vivificatio scientiarum*, in demostratione quod gloriosior et excellentior delectationum, cognitio Dei excelsi, et contemplatio vultus ejus (referring to *Ihia*, IV, 219). Et in libro qui dicitur *Trutina operum*, in capitulo probationis, quid sit beatitudo ultima. Hoc idem etiam confirmat Alpharabius in libro *de auditu naturali*, tractatu II circa finem, et in libro *de intellectu*. Ex his patet, quod etiam apud philosophos sarracenorum, beatitudo eterna consistit in cognitione et amore Dei, non in delectatione."

the so-called " precursors " of the Divine Comedy could the poet have found inspiration for his delicate picture. Whereas, to Dante paradise is pure light, and the life of the blessed, one of ecstatic contemplation and Divine Love, in the rude conception of most of his Christian predecessors—who were merely monks or *jongleurs*—life in heaven is but a grotesque exaggeration of the life of the refectory and the choir, or of the life at the court of a feudal lord.[1] Thus, the question of determining the values to be attributed to the conceptions of paradise current in the Middle Ages may in all fairness be reduced to the following terms : In the Moslem world two antithetical ideas flourished almost simultaneously—the coarse and sensual paradise of the Koran, and the spiritual picture of the philosophers and the mystics. In the Christian world, the same two ideas existed—the materialistic conception, equivalent to that of the Koran, which flourished prior to the Divine Comedy, and the spiritual picture, which was solely the work of the Florentine poet.[2] Dante himself appears to disdain the conceptions of his Christian predecessors when, in announcing his ascension to paradise, he says, " If God . . . wills that I may behold his court in a manner quite outside modern use."[3]

Once the mind is free from the prejudice, as common as it is ill-founded, that regards all Islamic conception of paradise as materialistic, it will the more readily grasp how it came about that Islam, as early as the eighth century of our era, conceived so spiritual a picture of heaven as that

[1] Cf. D'ANCONA, *Precursori*, 29 : " Hanno . . . tutte queste leggende carattere ingenuo, anzi fanciullesco, che di necessità ce le fa porre fuori della cerchia della vera poesia." *Ibid.* 31 : " Nè più alto e condegno è il comune concetto della sede celeste . . ." *Ibid.* 32 : " e per rappresentar le gioie del paradiso abbiano avuto ricorso a raddoppiare di più che mille milia il coro od il refettorio." *Ibid.* 88 : " Ma questa corte celeste . . . diventa la corte plenaria di un signore feudale." Cf. *Ibid.* 104–6.

[2] In Part III, Ch. VI, Moslem precedents will be shown for many of these materialistic Christian legends.

[3] *Purg.* XVI, 40. The hypothesis is D'Ancona's, who in note 2 to page 108 of his *Precursori* says : " Si potrebbe in Dante vedere giusto disdegno, anzichè ignoranza dei suoi predecessori." Cf. ROSSI, I, 140 : " Con codesta povera concezione . . . non è neppure paragonabile la concezione dantesca," and I, 147 : " Mentre i precedenti descrittori non avevano saputo se non trasferire nel soggiorno dei beati i più soavi diletti della vita terrena, per Dante il premio dei buoni è tutto nel intimo godimento che loro procura la visione e la cognizione di Dio."

found in Version C of Cycle 2 of the legend of the *Miraj*. The many striking features of resemblance borne by that description to the paradise of Dante were exhaustively dealt with in the first part of this work, and the wealth of coincidence afforded room for so minute a comparison that but little is now needed to complete the parallel.

4. To begin with the general scheme of the Paradiso, we know that Dante's paradise is formed of the nine astronomical heavens of the Ptolemaic system. In the first seven heavens it is only by chance that the poet sees the blessed, who are distributed according to their merits. Their real residence is in the Empyrean, or immobile sphere, which is thus the true paradise or theological heaven. There Dante pictures them as seated on thrones, benches or seats of light in the form of an amphitheatre, which gives the whole assembly the appearance of an immense rose of light, in the centre of which God stands revealed to the contemplation of His Chosen. The Empyrean is the celestial Jerusalem and lies in the vertical projection of the earthly Jerusalem, whilst beneath the latter opens the abyss of hell. The most perfect symmetry exists between the realm of reward and the realm of punishment. Both contain ten mansions and, just as the depth of each infernal mansion indicates the gravity of the sin punished therein, so does each degree of merit find its reward in a correspondingly high mansion in heaven.[1]

Most, if not all, of the architectural features of this plan have already been shown to exist in one or other of the versions of the legend of the *Miraj*. Thus, many of those versions represent the astronomical spheres as being inhabited by saints, prophets, and angels, who were seen to be allotted to the spheres according to their merit.[2] This conceit, though shared by Dante and Islam, had however no Biblical

[1] Cf. ROSSI, I, 141–2 and 147.
[2] It was also believed in Islam that the blessed meet in the heavenly mansions to converse together and welcome the newly-arrived souls, whom they ask for news of their friends and relations on earth. The *hadiths* on this subject may be found in *Tadhkira*, 17; *Kanz*, VII, 231, Nos. 2,568 and 2,571; and IBN MAKHLUF, II, 143. Dante describes many similar conversations of his with the blessed on the events and persons of his time, notably with Piccarda, Cunizza, Costanza, Folcheto, and Cacciaguida.

foundation; for neither the Old nor the New Testament definitely mentions the astronomical heavens as being the dwelling-places of the blessed. The idea can only have been derived either from the Cabbalists or some of the apocryphal Christian writers [1]; for the Fathers of the Church and the early ecclesiastical writers were careful not to attempt any specific localisation of the theological heaven.[2]

One outstanding feature of Dante's general scheme of paradise has been universally admired for its originality. The site of glory, or celestial Jerusalem, he places directly above the Jerusalem on earth, which according to the poet occupies the centre of our northern hemisphere.[3]

Exactly the same conception existed in Islam as early as the seventh century, that is to say, in the time of Mahomet himself. A legend attributed to the famous traditionist and companion of the Prophet, Kaab al-Akhbar, a Jewish convert who introduced many rabbinical myths into Islam, runs: " Paradise is in the seventh heaven, opposite Jerusalem and the rock (of the Temple); if a stone were dropped from paradise, it would surely fall upon the rock."[4] Similar rabbinical sayings, attributed to the same traditionist, or to

---

[1] Cf. VIGOUROUX, Dict. de la Bible, s.v. ciel.

[2] TIXERONT, s.v. eschatologie. Origenes (Ibid. I, 303) and St. Ephrem (II, 221) alone appear to mention the astronomical heavens. Accordingly PERRONE says (II, 110, n. 2):—
" Non levis inter aliquot ex antiquis Patribus dissensio occurrit, ubi agitur de statuendo loco, in quem justorum animae abscedentes a corpore deferantur. Alii coelum, alii sinum Abrahae, isti locum quietis, illi paradisum censent sive appellant. Paradisus ipse apud aliquos aut ipsum coelorum regnum significat, aut saltem in coelorum regione situs creditur; apud alios in ignota hujus terrae plaga. Sunt et paucissimi qui sub terra sive in inferis ..."
St. Thomas, in explaining the passage in the Gospel according to St. Matthew, V, 12, agrees with St. Augustine that " Merces sanctorum non dicitur esse in corporeis coelis " (Summa theol. 1-2ae, q. 4, a. 7, ad 3). Nor is mediaeval art any more precise, for in the French cathedrals Paradise is shown as the bosom of Abraham. Cf. MÂLE, 427.

[3] FRATICELLI, commenting on the passage of Inf. XXXIV, 112–115, says, " Imagina Dante che Gerusalemme sia posta nel mezzo dell'emisfero boreale "; and to Par. XXX, 124-8, he remarks, " E qui vuolsi notare che, come Gerusalemme (secondo il creder d'allora) è nel mezzo della terra abitata; così Dante imagina il seggio de'beati, la Gerusalemme celeste, soprastare a perpendicolo alla terrena. Cf. ROSSI, I, 141: " una stessa retta ... da Gerusalemme ... prolungata ... sale al centro della mistica rosa "; and I, 142: " così la Gerusalemme terrestre per una linea diritta ... si congiunge colla Gerusalemme celeste."

[4] MS 105 Gayangos Collection, fol. 117 r°,

another Jewish convert, Wahb ibn Munabbih, and sometimes to the kinsman of the Prophet, Ibn Abbas, must have contributed to spread the belief that paradise lay in the vertical projection of Jerusalem and its Temple. Indeed, geographical treatises of the tenth century describe Jerusalem as follows[1] :—

" Jerusalem is the navel of the earth. The Gate of Heaven stands open on its temple. In Jerusalem is the Divine Light and the Divine Fire. To visit Jerusalem is to enter heaven. God said of the rock (of the Temple), ' Thou art My lower throne ; from thee heaven rises unto Me ; underneath thee stretches the earth ; in thee lie My heaven and My hell.' From Jerusalem Jacob saw the ladder that rose to heaven. Jesus ascended into heaven from Jerusalem and thither He will descend again. That part of the earth that is nearest to heaven is Jerusalem."

It should be remembered that in several versions of the *Miraj* Mahomet began his ascension from the same rock of the Temple of Jerusalem, and this the commentators explain by quoting in a slightly altered form the legend mentioned above as told by Kaab al-Akhbar : " The Gate of heaven, named the Mount of the Angels, lies opposite Jerusalem."[2]

This obsession for symmetry in design is characteristic of Moslem eschatology, in which the world beyond the grave was conceived on the lines of this world. All versions of the Mahometan ascension tell of a temple in heaven called the " House of Habitation," which is but the counterpart of the Holy Shrine at Mecca ; and, as the Caaba is supposed to have been built by Abraham, so the latter is represented as residing near the heavenly temple. Moreover, in some legends this temple of paradise is supposed to lie in the vertical projection of the Caaba, just as the Celestial Jerusalem lies directly above the Jerusalem on earth. One of these legends Ibn Arabi quotes : " Were the House of Habitation to fall to the earth, it would assuredly fall on the temple of the Caaba."[3]

Nor does this desire for symmetry, which so imbued the

---

[1] Cf. HAMADHANI, 94–8. Also YAQUT, VIII, 111, s.v. Bayt al-Muqaddas.
[2] MS 105 Gayangos Collection, fol. 101 v°.   [3] *Futuhat*, II, 582.

minds of Moslem traditionists, end there. The realms of pain and of reward, hell and heaven, correspond in design just as perfectly as they do in Dante's design. This may be seen from the general plan that Ibn Arabi traces with almost mathematical precision.[1]

" The degrees of heaven are as many in number as the degrees of hell ; for each degree in the one has its counterpart in the other. This is but natural, for man can but comply, or fail to comply with any one precept. If he complies with it, he gains a degree of glory commensurate with his merit; but, if he fails to do so, he suffers condign punishment in hell. Thus, were a stone to fall from any one degree in paradise, it would of a surety fall in a straight line on the corresponding degree in hell."

5. The actual description of Dante's abode of glory is contained in Cantos XXX, XXXI, and XXXII of the Paradiso.[2] As the rays spread from the centre of Divine Light throughout the Empyrean, they create a number of luminous circumferences of immense diameter on planes that lessen in extent as they gradually descend. Each of these circles, like the tier of an amphitheatre, is formed of a row of seats, benches or thrones. The ranks thus formed Dante likens to the petals of an immense rose, each petal of the mystic flower representing a seat in glory, and the petals on one and the same plane, a circle or tier of the celestial amphitheatre. Dante also compares the abode of bliss to a realm, a garden, or a hill around which the blessed are

[1] *Futuhat*, II, 898. On the following page he inserts a geometrical design, in which, taking the five fundamental precepts of Islam by way of example, he shows how the grades of hell correspond symmetrically to the grades of paradise. This design, with a few unimportant omissions, is reproduced below. The dotted lines indicate the vertical projection of the grades of heaven above those of hell.

GRADES OF HEAVEN.

Reward of faith.	Reward of prayer.	Reward of almsgiving.	Reward of fasting.	Reward of pilgrimage.
Punishment of faith.	Punishment of prayer.	Punishment of almsgiving.	Punishment of fasting.	Punishment of pilgrimage.

GRADES OF HELL.

[2] The actual verses are *Par.* XXX, 100–132 ; XXXI, 1–54, 112–117; XXXII, 1–84, and 115–138.

grouped in ecstatic contemplation of the Divine Light; but the simile he mainly uses is that of the mystic rose, which, although he never actually employs the figure, he derived, no doubt, from the more graphic image of an amphitheatre.

The moral principle underlying the distribution of the blessed in the various tiers of the amphitheatre is applied with as strict a regard for symmetry as is shown in the geometrical design. All is governed by law and nothing is left to chance. The greater or lesser height of each circle corresponds to the greater or lesser degree of holiness attained by the souls, who, again, occupy a position on the left or right in each circle according to the nature of their faith before or after the advent of Christ. Further, the saints of the Old Testament are separated from those of the New Testament by subdivisions within each sector, some of which are in a vertical, others in a horizontal, sense. Men and women, children and adults, all are grouped in their respective classes in the various parts of the rose. Perfect symmetry marks the whole scheme throughout. Thus we find that Eve, the mother of human sinners, sits underneath Mary, the Mother of Christ the Redeemer; on the left of Mary sits Adam, the father of mankind, and on her right, St. Peter, the father of the Church. The blessed occupy their seats in Glory for one or the other of two reasons—either owing to their works plus grace, or to Divine grace alone; in the former category are the adults, in the latter, the children who were only saved through the faith of their parents. A third class, formed of the children and adults who sit in the places left vacant by rebel angels, might indeed be added. In conclusion, the spirits occupying the principal seats in the first circles, though not actually so classified by Dante, fall into three groups—the patriarchs and apostles, such as Adam, Moses, John the Baptist, St. Peter, and St. John the Evangelist; beneath them, the holy doctors of the religious orders, such as St. Francis, St. Benedict, and St. Augustine; and, still lower, the laymen and clergy who followed the teaching of these doctors.

In spite of these differences in degree, the life of the blessed is essentially one and the same. With their gaze fixed on the focus of Divine light, they contemplate God and know Him more or less perfectly according to the strength of their vision, which, in turn, depends on the purity and intensity of the Divine love they felt on earth. The difference in degree is made outwardly manifest by the greater or lesser brilliance each spirit emits ; but it does not imply any essential difference either in the vision itself or in the spiritual delight of the souls ; nor can it give rise to any desire on the part of those in the lower ranks to occupy a higher seat, and still less can it cause any feeling of envy, for this would be incompatible with the spirit of brotherly love that unites them in the love of God ; each, moreover, is aware that the joy experienced in the degree allotted to him is greater than he could possibly deserve.

6. Of this clearly defined scheme the Dantists have been able to trace but little to other Christian authors ; indeed, with the exception of the situation of paradise in the Empyrean, almost the whole of Dante's architecture of heaven has been attributed to the inventive faculty of the poet himself. Again, therefore, before pronouncing final judgment on the originality or otherwise of the conception, we would suggest that the Moslem sources be consulted. In this respect especial interest attaches to the works of the mystical writers of Islam, and more particularly to the detailed and picturesque descriptions of the realm of glory given by the Sufi of Murcia, Ibn Arabi.

The division of heaven into seven mansions, in diametric opposition to the seven stages of hell, dates from the early centuries of Islam. Ibn Abbas, in a *hadith* that is repeated again and again in the holy books of Islam, refers to these divisions indiscriminately as gardens, gates, mansions, stages or circular strata ; and with names derived from the Koran he enumerates them in the following order[1] : The first and highest is the mansion of the Divine Majesty ; the

---

[1] *Tadhkira*, 99. Gayangos Coll., MS 159, fol. 2 v° ; MS 64, fol. 25 v°.

second, the mansion of peace ; the third, the Garden of Eden ; the fourth, the garden of refuge ; the fifth, the garden of eternity ; the sixth, the garden of paradise ; and the seventh, the garden of delight. Other versions of the *hadith* change the order of the mansions, add one to their number, or vary the names given above.

As early as the tenth century a moral principle, in the form of a graduation of the bliss of glory, was introduced into the architectural scheme. The author of the *Corra*, who lived at Samarcand in that century, says that at intervals, according to their merits, God grants the Beatific Vision to His blessed ; they, for example, who mortified their flesh and gave their whole life to His service, shall enjoy the vision every Friday ; those who indulged in the pleasures to which youth is prone, shall behold it but once a month ; and they who only served God toward the end of their days, but once a year ; whilst such as spent their life in sin and only repented on their death-bed, shall see the vision but once throughout eternity.[1]

Other *hadiths* attempt to connect the seven or eight mansions of bliss with as many categories of blessed.[2] One such classification may serve as an example : The first heaven is reserved for the prophets, the envoys of God, the martyrs, and the saints ; the second for such as fulfilled the rites of prayer and ablution ; the third for men of holy meditation ; the fourth, for the devout in religious practice ; the fifth, for the ascetics ; the sixth, for those militant in the spiritual strife with passion ; the seventh, for pilgrims ; and the eighth, for those who were chaste and charitable towards their neighbours.

From these *hadiths* the mystics gradually elaborated their doctrine of the Beatific Vision, which, besides being originally Christian, was influenced by the neo-Platonic tradition of Moslem philosophy. Ibn Ayshun, of Toledo, who lived in the first half of the tenth century, describes the vision of the countenance of God as being like the contemplation of the

---

[1] *Corra*, 132.   [2] Gayangos Coll., MS 64, fol. 25.

sun or moon when unhidden by clouds.[1] Two centuries later, Shakir Ibn Muslim, of Orihuela, enumerates the different aspects in which God appears to the blessed according to his attributes of perfection, beauty, eloquence, mercy, bounty, wisdom, and kindness.[2] The author of the *Tadhkira*, in the middle of the thirteenth century, completes the doctrine by stating that even after each vision of the Divine essence the eternal light continues to reign in the souls of the blessed, so that the bliss of glory may be uninterrupted.[3] The Cordovan ascetic further establishes a difference of degree in the enjoyment of the vision, according to the merit of the soul ; to each precept of the Divine law there corresponds a degree of bliss that can only be attained by compliance with that precept.[4] In the twelfth century, the famous Oriental theologian and philosopher, Fakhr ad-Din ar-Razi, availed himself of the elements contained in the Koran and the *hadiths* to trace a general scheme of paradise showing eight main divisions, subdivided into a hundred degrees or stages.[5] Thus, in the centuries immediately preceding the Divine Comedy the structure of paradise, as conceived in the mind of Eastern and Western Islam, appears complete in outline and detail.

[1] Cf. Ibn Makhluf, II, 147. Abu Abd Allah Mohamed ibn Ayshun was a theologian and lawyer who also wrote poetry and compiled several books of *hadiths*. After being taken captive by the Christians, he was ransomed and died in his native town, Toledo, in 952 A.D.

[2] Cf. Ibn Makhluf, II, 151–154.

[3] Cf. Ibn Makhluf, II, 157.

[4] *Tadhkira*, 85.

[5] Ibn Makhluf, II, 58. The elaboration of this fantastic picture of glory was continued, more notably by the Spanish and African sufis between the twelfth and fourteenth centuries, until about the time the Divine Comedy was produced. Although Ibn Arabi's is undoubtedly the one that most nearly approaches the Dantean version, the following by Izzu'd-Din ibn Abd as-Salam of the fourteenth century, is also of interest :—

In heaven there are as many grades as there are virtues, and each of these is again subdivided into the lowest, the intermediate, and the highest grades. Thus, for example, the martyrs of Islam occupy the hundred highest grades as a reward for faith ; another hundred correspond to each of the other virtues ; then come a hundred grades for just rulers ; then a hundred for sincere witnesses, and so forth. If two of the elect are equally deserving by reason of faith (whether mystic or theological), both occupy the same grade ; but, if there is any difference in either the quantity or the quality of their faith, then they are placed apart. And so it is with the other virtues.

IX

THE CELESTIAL PARADISE OF ISLAM IN THE DIVINE COMEDY—(CONCLUSION)

1. Of the doctrine of paradise in general it may be safely said that nobody succeeded like the Murcian, Ibn Arabi, in blending all previous conceptions into one harmonious whole. Not only is Ibn Arabi's scheme embellished by the artistry of its author, but it is so illustrated by means of geometrical sketches that the general plan of his various heavenly mansions can be seen at a glance. This, from our point of view, is its most interesting feature.

In the cosmology of Ibn Arabi, the entire universe is represented by a circle or sphere[1] ; and the plan of the cosmos consists of a series of concentric spheres, which rise one above another with progressively increasing radii. At present we are only concerned with the units comprised between the earth and the Divine Throne. These, beginning at the bottom, are in turn[2] : the spheres of the earth, water, air and ether ; then, in the astronomical world, follow in succession the spheres of the moon, Mercury, Venus, Sun, Mars, Jupiter, Saturn, and that of the Fixed Stars ; still further is the sphere without stars or the *primum mobile*, where the astronomical world ends, and, finally, above all, shining like a focus of eternal light, the Throne of God Himself.

The paradise of the elect Ibn Arabi places between the heaven of the Fixed Stars and that of the *primum mobile*. Here, other eight concentric spheres, rising, as before behind and above each other, represent the eight mansions of the celestial paradise. These appear in the following order : 1. The abode of grace ; 2. The mansion of perseverance ; 3. The abode of peace ; 4. The garden of eternity ; 5. The garden of refuge ; 6. The garden of delight ; 7. The garden of paradise ; 8. The Garden of Eden.[3]

---

[1] A translation of the principal passages of the *Futuhat* relating hereto is given in the author's *Mohidin*, pp. 7–23.

[2] *Futuhat*, III, 579, and *passim*.

[3] *Futuhat*, I, 416; III, 552 and 567. Cf. *Al-Yawaqit*, II, 197. Cf. *Par.* XXX, 103, 125, and 130; XXXI, 67 and 115; XXXII, 26 and 36.

Each of these eight spheres[1] is divided into innumerable *grades*—Ibn Arabi, like Dante, claims that the number of these is considerably more than several thousand—which are grouped to form one hundred different categories. These in turn represent a still more limited number of classes of the chosen, which, if the followers of Mahomet only are considered, do not number more than twelve. Each grade contains countless individual *mansions* or *dwelling-places*.[2]

Fig. 1

2. Now, no great effort of imagination is required to trace the analogy between this fantastic conception and Dante's rose. True, Ibn Arabi does not employ the simile of the rose in his text ; but a mere glance at his plan, which, drawn with geometric precision, he himself has handed down to us, will at once suggest such a simile.

The figure given here (see Fig. 1) is as it appears in the *Futuhat*, III, 554, with the Arabic names translated. In its construction it is identical with the figure appearing under

---

[1] There are really only seven, as the first, being dedicated to Mahomet, must be associated with all the others.

[2] LANDINO, in discussing *Par.* XXXII on fol. 433 of his Commentary, arrives at the same number of *twelve* as that of the main degrees in Dante's realm of glory : " Onde sono sei dfferentie e ciascuna ha provetti e parvuli, che fanno dodeci." For the number of gradins, cf. *Par.* XXX, 113 : " piu di mille soglie."

the number 32 in Manfredi Porena's *Commento grafico alla Divina Commedia* as the plan of Dante's rose (see Fig. 2). Porena in his description compares it to an amphitheatre the tiers of which are occupied by the elect.

3. Apart from this similarity in geometrical design, there is a further affinity between Dante's rose and a Moslem myth whereby paradise is likened to a tree. Ibn Arabi, availing himself of a tradition very popular in Islam,[1] introduces into his plan a mighty tree depending from the heaven of the *primum mobile*, or roof of the abode of glory, whose foliage spreads throughout the seven celestial spheres and each branch of which penetrates one of the countless individual mansions of bliss. This tree he calls the tree of happiness, or bliss (see Fig. 1). Now, if this tree were to be depicted on Ibn Arabi's plan of the mansions of glory, the effect of its myriad branches extending to their set places on each of the seven strata of paradise would be to give the whole figure the appearance of seven concentric circles of leaves ; and this is exactly the impression one gets on looking into a rose.[2]

Nor does this mythical tree of Islam, growing downwards from the heaven of the highest sphere, appear to have been out of Dante's ken. His conception of the astronomical spheres (and they also from time to time serve as mansions of the blessed) is likewise that of a huge inverted tree, each one of whose branches corresponds to one of the astronomical spheres and whose roots are in the Empyrean. This image he forms when he reaches the sphere of Jupiter.[3] It must be admitted, however, that Dante's simile is not nearly so

---

[1] *Corra*, 118 : " And the Prophet said : In heaven is the tree of happiness whose root is in my dwelling-place and whose branches shelter all the mansions of heaven ; nor is there mansion or dwelling-place which holds not one of its branches . . ." (*Ibid.* 119). " Each of the blessed has his own branch, with his name inscribed upon it."

[2] A rough sketch of this Islamic tree is to be found in the illustration from the *Ma' rifet Nameh,* included by Carra de Vaux in *Fragments d'Eschatologie musulmane*, pp. 27 and 33. An amplified reproduction is here given (see Fig. 3).

[3] *Par.* XVIII, 28–33, on which Fraticelli comments :—
" Paragona il sistema de'cieli ad un albero che si fa più spazioso di grado in grado ; e fa che abbia vita dalla cima, in contrario de'nostri alberi, che l'anno dalle radici, perchè ei la toglie dall'empireo."

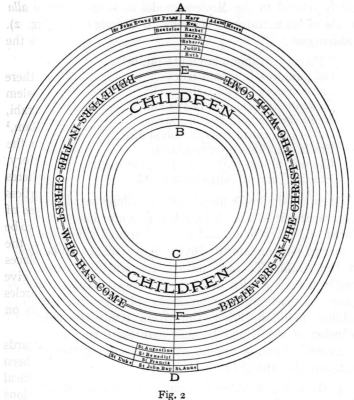

Fig. 2

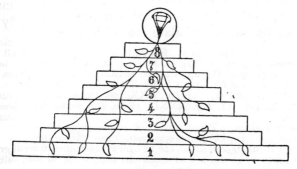

Fig. 3

closely related to the Moslem model as is the same simile of one of his imitators. We refer to Federigo Frezzi in his *Quadriregio*[1] :

> " Poscia trovammo la pianta più bella
> Del paradiso, la pianta felice
> Che conserva la vita e rinnovella.
> *Su dentro al cielo avea la sua radice*
> *E giù inverso terra i rami spande*
> Ov' era un canto che qui non si dice.
> Era la cima lata e tanto grande
> Che più, al mio parer, che duo gran miglia
> Era dall' una all' altra delle bande."

The other similes Dante uses in describing paradise—when he compares it to a walled garden, to a kingdom over which Christ and Mary reign, and to a hill around which the elect gather to contemplate the Divine light—are also to be found in Ibn Arabi. To him, indeed, the whole of paradise is simply a huge garden divided into seven circular parts by means of seven walls or luminous spheres[2] ; and its most sublime mansion, Eden, Ibn Arabi terms the palace or mansion of the King,[3] because here there rises a " hill of exceeding whiteness around which the elect gather to contemplate the Almighty."[4]

4. We will now proceed to compare the moral structure of Dante's paradise with that of Ibn Arabi. The outstanding feature of both works is the tendency of the writers to exaggerate the number of divisions and subdivisions of the various categories in which the elect are placed. Ibn Arabi, indeed, insists that " no good deed that ever was performed is without its own appropriate reward in paradise."[5] The

---

[1] In GRAF, *Miti*, I, 140, note 35 For particulars about Federigo Frezzi who composed his poem in 1394, cf. ROSSI, I, 264.

[2] *Futuhat*, I, 416 and III, 567. Cf. *Par.* XXXII, 20 and 39 ; XXXI, 97.

[3] *Futuhat*, I, 416 and III, 577. Cf. *Par.* XXXI, 25, 115, and XXXII, 61.

[4] *Futuhat*, I, 416 and 417. Cf. *Par.* XXX, 109, and XXXI, 121.

[5] *Futuhat*, I, 415. Cf. *Par.* XXXII, 52–60, and Fraticelli's comment thereon :—

" In questo così ampio Paradiso non può aver luogo un *punto*, un seggio, dato a caso . . . Poichè *quantunque vidi*, tutto quello che qui vedi, *è stabilito per eterna legge* in modo, che ad ogni grado di merito corrisponde un ugual grado di gloria, a quel modo che *dall' anello al dito*, al dito corrisponde proporzionato anello."

chief categories are eight in number, just as in the human body there are eight organs, controlled by the soul : the eyes, ears, tongue, hands, stomach, pudenda, feet, and heart. It will be remembered that this principle formed the basis of the moral structure of hell, for Ibn Arabi, as well as Dante, held that the strictest symmetry should be observed in the conceptions of the two worlds of the after-life. Of the eight categories in question, then, each has its reward in one of the eight spheres or strata of the celestial paradise.

Further, these eight rewards are subdivided into a multiplicity of grades, each one of which is assigned to a specific virtuous deed. The age of the blessed—to cite but one example, which is eminently Dantean—is taken into consideration when the rewards are administered, so that an old man, who has led a sinless life in the faith of Islam, is appointed to a higher grade than a younger man of equal innocence, even although both may have been distinguished for the same virtue.

Another striking similarity between the two works is to be found in the allotment of the various places that the elect occupy in each of the eight spheres of glory. According to Ibn Arabi, three reasons determine the allocation : the first, grace alone, in which category are placed children who died before reason came and adults who lived according to the natural law ; the second, personal virtue or good deeds performed by adults ; and the third, inheritance of the celestial mansions left unoccupied by the damned.[1] To strengthen the parallel, Ibn Arabi points out that the second reason does not imply that the happiness of glory is only the due reward for good done on earth. It is, he explains, something much greater than a mere recompense.[2]

By way of exemplifying how the elect are distributed, Ibn Arabi enumerates four of the principal categories in the

---

[1] Cp. *Futuhat*, I, 414, with *Par.* XXXII, 42–47 and 73–74. Also *Futuhat*, I, 415, with *Par.* XXX, 131–132.

[2] *Futuhat*, III, 8 : ' Divine mercy is greater than Divine anger. The damned, then, are punished for the sins they have committed only, but the elect enter heaven through grace and experience such bliss as by their good works alone they would not deserve.' Cf. *Par.* XXXII, 58–66.

higher grades : first, the prophets or God's messengers, who occupy pulpits in the highest grade ; secondly, the saints, who, as disciples of the prophets, are seated on thrones in the next grade ; thirdly, the wise men, who, having in life acquired a scientific knowledge of God, are placed in chairs in a still lower grade ; and fourthly, the pure in heart, who, having only gained a knowledge of Divine things through revelation, occupy gradins beneath the others.[1] Dante's distribution is on the same lines. In the highest seats he places the prophets, such as Adam and Moses, and the apostles, St. Peter, St. John, and so forth ; beneath these, the doctors of the religious orders, St. Francis, St. Benedict, and St. Augustine ; and lastly, the faithful, who obeyed the commandments.[2] It is also worthy of note that Dante in his description of the seats of the blessed uses the same terms as Ibn Arabi, namely, *thrones* or *chairs, gradins* or *forms.*[3]

In the four general categories in question Ibn Arabi again distinguishes, although somewhat vaguely, between the Moslem elect and those who, before Islam, professed the other religions revealed by the prophets of Israel, of whom, according to Moslem theology, Christ was one.[4] This vagueness is surprising, seeing that the Dantean division of the two elects had been established in Moslem tradition long before Ibn Arabi's time. A *hadith,* attributed to Ali, son-in-law of the prophet, clearly defines it[5] :

" At the Divine Throne are two pearls, one white and the other yellow, each of which contains 70,000 mansions. The white pearl is for Mahomet and his flock ; the yellow for Abraham and his."

[1] *Futuhat,* I, 417 ; II, 111 ; and III, 577.
[2] LANDINO, on fol. 432 v° of his Commentary, explains this point very clearly.
[3] Cp. *Par.* XXXI, 69 ; XXX, 133 and XXXII, 7 ; XXXI, 16 ; XXX, 115 and 132, with the passages of the *Futuhat* quoted under (¹).
[4] In Ibn Arabi, as will shortly be shown, the difference in the intensity of the Beatific Vision depends, as in Dante, on the nature of the faith the elect professed on earth.
[5] IBN MAKHLUF, II, 59–60. In Islam Mahomet is regarded as the Prophet who renewed the teaching of the one true religion as revealed by God to Abraham ; and, just as Abraham is the patriarch of the Old Testament, so Mahomet may be said to be the patriarch of the new Testament of the Moslems.

The analogy between this idea and Dante's distribution is obvious. In the mystic rose the prophets, patriarchs and saints of the Old Testament are placed in the left sector and those who lived after Christ in the right.[1] The similitude, however, extends to the actual details. Just as Ibn Arabi couples Mahomet with Adam in the same degree of the Beatific Vision, so does Dante place Adam with St. Peter in the mystic rose.[2]

5. Let us now study awhile the scene of the glorious triumph of the elect as depicted by the Murcian mystic. Briefly, the *Futuhat* description is as follows :

" The blessed gather around the snow-white hill to await the epiphany of the Lord. As they stand, each in his respective grade and place and magnificently arrayed,[3] a dazzling light shines forth before which they fall prostrate. Through their eyes into the inmost recesses of their bodies and souls the light penetrates, so that each of the blessed becomes all eye and ear and sees and hears with his entire spirit, such is the virtue conferred on them by the light. Thus are they prepared for the presence of the Almighty. And then the Prophet appears before them, saying, ' Prepare, then, ye chosen, for the manifestation of the Lord.' The three veils that enshroud the Almighty—the veils of glory, majesty and power—are drawn aside at His will, and the truth is revealed, one vision, yet in the dual epiphany of the two names, the beautiful and the good. The magnificence of the Lord leaves the elect spellbound, and the brilliance of the wonderful vision pervades their beings."

" This vision, although in itself one and the same so far as the elect are concerned, has, nevertheless, different aspects.[4] Those prophets, who only acquired their knowledge of God through the faith received from God Himself and did not increase that knowledge by reason and contemplation, will behold the vision through the eye of faith. The saint whose faith in God was inspired by a prophet will see it through the mirror of that prophet. If, however, he also gained a knowledge of God through contemplation, then will he have two visions, one of science and the other of faith.

---

[1] *Par.* XXXII, 19–27.   [2] *Futuhat*, II, 113, and *Par.* XXXII, 118.
[3] *Futuhat*, I, 417–420.   [4] *Futuhat*, II, 111.

And so also will it be with the prophet. Similarly, the saint who, unenlightened by any prophet, acquired his knowledge, either through his own reason or direct from the Almighty, or in both of these ways, will be ranged in the Beatific Vision with the men of science or those of simple faith, or with both of these classes. Those who obtained from God the mystic intuition only will occupy a grade in glory apart from all the other elect. To sum up, the three aspects which God presents to the elect correspond to the different ways in which a knowledge of Him was gained on earth; and he who acquired that knowledge in all three ways will witness three Divine manifestations in the same instant. The visions of the elect in these three categories are graded thus : the prophets who received supernatural inspiration from God excel those saints who followed their teaching ; while those who were neither prophets nor their disciples but simply saints and friends of God will, if they achieved the desired end by rational contemplation, be inferior in the Beatific Vision to the mystics, because reason, like a veil, will intervene between them and the Divine truth, and their efforts to raise it will be of no avail. In like manner the followers of the prophets will be unable to raise the veil of prophetic revelation. And so it is that the Beatific Vision, pure and unalloyed, will be the heritage exclusively of the prophets and those mystics who, like the prophets, received Divine inspiration on earth."

" In each grade of vision a relative degree of bliss will be experienced.[1] Thus, the joy of some of the saints will be purely intellectual and that of others, emotional, physical, or imaginative, as the case may be. As for the mass of the faithful, the enjoyment derived by each from the Beatific Vision will also be proportional to his capacity for understanding the theological dogmas of his master. Further, as the mentality of the multitude is chiefly imaginative, so will be their knowledge of God and their participation in the Beatific Vision. This, too, will be the lot of the majority of the men of rational science, few of whom, although superior to the multitude, are on earth able to conceive the absolute abstraction from all matter. Hence it is that the greater part of the truths revealed by God through religion have been presented to the multitude in a form adapted to its understanding, though invariably accompanied by vague

[1] *Futuhat*, II, 112–113.

allusions, which are intelligible only to a select few of those of superior intellect."[1]

Continuing, Ibn Arabi from time to time gives further interesting details[2] :

" In the Beatific Vision God manifests Himself to the elect in a general epiphany, which, nevertheless, assumes various forms corresponding to the mental conceptions of God formed by the faithful on earth. There is, then, one single epiphany, which is multiple only by reason of the difference of forms in which it is received. The Vision impregnates the elect with Divine light, each experiencing the Vision according to the knowledge of the Divine dogma or dogmas gained by him on earth."

" The Divine light pervades the beings of the elect and radiates from them, reflected as if by mirrors, on every-thing around them. The spiritual enjoyment produced by the contemplation of this reflection is even greater than that of the Vision itself. For, at the moment when they experi-ence the Beatific Vision, the elect are transported and, losing all consciousness, cannot appreciate the joys of the Vision. Delight they feel, but the very intensity of the delight makes it impossible for them to realise it. The reflected light, on the other hand, does not overpower them, and they are thus able to participate in all its joys."

The fact of there being different grades of glory engenders no bitter feeling, much less envy, in the minds of those of the elect that occupy the lower grades. Ibn Arabi makes this point clear.[3]

" Each knows his allotted grade and seeks it as a child seeks its mother's breast, and iron, the lodestone. To occupy or even aspire to a higher grade is impossible. In the grade in which he is placed each sees the realisation of his highest hopes. He loves his own grade passionately and cannot conceive that a higher could exist. If it were not so, heaven would not be heaven but a mansion of grief and bitter dis-illusion. Nevertheless, those in the superior participate in the enjoyment of the lower grades."

[1] This latter thesis was propounded by Averrhoes and adopted by St. Thomas. Cf. Asín, *Averroismo*, 291 *et seq.*
[2] *Futuhat*, III, 578.   [3] *Futuhat*, III, 577.

6. From this description, so rich in detail, in picturesque images and in philosophico-theological ideas, we may now select those cardinal theses that are prominent in Ibn Arabi and compare them with Dante's ideas.[1]

Firstly, the life of glory, according to the Murcian mystic, consists fundamentally in the Beatific Vision, which is conceived as a manifestation, revelation, or epiphany of the Divine light. God is a focus of light, the rays of which serve to prepare the elect to look upon the Almighty.

The parallel between this conception of Ibn Arabi and that of Dante need not be insisted upon ; both in idea and artistic execution the two are identical.[2] For the latter, mediæval Christian literature furnishes no precedent whatever. The former, however, the idea or theological thesis of the necessity of a Divine light with which to behold the Almighty, had been conceived and discussed by the scholastics long before Dante's time. St. Thomas Aquinas freely refers to a *lumen gloriae*, which strengthens the human understanding for participation in the Beatific Vision.[3]

At the same time it is certain that St. Thomas Aquinas himself admits seeking inspiration, not among the Holy Fathers and scholastic theologians, but among the Moslem philosophers.[4] It is the authority of Alfarabius, Avicenna, Avempace and Averrhoes that he quotes, when he attempts to explain the Beatific Vision in terms of philosophy, and it

[1] Before entering on this comparison we may be allowed to point out a curious coincidence in the chronology of Dante's ascension and that assigned in the *hadiths* to the ascension of the blessed souls to enjoy the Beatific Vision. Dante undertook his ascension " nel mezzo del camin di nostra vita " (*Inf.* I, 1) or, according to the commentators, " a trentacinque anni," or " dell'età di 32 o 33 anni " (Cf. Scartazzini). A *hadith* in the Gayangos Coll., MS 105, fol. 140 r°, attributes to Mahomet the statement that the blessed will enter paradise " at Jesus' age, or the age of thirty-three." Further, Dante ascends to heaven on Good Friday (cf. Fraticelli, pp. 622–3) and the *hadiths* state that the Beatific Vision takes place on Friday, the holy day of Islam (cf. *Kanz*, VII, 232, Nos. 2,572 and 2,641).

[2] Cf. *Par.* XXX, 10, 106, 112, and 115 ; XXXIII, 76 and 82 with *Futuhat*, I, 417, last line ; 418, line 8.

Further, just as St. Bernard bids Dante be prepared for the Divine light (*Par.* XXXII, 142, and XXXIII, 31), so does the Prophet, in Ibn Arabi's description, warn the elect (*Futuhat*, I, 418, line 12).

[3] *Summa contra Gentes*, lib. III, ch. 53 and 54. Cf *Summa theol.* part 1, q. 12, a. 5. [4] *Summa theol.*, suppl. part 3, q. 92, a. 1.

is the theory of Averrhoes, of the vision of the substances separated by the soul, that he accepts as the one most suitable for the elect's vision of God.[1]

That Aquinas should not have recourse to patristic or scholastic literature was but natural, seeing he would find there little or no information about so abstruse a theme. The chroniclers of dogma recognise that the philosophic explanation of this article of the Christian faith is not to be found in the Holy Fathers nor in the early theologians. St. John Chrysostom even denies the vision of the Divine essence. St. Ambrose, St. Augustine, and with the latter all the Latins up to the eighth century, placed the blessed, according to the Scripture, *face to face* with the Divinity in the Vision ; and they make the least possible comment on the sacred text to avoid falling into any anthropomorphic error, maintaining that it is impossible for the human eye to look upon the Vision.[2] Those that go more deeply into the subject, like St. Epiphanes, merely arrive at the conclusion that the soul requires assistance before it can look upon God.[3] What the nature of this assistance is, neither the Scriptures nor the Holy Fathers have determined. This is admitted by Petavius. Although the sacred texts tell of a Divine *lumen*, this has no bearing on the scholastic theory of the *lumen gloriae*. St. Thomas, indeed, held that the *lumen gloriae* is a principle of vision, as it were a habit or faculty of seeing (akin to the sensitive faculty inherent in the eye), by means of which principle the human mind is trained to behold God. On the other hand, the *lumen* of the Psalms (XXXV, 10), " In lumine tuo videbimus lumen," was regarded by Origenes, St. Cyril, the pseudo-Dionysius, and St. Augustine, as a synonym of Christ, in Whose light we should see the Father. From which Petavius concludes

---

[1] *Loc cit.*, at the end of the body of the article :—

" Et ideo accipiendus est alius modus, quem etiam quidam philosophi posuerunt, scilicet Alexander et Averroes (3. *de Anim. comm.* 5 *et* 36) " ..." Quidquid autem sit de aliis substantiis separatis, tamen istum modum oportet nos accipere in visione Dei per essentiam."

[2] TIXERONT, II, 201, 349, 435 ; III, 431.

[3] *Haeres.*, 70, in PETAVIUS, *De Deo*, lib. VII, ch. 8, §1 : " Vi sua imbecillitatem corroborare dignatus est."

that the theory of the *lumen gloriae* is a novelty introduced by the scholastics.[1] He finishes by citing Plotinus as the only thinker that saw even vaguely the necessity, for the Vision of God, of a *lumen* which is God Himself. Had there only been added to his great store of patristic learning some knowledge of Moslem theology (which was unknown in his century), he would have completed the cycle of his historical investigations and filled the gap of centuries that separates Plotinus from the scholastics.

He would have found, indeed, in Algazel and in the Spaniards, Ibn Hazm and Averrhoes—to mention but three great theologians—the roots from which the theory of the *lumen gloriae* sprouted. Algazel dedicates a complete chapter of his *Ihia* to the development of this theory.[2] Long before St. Thomas, he defined the Beatific Vision as a perfection of the understanding and, in order to convey an idea of the vision of glory, he establishes a complete, although metaphorical, parallel between it and the physical vision. He says ·

As the physical vision is a complement and perfection of the fantastic representation of the object, the Beatific Vision is a clearer and more perfect perception of God as He appears to the mind in this life. He proceeds[3] : " God will reveal Himself to the elect in all the splendour of His manifestation. This epiphany, compared with the knowledge of God possessed by the elect, will be like the manifestation of an object in a mirror compared with a fantastic representation of it. That epiphany of God is what we call the Beatific Vision. It is, then, a real vision, provided it is clear that here we do not understand by *vision* a complement of the imaginative representation of the imaginable object, represented in a concrete form, with dimensions, site, etc. The knowledge which you have gained of God on earth will be completed in

---

[1] PETAVIUS, *loc. cit.*, §4 : " Quocirca de illo lucis officio et usu, qui in scholis percrebuit, nihil apud antiquos expressum habetur, nisi quod vis quaedam naturali superior et auxilium requiri dicitur quo mens ad tantam contemplationem possit assurgere. Quale autem sit necessarium illud auxilium, sive lumen gloriae, quo ad Deum videndum natura fulcitur, nemo liquido demonstravit, minime omnium efficientis quoddam genus esse causae, ac velut habitum."

[2] *Ihia*, IV, 222. Cf. *Ithaf*, IX, 581. [3] *Ihia*, IV, 223, line 14 inf.

heaven and will become presence or experience. Between this presence in the future life and the knowledge acquired on earth there will be no more difference than what comes from a greater manifestation and clearness."

Ibn Hazm, the great eleventh-century theologian of Cordova, expounds a similar doctrine :

" We do not admit the possibility of seeing God with a sort of human vision. We simply maintain that God will be seen by means of a power distinct from that which we have in our eyes, a power that will be inspired in us by God. Some people call it a *sixth sense*. And the proof lies in the fact that, as we now know God with our souls, which in this life He has strengthened to that end, so afterwards God may strengthen our vision in order that we may behold Him."[1]

We have already seen how Averrhoes' theory was accepted by St. Thomas as an explanation of the Beatific Vision. But he goes further. In one of his theological treatises,[2] dealing with the texts of the Koran which compare God to a light, he says :

" God, being the cause of the existence of all beings and the cause of our being able to see them, has rightly been called *Light* ; for the same relation exists between light and the colours, that is to say, light is the cause of their existence and also of our being able to see them. Nor can any doubt exist about the dogma of the vision of God, which is a light, in the life to come."

And after refuting all objections, he concludes, like Algazel, by asserting that the Vision will consist in an increased knowledge of the Divine essence.

7. The analogies, however, between Dante's conception and that of Ibn Arabi are not limited to the general theory of the *lumen gloriae*. Other even more striking similarities are :

Secondly. In both descriptions the elect are in the same attitude, their gaze fixed on the focus of Divine light.[3] The different grades in the Beatific Vision depend, according to Dante, on the degree of love that each of the elect shows for

---

[1] *Fasl*, III, 2–4. [2] *Kitab falsafat*, 53.
[3] Cp. the passages from the *Futuhat* translated above, on pp. 157–159, with *Par.* XXXI, 27, and XXXIII, 43, 50, 52, 79, and 97.

God, whereas in Ibn Arabi it appears to be the nature of the knowledge that the souls possessed of the Divinity that counts.[1] It would seem, then, that Dante adopted the point of view of a voluntaryist, and Ibn Arabi, that of an intellectualist. The difference, however, is more apparent than real. For Dante frequently appears to adopt Ibn Arabi's standpoint as an intellectualist ; on several occasions he attributes the grade of glory to the nature of the faith or the illuminating grace with which the soul knew God.[2] Further Ibn Arabi, like all Moslem mystics, is essentially a voluntaryist ; virtue, in his opinion, is based, not on theological knowledge or dead faith, but on divine love, at once the cause and the fruit of the knowledge that the soul has gained of God. He therefore reserves a prominent grade in the Beatific Vision for the contemplative mystics and places in an inferior position such saints as were also philosophers.[3] This doctrine was expounded by Algazel before Ibn Arabi. The happiness of heaven—he writes in his *Ihia*[4]—will be proportionate to the intensity of the love for God, just as this love will be commensurate with the knowledge of God gained by the elect on earth and called by Revelation, faith.

Thirdly. The difference in grades is shown, not in the Beatific Vision itself, but in the variety of forms in which the Divine light is made manifest to the elect and in the greater or lesser brilliance of the light they receive and reflect.[5] These three ideas of Ibn Arabi have also their respective parallels in Dante's conception. In *Par.* XXX, 121, he says : " There, distance makes no difference, for where God governs the natural law has no power whatever." In this way Dante establishes the essential unity of the vision in its different grades. If in these grades there is any difference, it is not in the thing seen but in the way of seeing

---

[1] Cf. Rossi, I, 147. " Per Dante, il premio dei buoni è . . . vario di grado, secondo la purezza e l'intensità dell'amore divino." Cf. *Futuhat*, I, 418, line 7.

[2] *Par.* XXXII, 19, 38, 74. Cf. *Futuhat, loc. cit.* ; also I, 419, line 9 inf. ; II, 111, line 8 inf. ; II, 113, line 10 inf.

[3] *Futuhat*, II, 111, line 9 inf. and 1 inf.

[4] *Ihia*, IV, 224, line 15.   [5] *Futuhat*, III, 578, line 2.

it. Accordingly, in *Par.* XXXIII, 109, he adds: "Not because there were more than one aspect of the light I saw, which itself is immutable, but because my vision, strengthened by its contemplation, was able to see it in another manner."

Finally, that the light acquired is reflected by the elect, and its greater or lesser brilliance distinguishes their greater or lesser glory, are points frequently alluded to by Dante in the Paradiso.[1] The Dantists have explained this theme by the Thomist doctrine of the endowments of the glorious body, one of which is the radiance it derives from the glory of the soul.[2] Now, we have already seen how Ibn Arabi, before St. Thomas, likewise explains the radiance of the elect by the superabundance of Divine light, which pervades the body of each blessed and is reflected from all around it. Nor was this an original idea of Ibn Arabi's, but merely a repetition of the doctrine of the *Ishraqi* mystics. Indeed, in the tenth century of our era, the author of the *Corra*, having discovered it in some *hadiths* of a still earlier date, used the theme in his description of paradise. In those pictures of the glorious life, the external brightness of the elect indicates the grade of glory of each. The following passages put the matter beyond all doubt[3]:

"He who belongs to the highest category of the elect so illumines the others that the whole of heaven is bright with the radiance of his face." Again, it is stated that "the

---

[1] Rossi, I, 147: "Il vario grado di lor beatitudine è appunto rappresentato dalla varia luminosità e dalla loro distribuzioni pei sette primi cieli." Cf. *Par.* XXX, 12, and XXXI, 59; also *Par.* XIV, 43–60.

[2] *Summa theol.*, suppl. 3ae part., q. 85, a. 1:
"Ideo melius est ut dicatur quod claritas illa causabitur ex redundantia gloriae animae in corpus . . . ; et ideo claritas quae est in anima spiritualis, recipitur in corpore ut corporalis; et ideo secundum quod anima erit majoris claritatis secundum majus meritum, ita etiam erit differentia claritatis in corpore."

[3] *Corra*, 102, 104, 106, 114, and 117. Cf. *Kanz*, VII, 232, Nos. 2,575, 2,588, 2,608, 2,616, 2,629, and 2,658. In Nos. 2,616 and 2,658, moreover, the bodies of the women of heaven are said to be "translucent like crystal or precious stones," an idea that reappears in *Par.* XXXI, 19, and XXIX, 124. The sufis, and particularly Ibn Arabi, held that the souls, until the resurrection of their bodies, lived in bodies of the world beyond the grave, similar in nature to the forms we see in dreams (cf. Asín, *La Psicología*, 45). This theory may have given rise to Dante's conception of the spirit-bodies, which cast no shadow. Cf. *Purg.* III, 16–30. The same property was attributed to the body of Mahomet in this world. Cf. MS 64 Gayangos Coll., fol. 114.

elect see one another in paradise as we see stars shining in the sky " ; that " if one of the elect were to descend to earth, he would eclipse the light of the sun " ; that Fatima, the daughter of Mahomet, is called the Brilliant, the Splendid, on account of the intensity of her light ; that " the robes of the blessed reflect the Divine light " ; that " when the Almighty appears in the Beatific Vision and the light of the Divine countenance falls on the faces of the elect, it causes them to shine with such brilliance that they appear transfigured with ecstasy " ; and, lastly, that after the Beatific Vision the elect marvel at their own greater brilliance, increased by the reflection of the countenance of God.

Fourthly. The Beatific Vision will engender joy or delight, proportional to the various grades of the Vision, but so intense as to produce ecstasy in the soul. As is well-known, this idea of Ibn Arabi's reappears in full in Dante's work.[1] The idea of proportion may, it is true, have been taken from the Thomist doctrine rather than from Islamic sources.[2] Not so the idea of the ecstasy ; of this there is not a word in the Thomist doctrine, which confines itself to an explanation of the philosophic origin of the three endowments of the blessed soul : vision, delectation, and comprehension of the Divine essence. Whereas, if the ecstasy in Dante be psychologically analysed and compared with that in Ibn Arabi, various constituent elements common to both will be found : loss of memory, somnolence or semi-consciousness, produced on the soul by the intensity of delight.[3]

Fifthly. The fact of there being different grades in the Beatific Vision excites no feeling of envy or sadness among those in the lower grades. Each accepts his share of the glory as if it were impossible even to desire anything greater. And this is so, because all love the grade they occupy ; and, further, because, if it were not thus, heaven would not be a mansion of peace and delight.[4]

---

[1] *Par.* XXX, 40. Cf. *Futuhat*, II, 112, line 11 inf.

[2] *Summa theol.*, suppl. 3ae part., q. 95, a. 5.

[3] *Par.* XXXIII, 57 and 94. Cf. *Futuhat*, I, 419, line 7 inf. ; III, 578, line 11. See also the comparison *supra*, pp. 31 and 32.

[4] *Futuhat*, III, 577, line 10 inf. This point is frequently brought out by Moslem theologians and is based on two passages in the Koran (VII, 41, and XV, 47), in which it is said that God will remove all envy and resentment from the hearts of the blessed.

Dante puts the same explanation in the mouth of Piccarda[1]: " Our desires, awakened only by the love of the Holy Spirit, are satisfied in the way that He determined." To Dante's inquiry whether there is no desire on the part of the souls to attain to a higher place, Piccarda replies : " Brother, a feeling of charity quells such a desire, and we long for nothing more than what we have. Were we to aspire to a higher sphere, our wish would be at variance with the will of the Almighty, and such disagreement does not exist in the kingdom of heaven." Dante, satisfied with the explanation, concludes : " Then I understood why in the heavens all is paradise, notwithstanding the different degrees of bliss."

8. The identity thus established between the five fundamental theses of the Murcian Ibn Arabi on the Beatific Vision and Dante's is strong enough to render comment unnecessary. In comparison, the other similarities, such as picturesque details and artistic devices, used in both descriptions in an attempt to delineate by geometrical figures the Divine truth as seen in the glorious vision, are vague.

The analogy that was revealed in the discussion of Version C of the second cycle of the *Miraj*[2] between the apotheosis witnessed by Mahomet and that described by Dante need not be dwelt upon. It is as well to recall, however, that the image representing the Divinity in that version, which dates back to the eighth century, is identical with that employed by Dante : a focus of light, surrounded by concentric circles, composed of tiers of resplendent angels. This description was perpetuated in Islam, and Ibn Arabi frequently reproduced it in his *Futuhat*, notably in his portrayal of God at the final judgment.[3]

But the similarity extends further. Dante, having arrived at the spiritual cusp of his glorious ascension, attempts to explain the mystery of the Trinity by means of the same

---

[1] *Par.* III, 52, 64, 70, and 88. Cf. Par. XXXII, 52 and 63.
[2] Cf. *supra*, pp. 31 and 32.
[3] *Futuhat*, III, 574, and I, 402. In III, 556, the apotheosis is shown graphically, though on account of the difficulty of design the rows of angels are not represented by circles.

geometrical circular symbol : three circumferences, of equal
size and multi-coloured, the first two of which seem to be
a reflection of the other, after the manner of two rainbows,
and the third as of fire, emitted by the other two.[1] Now,
the more shrewd among the commentators, although
acknowledging the ingenuity shown by Dante in his conception, admit that this geometrical symbol of the three
circles, as a representation of the persons of the Trinity, is
more of an enigma than it is explanatory. No details are
given of the colour of the first two circles or of the geometrical relationship between the three, whether they are
concentric or eccentric, whether they are tangent to or cut
each other—in fact, no help whatever to interpret the symbol
is given.[2] One fact, however, stands out : Dante uses the
symbol of the circle to represent God in all His aspects—
as One in the Essence, as the Father, as the Son, and as the
Holy Ghost. Thus, the symbol of the circle represents God
conceived both as the principle of emanation and as the
emanation itself.

Now, it is well known that the same use of the circle as a
symbol of the Divinity was made in the Plotinian metaphysics.[3] The *Apocryphal Theology* of Aristoteles, as also
the apocryphal book of Hermes Trismegistus and the *Liber
de Causis*, made this symbol known to the Moslems and the
scholastics ; but it was the Moslems, the *Ishraqi* mystics
in particular, who had recourse to the circle on every possible
occasion to explain their ideas on emanation, both in their
metaphysics and their cosmology.[4]

The Murcian Ibn Arabi, more than any of the *Ishraqis*,
employs circles, concentric and eccentric, secant and tangent,
to represent the Almighty, whether in His abstract indi-
viduality, in His attributes, names and relations, in His

[1] *Par.* XXXIII, 115.
[2] Cf. E. Pistelli, *L'ultimo canto della D.C.* (in Scartazzini, *Par.* XXXIII,
120) :—
" Noi non tenteremo di seguirlo (*i.e.* Dante) e di rappresentarci sensi-
bilmente i tre archi di due dei quali, tra le altre cose, neppure ci ha detto
il colore. Che Dio sia fuori delle leggi dello spazio e del tempo, sta bene ;
ma noi le leggi dello spazio non consentono di veder distinti tre cerchi
chè in realtà sono uno solo e anche per questa via ricadiamo nel mistero."
[3] *Enneades*, VI, 8, 18.   [4] Cf. Asín, *Abenmasarra, passim.*

manifestations *ad extra*, or in His emanation.[1] A circle of white light on a red background, also of light, with two radii projecting from it, as it gently moves but never changes, is the symbol by which he represents the individual essentiality of God.[2] The procession of the beings who emanate from God the essence is also symbolised in the *Futuhat* by a circle.[3] The centre, like a focus of light, is God, from Whom the contingent beings emanate, just as the radii of a circle proceed from one central point to terminate in a series of points which, when joined together, form the circumference, symbolical of the cosmos ; and just as these points are in their essence indistinguishable the one from the other, so also in the emanation of God is there a unity of substance and a multiplicity of epiphanies ; the beings are merely the aspects, or the names and forms under which the Divine light appears.

These emanations likewise are represented by circles[4] ; at the innumerable points on the first circumference, the centre of which is God, an infinity of other circumferences cut the circle ; and these in turn produce other circles, secant as before, and so on *ad infinitum*. As the circles multiply, the centre of their origin, God, becomes hidden, nevertheless, all reflect the light of His first epiphany. All the ingenious and paradoxical similitudes which Ibn Arabi deduces from this symbol of the Divine emanation are founded upon one main idea, the basis of his pantheism, half emanative, half immanent. God and the creatures are one 'and the same substance ; the multiplicity of the emanations in no wise changes the essence of their origin ; and these emanations are merely distinct affinities, who represent the immanence of the origin from which they spring.

This general plan of the Divine emanation becomes less involved when Ibn Arabi proceeds to represent the onto-.

---

[1] His book, *Formation of tables and circles*, is specially devoted to this subject. Cf. *Futuhat*, III, 523.
[2] *Futuhat*, II, 591. Cf. Asín, *La Psicología*, 69.
[3] *Futuhat*, III, 158, 363, and 589. For a translation of the passage on 363, see Asín, *Mohidin*, 7–13.
[4] *Futuhat*, I, 332, translated in Asín, *Mohidin*, 13–17.

logical categories alone by the symbol of concentric circles.[1]
The supreme series of these consists of three substances,
hypostases or emanations from the One Absolute : first,
the Spiritual Substance, from which proceed all those
beings who are not God ; secondly, the Universal Intellect,
which is the Divine light by which the beings of the Spiritual
Substance receive objective reality ; thirdly, the Universal
Soul, likewise an emanation from the One, through the
Intellect.[2] This triad of substances, which to Ibn Arabi
represents the essence of God, is shown in the *Futuhat* by
a geometrical figure composed of three circles : the largest,
which encircles the whole figure, represents the Spiritual
Substance ; inside, two smaller eccentric circles, almost
tangent to one another, symbolise the Intellect and the
Soul. Ibn Arabi gives no reasons for these graphic details
of his plan, but the mere fact of his using the three circles
as a symbol for the three hypostases of his Trinity, to wit,
the principle of prime aptitude for the existence of all beings,
the principle of active potency to give such existence, and
the principle of life of the cosmos, is in itself an interesting
point and one that will repay the study of those who, while
appreciating the subtle ingenuity of the Florentine poet, are
not content merely to admire his artistic creations but are
eager to find out whence he derived his ideas.[3] For, in spite
of there being an abyss of differences between the pantheistic
triad of Ibn Arabi and the Catholic dogma of the Trinity,[4]
this in no wise affects the symbolical representation of the

[1] *Futuhat*, III, 560.

[2] For a fuller exposition, see AsÍN, *La Psicología*, 25–39, and *Abenmasarra*, *passim*.

[3] The figure is given on p. 553, and explained on pp. 560–2, of vol. III of the *Futuhat*. It is essentially as represented hereunder, A being the Spiritual Substance, B the Universal Intellect, and C the Universal Soul.

[4] Ibn Arabi admits, however, a certain trinity of relations as essential to Divine unity. The metaphysical reason of his opinion is to be found in the Pythagorean conception of the number three as being the origin of odd numbers (cf. *Futuhat*, III, 166, 228, 603). In *Futuhat*, II, 90, he applies the doctrine to theology and, in order to explain the origin and existence of the Cosmos, he establishes three Divine elements : the Essence, the Will, and the Word. In *Dakhair*, 42, he attempts to establish analogies between the Christian doctrine of the Trinity of Divine Persons and the trinity of Divine names as taught in the Koran—God, the Lord, and the Merciful.

two conceptions by a geometrical plan. To adapt this plan to a representation of either conception would constitute neither an absurdity in metaphysics nor a danger from the point of view of dogma, provided that the key to the enigma were kept discreetly hidden and concrete details in its interpretation were omitted ; and this is exactly what Dante did. In describing his symbol of the three circles, he con-

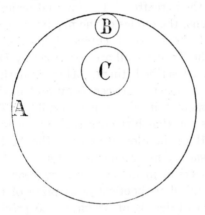

fines himself to stating that the three are one only as regards " continenza," i.e., substance, and that they are of different colours, to distinguish the Three Divine Persons, in the unity of essence.[1]

X

SYNTHESIS OF ALL THE PARTIAL COMPARISONS

1. The many minute comparisons made in this second part of our work will now enable us to present, in the form of a synthesis of the partial results, the following conclusions :

A considerable number of the details and topographical

---

[1] Ibn Arabi's symbol is as difficult to interpret ; for besides the three circles representing God in His three manifestations of spiritual matter, intellect, and soul, he speaks of the manifestation of God through three veils, or under three names (*Futuhat*, I, 418). Again, the manifestations of the Divine names he symbolises by eccentric circles of diverse radius (*Futuhat*, III, 558). Ibn Arabi does not mention the colours of these Divine epiphanies, but in the *Corra*, 125, the Divinity is said to appear to the elect wrapt in a white light with shades of green, red, and yellow.

descriptions in the Divine Comedy, although they have no parallels in the *Miraj*, have, nevertheless, their precedents in Islamic literature, whether it be in the Koran, in the *hadiths*, in the Moslem legends of the final judgment, or in the doctrine of the theologians, philosophers, and mystics.

2. Among all the Islamic thinkers, the Murcian Ibn Arabi stands out as the most likely to have furnished Dante with his model for the hereafter. The infernal regions, the astronomical heavens, the circles of the mystic rose, the choirs of angels around the focus of Divine light, the three circles symbolising the Trinity—all are described by Dante exactly as Ibn Arabi described them. This similarity betrays a relation such as exists between copy and model. That it should be a mere coincidence is impossible. The historical facts are these: in the thirteenth century, twenty-five years before the birth of the Florentine poet, Ibn Arabi introduced into his *Futuhat* plans of the hereafter, all of which were circular or spherical in design. Eighty years after, Dante produces a marvellous poetical description of the after-life, the topographical details of which are so precise that they enabled the poet's commentators in the twentieth century to represent them graphically by geometrical plans; and these plans are essentially identical with those designed by Ibn Arabi seven centuries before. If imitation by Dante can be disproved, the manifest similarity is either an insolvable mystery or a miracle of originality.[1]

3. Over and above this identity in construction there is a striking analogy in decoration. Indeed, the Aaraf seems to be the prototype of the limbo: the Gehenna, the model of the Inferno; the Sirat of the Purgatorio; the meadow between purgatory and hell, of the Terrestrial Paradise; and the eight gardens, of the Mystic Rose or Dantean Paradise.

---

[1] Had Vossler known of Ibn Arabi's plans, he would certainly not have sought in the symmetry of Dante's three realms a symbolical application of the Ptolemaic system to purgatory and hell. Vossler, after lengthy explanations and subtle interpretations of this theory, exclaims (I, 252) :—

" Chi può decidere ove graviti il centro di tali simboli, se nella poesia o nella scienza ? " . . . " Noi non conosciamo nella letteratura mondiale alcun altro laboro artistico, che sia così profondamente penetrato di filosofia."

4. The same unity in architectural design and the same hankering after symmetry, physical as well as moral, are exhibited in both descriptions. Jerusalem is the pivot on which the other world revolves ; beneath it is hell, in the last storey of which Lucifer is imprisoned ; vertically above Jerusalem is the theological heaven, where dwell the Divinity and the elect ; here, the number, as well as the subdivision, of the mansions is identical with that of the infernal regions, with the result that each place in hell has its antithesis in heaven.

5. The likeness between the two extends to many of the episodes and scenes, some of which are literally identical. For instance, the classification of the inhabitants of the limbo and their moral suffering are analogous to those of the Aaraf ; the black tempest of the adulterers is the Koranic wind of Ad ; the rain of fire that beats down upon the Sodomites, who are driven round in a circle ; the punishment of the soothsayers, whose heads are reversed ; Caiaphas, crucified upon the ground and trampled upon ; the robbers, devoured by serpents ; the authors of schism, with their bowels protruding and their arms cut off, or with their head, talking, in their hands ; the giants, whose abnormal proportions are described in parallel terms ; the torture of the ice, which is the Moslem *zamharir*, suffered by traitors ; the picture of Lucifer, fast in ice like the Islamic Iblis ; the dense smoke that envelops the passionate in purgatory, identical with that which, according to the Koran, will appear on the Day of Judgment ; the double ablution in the two rivers of the earthly paradise, and the meeting of Dante with Beatrice, which is a parallel scene to that of the entry of the soul into the Islamic paradise, after ablution in two rivers, and of the meeting with its heavenly bride ; and, lastly, the description of the Beatific Vision as a Divine *lumen*, which produces outward brilliance, intellectual clarity, and ecstatic delight.

6. If to all these analogies of architecture, topography, and setting, are added those that were brought out in full relief in the first part of this work, it will be apparent that the religious literature of Islam alone, in the sole theme of the

after-life—a theme mainly developed around the *Miraj*—offers to investigators a more abundant harvest of ideas, images, symbols, and descriptions, similar to those of Dante, than all the other religious literatures together that have up to now been consulted by Dantists in their endeavours to explain the genesis of the Divine Comedy.

7. And here our study might be concluded, were it not for one important doubt that may assail the mind of the investigator.

The artistic devices and theological-philosophic conceptions introduced by Dante into his poem are attributed by Dantists to the poet's own inventive genius, stimulated to a certain extent by his acquaintance with sundry popular legends that were broadcast throughout Europe in the centuries immediately preceding his appearance. These mediæval legends are technically referred to as the " precursors of the Divine Comedy."

Now, it is certain that none of these furnishes the same explanation for so many elements of Dante's work as does the legend of the *Miraj*, and, taken altogether, they fail to throw light upon many details which the *Miraj* and Islamic literature in general explain in full. Further, the analogies between the Divine Comedy and its precursors are too slight to establish any relation such as exists between model and copy.

In spite of all this, however, it might be possible to ignore the hypothesis of Moslem influence over Dante's poem and fall back on the theory that the poem was conceived in the womb of Christian literature and evolved from the seeds of eschatology contained in its mediæval precursors. To rebut this theory and render the argument in favour of our hypothesis conclusive, further investigation is, therefore, necessary. The origin of the eschatological elements in the precursory legends must be inquired into, in order to ascertain whether they were indeed all of native Christian growth, or whether they do not also show signs of Moslem ancestry such as the Divine Comedy has revealed to us.

PART III

MOSLEM FEATURES IN THE CHRISTIAN LEGENDS
PRECURSORY OF THE DIVINE COMEDY

PART III

MOSLEM FEATURES IN THE CHRISTIAN LEGENDS PRECURSORY OF THE DIVINE COMEDY

I

INTRODUCTION

1. THE belief in the immortality of the soul and the natural desire of man to lift the veil shrouding the mysteries of the after-life appear to have been the psychological motives that inspired the authors of the many legends, popular throughout mediæval Christian Europe, the main theme of which is the picturesque description of a fantastic journey to the realms beyond the grave. These are the legends that, in the opinion of the scholars, provided Dante with the raw material for his poem.[1] Accordingly, they have been collected and analysed with scrupulous care by the leading critics, who, needless to add, consider them to be of purely Christian origin, either the spontaneous outcome of popular imagination or the result of centuries of monastic learning embellished by the artistic fancy of the troubadour.[2] The main centre from which these legends radiated over Europe appears indeed to have been the monasteries of Ireland. But it is interesting to note the marked difference between the legends that appeared before and those that appeared after the eleventh century. The monastic tales prior to that century are so poor in material and inartistic in treatment, the scenes representing the future life of the soul so trivial and at times coarse that, even had Dante known of their existence, they could scarcely have served as models for his work. This is

[1] D'ANCONA, 13, 107. Cf. also LABITTE, OZANAM, and GRAF.
[2] D'ANCONA, 9, 25, 26, 27, 38, 70, 84, and *passim*.

admitted by D'Ancona himself. Later on, however, fresh tales appear, revealing a more fertile imagination and greater refinement on the part of the authors. These D'Ancona calls " veri abbozzi e prenunziamenti del poema dantesco."[1]

2. How is this sudden change in the development of the eschatological theme in Western Christian literature to be accounted for ? The hypothesis of the influence of elements, foreign to Western culture but adaptable thereto—inasmuch as their origin may in the end be traced back to the same early Christian stock—would not appear to be extravagant. Graf has observed that many particulars of the universal myth of paradise, although omitted from the Biblical narrative, reappear in these Christian legends ; and he adds significantly that *it is not known whence they came nor by what means they were transmitted.*[2] Yet Graf made most methodical use of all the sources available to modern European erudition. The eschatological literature of Islam alone seems to have escaped the attention of this keen critic, for the Arabic texts, when not translated into some European tongue, were as a sealed book to him. In the following pages an attempt will be made to fill this gap by examining the Moslem legends for evidence of poetic features that may have influenced the Christian legends and thus explain their remarkable efflorescénce in the eleventh century.

3. General evidence of such influence may be found in a feature observed by Graf himself. He notes that in many of the more popular legends of that date the souls of the deserving, before being admitted to eternal bliss, are led to a place other than the theological heaven, there to await the day of resurrection and judgment. But, as Graf states, from the fifth century onwards it was a dogma of the Church that the righteous were straightway admitted to the Beatific Vision, and any doctrine to the contrary was accursed.[3] Can stronger evidence exist of the non-Catholic origin of those legends ? Islam, on the other hand, holds that from the time of death until the day of resurrection the souls of the

[1] D'ANCONA, 42.   [2] GRAF, *Miti*, I, Introduction, XXII.
[3] GRAF, *Miti*, I, 66–67.

just await judgment either in their graves, miraculously transformed into dwellings of temporary bliss, or in a garden of happiness lying apart from heaven.[1] The souls of martyrs alone appear to be immediately admitted to heaven, or rather to a Divine bower at the gate leading to the theological heaven. As will be shown hereunder, the scenes of this life of bliss prior to judgment bear a strong resemblance to several episodes of the Christian legends ; and this similarity in descriptive detail, added to the coincidence of dogmatic belief, would seem to confirm the hypothesis of the Moslem origin of those legends. Nor is this belief, which, while still alive in Islam, had long been abandoned as heterodox by Western Christianity, the only proof of Moslem inspiration. Ozanam and D'Ancona state that many of the more poetic and edifying of these legends never received the official approval of the Church,[2] as if the latter had divined the existence, beneath the veil of poetic adornment, of a doctrine not altogether compatible with the orthodox creed. Indeed the palpable evidence of Islamic influence that will be found in many of these mediæval legends fully justifies that attitude.

4. In the following chapters the comparison of these legends with the Moslem tales is based—be it frankly admitted—not upon their entire texts, but upon the summaries furnished by the critics. Less minute, therefore, than the comparison aimed at in the two former parts of this work, it will serve to give a brief survey rather than a definite solution of this interesting literary problem.

Nor is any attempt made to group the Christian legends according to any new system. Where not already collected in cycles, they will be considered separately, even at the risk of repetition. Such repetition will not extend, however, to particulars the Islamic origin of which has already been proved. To these brief allusion only will be made and special attention paid to new features for which no Moslem precedent has so far been found.

[1] Cf. *Sudur*, 96–109 and IBN MAKHLUF, I, 57, and *passim*.
[2] OZANAM, 458 ; D'ANCONA, 33.

LEGENDS OF VISIONS OF HELL

1. *Legend of the Three Monks of the East or of St. Macarius.*[1] —Labitte and D'Ancona ascribe this legend to the sixth, seventh or eighth century ; but Ozanam maintains that it must be later than Islam, seeing that in the epilogue the saint inquires of his guests what news they have of the Saracens. Graf considers it to be of Græco-Christian origin, but the mystery surrounding the person of the saint himself contributes to render the origin of the story still more obscure.

2. We will briefly examine the descriptive features that may point to a Moslem origin.

In the course of their long and adventurous pilgrimage the three monks cross Syria, Persia and Ethiopia. Passing through a country inhabited by dog-headed men, they traverse a land of pygmies and reach a territory swarming with dragons, basilisks, asps and other venomous creatures. Pursuing their way, they cross a desert region strewn with stones and rocks and, passing through the country of elephants, finally come to a land of deep shadow, behind which rises the monument erected by Alexander the Great as a boundary marking the end of the world.

The early Moslem tales referred to in a former chapter as being the remote prototypes of Dante's hell, and notably a *hadith* of the time of Mahomet, give a similar division of the earth into seven regions, some of which are identical with those of the legend. Thus, the dog-headed men appear in the third earth of the *hadith* ; the fifth is full of serpents and scorpions ; and the fourth is formed of sulphurous stones.[2] Finally, the region of darkness recurs in all the versions of the tale of Dulcarnain, who in Arabic legend is identified with Alexander the Great ; and the monument appears as a wall built, according to the Koran, by Dulcarnain as a protection against the peoples of Gog and Magog, who,

---

[1] LABITTE, 103 ; OZANAM, 434 ; D'ANCONA, 38 ; GRAF, I, 84.
[2] Cf. *supra*, p. 88.

according to a version of the Islamic legend—like the pygmies of the Christian legend, whose stature was only an ell—measured but a hand and a half in height.[1]

The three monks then penetrate into the infernal regions and there witness tortures, some of which are noteworthy for their resemblance to Moslem punishments already mentioned. Thus, as in all the versions of the *Miraj*, sinners are seen tormented by serpents in a lake of burning sulphur ; further on, the monks behold a giant chained in the midst of flames—a figure that also appeared in the *hadiths* depicting hell[2] ; again, a woman is shown tormented by an enormous serpent in a manner as horrible as that of the Moslem tortures[3] ; and so on.

3. The Moslem character of the tale, however, is most apparent from the following episode :

The pilgrims have left hell behind them and now enter a wood of lofty trees, upon the branches of which sit a multitude of souls reincarnate in the form of birds. These cry out to God with the voices of human beings begging Him to forgive them their sins and explain to them the wonders they have witnessed.

Graf, in seeking to account for the frequent occurrence of this myth in mediæval legend, finds no precedent but that of early Christian symbolism, in which the soul is represented in the form of a bird. But in Christian symbolism the dove alone represented the Holy Ghost and only very occasionally, on the monuments of the Catacombs, the souls of the faithful. Moreover, the legend does not speak of symbols, but of the reincarnation of souls in birds, which live in a wood close, it is precisely stated, to paradise—features that will be seen to have a more satisfactory explanation in Moslem *hadiths*.

From early times it was a general belief in Islam that the spirits of men who fell in Holy Warfare and, occasionally, the souls of the faithful lived, incarnate in birds such as starlings, in a garden or wood at the gates of paradise, awaiting the day of resurrection. These birds, some of

---

[1] *Qisas*, 225–232. [2] *Supra*, pp. 89 and 106. [3] *Supra*, p. 103.

which are white and others green, fly freely through the garden and rest on the branches of the trees, the fruits of which they eat. They drink of the waters of the rivers flowing through the garden and spend their time in converse with God. The souls of Moslem children are likewise transferred to little birds, which fly about among the others. All these birds know and speak to one another. According to other *hadiths*, they are as white as doves or of a brilliant white like foam.

Some *hadiths* quote the colloquies God is supposed to hold with these birds, and the text remotely resembles the words attributed to the human birds in the Christian legend Thus[1] :

God asks them, " Know ye perchance of a better fate than that reserved unto you ? " and they answer, " No. Our sole desire were that our spirits might return to our bodies once more to fight and be sacrificed in Thy service." In other *hadiths*, the birds in which live the souls of the faithful other than martyrs, are made to utter the prayer, " Gather us, O Lord, to our brethren and grant us that which Thou hast promised unto us."

This belief was so deeply rooted in Islam that it gave rise to other holy legends as well as to theological polemics.[2] In the legends, a bird incarnating the spirit of an ascetic or mystic is supposed to appear on earth. In their polemics, the theologians in all earnestness discuss the nature of this being, which in the body of a bird harbours the mind of a man.

4. *Vision of St. Paul.*[3]—The passage in the Second Epistle to the Corinthians (XII, 2-4), in which the Apostle refers to his being wafted to the third heaven, was the nucleus round which this legend grew. It first appeared in the form

---

[1] *Sudur*, 96 and 98. It should be noted that the garden in which the birds live, lies at the gate of heaven ; this explains their request to God that, in accordance with His promise, He should allow them to enter the realm of Glory and taste the reward, of which as yet they only catch glimpses. The same request appears to be made by the human birds of the Christian legend in their prayer : " Ostende nobis ista quae vidimus, miracula tua, quoniam ignoramus quid sint." Cf. *Acta Sanctorum*, X, 563.
[2] *Sudur*, 102, 107, 108, 121, etc. [3] OZANAM, 399 ; D'ANCONA, 45 ; GRAF, I. 245.

of an Apocalypse written in Greek about the fourth century, and does not seem to have spread to Western Christianity before the ninth century. Indeed, as a vision it only dates from the twelfth, and in its more literary forms from the thirteenth century. In transmission from East to West it underwent considerable changes, which have not yet been explained.[1] A comparison of the later texts with similar Moslem legends may therefore be of interest as pointing to the hidden channel by which the tale reached Western Europe.

5. As in the *Miraj*, Mahomet was accompanied by Gabriel, so St. Paul in his nocturnal ascension is led by the Archangel Michael.

The first torture of hell witnessed by St. Paul—that of the avaricious, hanging by their feet, their tongues, or ears from the branches of trees—is evidently an adaptation from the Isra ; and it must be confessed that in the Moslem story there exists a relation between the sin committed and the member tortured that is altogether lacking in the Christian legend.

Over a turbid river, in the Pauline vision, stretches a bridge *as fine as a hair*, connecting this world with paradise ; this bridge the righteous souls cross with ease, but the wicked fall into the river. Here the plagiarism is flagrant ; for this is clearly a copy of the " sirat " or Moslem bridge crossed on the Day of Judgment, according to a Koranic myth, the Persian origin of which has been explained above.[2] Indeed, one of the early traditionists, Abu Said al-Khadari, in describing the " sirat " as being *finer than a hair*, uses the very same simile as the author of the Pauline vision.[3] It need hardly be pointed out that the position of this bridge, stretching from the earth to heaven across hell, is the same in both Christian and Moslem legends.

A wheel of fire that in ceaseless rotation torments the sinners is another instance of a torture copied from Islam. It will be remembered that in several *hadiths* a precedent was

---

[1] Cf. BATIOUCHKOF, *Le débat de l'âme et du corps*, 41–42, 514, 517, 518. 558, 559.   [2] *Supra*, p. 115 *et seq*   [3] *Tadhkira*, 58, line 3 inf.

found for the torture appointed by Dante to Sodomites[1] ;
among them is one dating from the eighth century that
says, " In hell there are people bound to flaming wheels,
the wheels of wells that turn in ceaseless rotation."[2]

6. Although other picturesque features may be passed over
as of minor importance,[3] the end of this apocryphal vision
is remarkable for two scenes of singular poetic beauty.   In
the first of these, St. Paul from hell sees angels leading a
righteous soul to paradise, while demons drag off a wicked
soul to torture.   All the religious books of Islam devote a
chapter to this subject.   Thus, the author of the *Tadhkira*
comments at length on a *hadith*, in which the death of the
righteous man is contrasted with that of the sinner ; and
the fate of their souls, as they are led by angels or demons
to heaven or hell, is depicted in awe-inspiring scenes.[4]   But,
as this scene of the Pauline vision recurs in many other
Christian legends, all bearing upon the same struggle between
angels and devils for the possession of the soul, its study
may be held over until later, when these particular legends
will be dealt with in detail.

The final vision of St. Paul is summarised by D'Ancona as
follows :

The sinners humbly beg the Apostle to intercede on their
behalf.   The *Miserere*, uttered by millions of souls, fills the
four heavens and reaches to the throne of Christ, Who
thereupon descends and sternly rebukes the reprobates.   For
the sake of His disciple, however, He grants them a weekly
respite from torture, from the ninth hour of Saturday to
the first hour of Monday.

In the summary of the Greek Apocalypse, given by Graf,
the analogous scene is as follows :

The Archangel Gabriel descends with the heavenly hosts,
and the damned implore his assistance.   St. Paul, who has

---

[1] *Supra*, p. 99.
[2] *Tadhkira*, 74, line 1 inf., and IBN MAKHLUF, II, 37, line 16.
[3] For instance, the graduation of the torture of fire according to the
degree of sin, the sinners appearing immersed in fire up to their knees,
their belly, navel, eyes, etc.   Cf. *supra*, p. 107, for the Islamic parallel
to this scene.
[4] *Tadhkira*, 18-19.   Cf. *Sudur*, 22.

wept over the indescribable tortures he has just witnessed, joins the angels in their intercession on behalf of the sufferers. Christ appears and, moved to pity by their prayers, grants the sinners an annual respite on Easter Sunday, the anniversary of His resurrection.[1]

Graf has pointed out that the main difference between the Greek Apocalypse and the Western *Visio Pauli* lies in the fact that, whereas in the former the respite from torture is annual, in the latter it is weekly.[2] When and by whom was this change introduced ? Islamic legends prior to the *Visio latina* show the same belief in a weekly day of rest for the damned, extending from the eve of Friday to the morn of Saturday. The point will be more fully dealt with when the cycle of Christian legends on this subject of a respite comes under discussion. Meanwhile, the conclusion to be drawn is, that the *Visio Pauli* reached Western Europe through Moslem adaptations of the Greek Apocalypse. A brief survey of these Islamic legends will complete the comparison.

One, current in the ninth century, forms but a new episode in the legend of Mahomet's ascension.[3]

Mahomet from heaven hears the cries of pain uttered by the undutiful children in hell and, moved to pity, intercedes with God on their behalf ; but God refuses to grant his request, unless the parents join him in his prayers. After witnessing the torture of the children, Mahomet returns weeping to the Throne of God and thrice repeats his entreaties, only to meet with the same answer. The Prophet then appeals in pleading tones to the parents, who are in heaven ; but they, remembering the ingratitude of their children, are loth to act. However, in the end he succeeds in softening their hearts and obtains permission to lead them to hell, where at the sight of their tortured children they burst into bitter tears. The sinners reply with cries for mercy, and the entreaties of the parents, added to those of the Prophet, finally obtain the pardon of the sinners.

A similar legend, telling of the delivery from hell of the

[1] D'ANCONA, 47 ; GRAF, I, 245. [2] GRAF, I, 247. [3] *Corra*, 92–99.

Moslem sufferers through the intercession of the Prophet,
is given in the *Tadhkira*.[1]

From the bottommost pit of hell the damned, with cries
of anguish, call on Mahomet to intercede on behalf of his
flock. At the same time they beg the Lord to forgive them
their sins, addressing Him in terms similar to those of the
Miserere of the Pauline vision, " Have mercy upon us, O
Lord ! " God grants their pardon and sends Gabriel to
deliver the believers from hell.

III

LEGENDS OF VISIONS OF HELL—*continued*

1. *Legend of Tundal.*[2]—As the protagonist lived in 1149,
there is no doubt that this legend dates from the second
half of the twelfth century. The author of the Latin version,
an Irish monk, states that he composed it from a text written
in a barbarous tongue.[3] Was this an Arabic text ? The
great number of Moslem features, several of them very
striking, would seem to suggest it.

The legend tells of a journey, undertaken by the soul of
Tundal upon his apparent death, to the realms beyond the
grave, and describes many scenes the Moslem origin of which
has already been sufficiently proved—the tortures by fire,
by intense cold, and by the fiends wielding red hot prongs ;
the river of sulphur, the narrow bridge that only the righteous
succeed in crossing, and many others.

2. But there are other more interesting visions. Thus,
at the further side of the bridge of hell is a monster, named
Acheronte, which, with its mighty jaws opening wide, is
seen devouring two sinners. The literary device whereby
hell is represented as a monstrous fiend rather than as a
place of torture is to be found in Islam many centuries

---

[1] P. 82. Another similar tale is given in the Gayangos Collection, MS 234,
fol. 101 :
   Gabriel descends to hell and, moved by the prayers of the damned
that he should obtain the intercession of Mahomet on their behalf, returns
to heaven and appeals to the Prophet. The latter intercedes with God
and the sinners are pardoned.

[2] D'ANCONA, 53–59.   [3] Cf. BLOCHET. *Sources.* III.

earlier.   The Moslem *hadiths* on the final judgment describe
a monster, called Gehenna, which, according to some versions, with its many mouths devours three sinners.[1]

Tundal further tells of a place of expiation for souls that,
being neither good nor wicked, are spared the torments of
hell, but are not worthy of association with the saints.   The
prototype of this region has been shown to be the Moslem
Aaraf.[2]

In another part of hell Tundal sees demons, who with
heavy hammers deal furious blows at sinners stretched upon
anvils. This vision is evidently an adaptation of the Moslem
scene of the *punishment in the grave*.[3]

Two demons, black and of sinister and repulsive mien,
appear before the sinner as soon as he is buried.   So misshapen are they that they cannot be likened to angels, men,
or animals.   In his hands each bears, for the purpose of
Divine vengeance, an iron hammer, so heavy that not all
the men in the world could lift it.   In thunderous tones they
begin to question the soul on the sincerity of his belief in
God and the Prophet. Paralysed with terror at the sight of
the monsters, whose eyes flash like lightning in the darkness
of the grave, the sinner is too conscious of his guilt to give
a ready reply to the fiends, who at each faltering answer
bring down their hammers with terrific force seven times
alternately upon the wretch's head.

The picture is so vivid that the story must undoubtedly
have created a profound impression ; and, indeed, it is to
be found in an adapted form in many a mediæval legend.
Thus, the tale of Hugh, Margrave of Brandenburg, tells
how, when hunting in a wood, he came across some men
of a black colour and deformed shape torturing souls by
beating them with hammers as they lay stretched on anvils.[4]
This picture agrees even more literally with the Islamic
model than does the scene in the legend of Tundal.

3. There remain three episodes that unquestionably are

---

[1] *Supra*, p. 109.   [2] *Supra*, p. 83.
[3] Cf. *Tadhkira*, 31–33, which gives *hadiths* on this subject that, being
vouchsafed for by Bukhari, are at least earlier than the ninth century of
our era.   [4] D'ANCONA, 78, and GRAF, I, 107.

copies of Islamic descriptions. These are the very three scenes that prompted D'Ancona to remark,[1] " Never perhaps has man shown such wealth of imagination in the invention of infernal tortures as did the anonymous monk that composed this legend "—a remark that the eminent critic would surely not have hazarded, had he known of the existence of the Moslem originals. The first of these scenes depicts Lucifer.

Surrounded by demons and chained to a red hot grill, he roars in agony ; and, as if seeking vengeance for his own suffering, with his hundred hands he clutches at innumerable souls and crushes them between his fingers even as a man would crush a bunch of grapes. The mangled bodies are then to be seen floating in the fiery vapour of his breath, alternately attracted and repelled by the respiration of the monster.

The posture of Lucifer, chained down amidst his fiendish host, is a Moslem feature that has already been referred to.[2]

The idea of the alternate attraction and repulsion of the bodies by his breathing appears to be taken from the scene of the *Isra* in which the bodies of the adulterers are shown floating up and down in the heat of the furnace. The most striking feature—that of Lucifer crushing the bodies of the sinners in his numerous hands—is modelled upon a *hadith* of the eighth century, which reads as follows :

" God has created an angel with as many fingers as there are sinners condemned to fire, and each sinner is tortured by a finger. I swear by Allah that the firmament would melt with heat, were that angel to place but one of his fingers upon it ! "[3]

4. The second episode is prefaced by D'Ancona with the following remark :

" The sole aim of the legend of Tundal is to provoke terror. With a refinement of torture truly mediæval, the souls of the damned are first taken to see the delights of the life led by the elect, in order that their suffering be all the greater : *ut magis doleant*."[4]

---

[1] D'ANCONA, 56.   [2] *Supra*, p. 89.   [3] *Tadhkira*, 73, line 16.
[4] D'ANCONA, 57.

This pathetic scene is frequently to be found in the religious works of Islam. According to the Moslem creed, identical on this point with the Christian, the moral suffering of sinners is intended to be far greater than their physical suffering. Algazel develops this theme in his *Ihia*. The grief of the sinners over their exclusion from heaven, he avers, would not be so intense were it not that God, to add to their punishment, has ordered them to be shown paradise from outside.[1] In proof, he quotes the following *hadith* :

On the day of judgment God will ordain that some of the damned be led to heaven ; but, when they are near enough to inhale the delicious perfumes with which the air is laden, and behold the castles of paradise and the delights awaiting the blessed, a Voice will of a sudden be heard saying : " Withdraw them, for they are unworthy of a place in heaven " ; and as they are turned away, they will be filled with a sorrow such as no one yet has felt or ever will feel. Then will they cry out, " Oh, Lord ! Hadst Thou but cast us into hell without showing us the rewards prepared for Thy chosen, it had been easier for us to bear our torment " ; and God will answer, " To-day shall ye taste the pain of torture, ye to whom I have denied the prize."[2]

This scene, in which cruelty is blended with sarcasm, shows no trace of the sweet message of pity preached by the Gospel, but rather breathes the spirit of vengeance that is characteristic of the Old Testament and is transparent in more than one passage of the Koran. Some of these passages are glossed in the *Tadhkira* with other *hadiths*, attributed to the converted Jew, Kaab al-Akhbar, describing various practical jokes played upon the sinners. Thus, the gates of hell are opened, as if to let the sufferers escape, to be quickly closed again whenever an attempt is made to pass through them ; or, a pretence is made of allowing the sinners to enter paradise, the gate of which is then slammed in their faces. Under the heading of " Tricks played upon the Damned," these cruel hoaxes prove that the comic and

---

[1] *Ihia*, IV, 383. Cf. *Ithaf*, X, 520.
[2] *Ihia* and *Ithaf*, loc. cit. Cf. *Tadhkira*, 83.

grotesque element found in many of the pre-Dante Christian legends was not wanting in the tales of Islam.

5. The last episode in the legend of Tundal that may be said to be of Moslem origin forms a striking picture :

The protagonist confesses to having stolen a cow from a fellow-priest and, as a punishment, his angel-guide obliges him to cross the narrow bridge leading to paradise at the same time warding off the attacks of that very cow.

D'Ancona points out a similar scene in the vision of the usurer Gottschalk, in which the Burgrave of Reiningen is condemned to be tossed and trampled upon by a mad cow, of which he had once robbed a poor widow.[1]

The episode appears to be a copy of an early Moslem *hadith* :

" I swear by Him in whose hands lies my soul that every owner of a sheep, a cow, or a camel, who has omitted to pay the ritual tax, will be confronted on the day of judgment by the animal in the fiercest form it ever assumed on earth ; it will gore him with horns of fire and trample upon him until his ribs are broken and his belly split in twain ; in vain will he cry out for help, for in the form of a wolf or a lion the beast will continue to torment him in hell."[2]

6. *Legend of Purgatory of St. Patrick.*[3]—This legend appeared in Ireland in the second half of the twelfth century and rapidly became popular throughout Christendom. Calderon immortalised it in his drama of the same title, and there is hardly a nation in Western Europe that has not drawn upon the legend for some literary purpose or other. The theme is a journey to the realms of the after-world by one Owen, an Irish knight, who is bold enough to penetrate into the cave by which, according to tradition, St. Patrick communicated with the other world. As D'Ancona observes, the legend is not remarkable for originality. " The visionaries," he says, " begin to copy one another, and this is but natural, seeing that their imaginative powers have become exhausted." The remark is very true and applies exactly

---

[1] D'Ancona, 58.

[2] *Corra*, 66. Cf. also Ibn Makhluf, II, 13, and *Kanz*, III, 250–252, Nos. 3,984–4,020.   [3] D'Ancona, 59–63 ; Labitte, 126.

to the present thesis ; for most, if not all, of the picturesque
features of this legend existed in Moslem eschatology.

7. Thus, Moslem models exist for the following scenes,
common to so many of the legends : the torture by serpents ;
the submersion of sinners in a river of molten metal, on the
banks of which stand demons ready to harpoon them ; the
passage of the narrow and slippery bridge ; the monster whose
breath alternately attracts and repels the bodies of the
sinners ; the wheel of fire ; the pit of sulphur ; the sinners
hanging by their eyelids or nostrils, or head downwards,
over flames of sulphur.

Other features of greater interest also appear to be of
Islamic origin. Thus, the sinners lying crucified to the
ground existed, as was shown in connection with Dante's
picture of Caiaphas, in the Moslem hell.[1]

The blast of bitterly cold wind to which other sinners are
exposed, is but the *zamharir* of Islam in one of its accepted
meanings.[2]

Finally, the burning sepulchres in which some of the
sinners lie buried, and the garments of fire covering others,
have been shown to be of Islamic origin.[3]

IV

LEGENDS OF VISIONS OF HELL (CONCLUSION)

1. *Vision of Alberic*.[4]—This legend is here included, not
because the scenes depicted in it are in any way original,
but because ever since the first publication of the Latin
text in 1824 by the Abbé Cancellieri the Dantists have considered it to be one of the most important precursors of the
Divine Comedy. Like the vision of St. Patrick, it dates from
the thirteenth century, but was written in Italy, at the
monastery of Montecasino. The monk, Alberic, is the protagonist and narrator of this journey to the realms of the

---

[1] Cf. *supra*, p. 101.
[2] *Supra*, pp. 106–107. Cf. OZANAM, 394 : " un soufle d'un vent d'hiver."
[3] Cf. *supra*, pp. 13 and 101.   [4] D'ANCONA, 63–69 ; LABITTE, 125.

after-life, which he is represented as having made in his childhood while unconscious during an illness.

The main episodes of the vision are those that have repeatedly been shown to be of Moslem origin. Thus, the lascivious are punished by being submerged in ice ; apostates are shown devoured by serpents ; murderers lie in the traditional lake of boiling blood ; wicked mothers hang by their breasts from hooks, while adulteresses hang over fires. Then there is the scene of the monster whose breathing attracts and repels bodies, and that of Lucifer bound with heavy chains in a deep pit in the centre of hell. Finally, we have the most common scene of all, the narrow bridge that leads to heaven.

2. *The Song of the Sun in the Edda.*—Among the fore-runners of the Divine Comedy, Ozanam includes the famous Solar Liod contained in the Edda Saemundar.[1] Remote as the origin of these tales may be, the Solar Liod itself does not seem to be much older than the eleventh century. Ozanam himself observes that the poet depicts the realms of the after-life in a manner differing from the pagan traditions of his country. Moreover, the picture contains three distinctly Moslem features. In the first place, the lower world is divided into seven regions, as in the Islamic tales. Secondly, the souls in hell are represented as birds whose plumage is blackened by smoke. Now, just as in the discussion of the legend of St. Macarius it was shown to be a common feature of Moslem tales to depict the souls of the righteous as incarnate in birds of white or green plumage, so in a later chapter it will be shown that the incarnation of the souls of the wicked in birds of black plumage is an idea also prevalent in Islam. Lastly, the author of the Solar Liod depicts thieves as moving in groups in hell, laden with burdens of lead. Surely this scene also is derived from a Moslem *hadith*, which says : " On the day of judgment the rich man who failed to serve God shall be obliged to carry his riches on his

---

[1] OZANAM, 403. Regarding the antiquity and religious character of the Edda, cf. CHANTEPIE, *Hist. des relig.*, pp. 675 *et seq.*, particularly p. 685.

back and at the passage of the bridge he shall stagger under his burden."[1]

3. *Vision of Turcill.*—This thirteenth-century vision contains, in addition to many Moslem features common to other legends, the scene in which a lawyer is forced to swallow his illicit gains.[2] The ninth century legend of Wettin showed the powerful of this world similarly expiating their crimes of rapine.[3] But this striking punishment was found in the *Isra*, where at one stage the faithless guardians and usurers are tortured by having stones of fire and darts of iron, symbolic of their ill-gotten gains, thrust down their throats, and in another scene lie helpless on the ground, their bellies swollen with the proceeds of their usury. The great age of the *hadiths* relating this torture is confirmed by Tabari in his ninth century commentary.[4]

4. *Vision of the Abbot Joachim.*—This twelfth-century vision contains the scene, so common in Moslem *hadiths*, of the narrow and slippery bridge leading across a river of burning sulphur that runs through hell. The souls of the righteous cross this bridge *with the swiftness of an eagle.*[5] The same simile occurs in a *hadith* which reads : " Some will cross the bridge with the speed of lightning, others like the wind, *others again like birds.*"[6]

At the farther side of the bridge rises a wall, upon which the garden of paradise is built. This picture appears to be a copy of the Aaraf, which is represented in the Koran as a garden and a wall rising between hell and paradise.[7]

5. *Vision of the Bard of Regio Emilia.*—This is an apocalyptic treatise composed in the thirteenth century in verse and in the vulgar dialect. Vossler states that it is difficult to understand how a nameless travelling minstrel could by his own unaided efforts have conceived so clear and comparatively logical a system of the after-world ; and this very symmetry leads the critic to attach prime importance to this vision as being a prototype of Dante's conception.[8]

---

[1] *Kanz*, VIII, 224, No. 3,552.   [2] D'ANCONA, 68, footnote.
[3] D'ANCONA, 58, footnote ; LABITTE, 112.
[4] *Tafsir*, XV, 11. Cf. MS 64 Gayangos Coll., fol. 113.   [5] OZANAM, 445–6.
[6] *Tadhkira*, 58, line 7 inf.   [7] Cf. *supra*, p. 83.   [8] VOSSLER, II, 201.

The troubadour imagines hell as divided into eight regions, each of which has a name and distinctive features of its own.

The first, called Ago, is full of fire ; the second, Tartaro, is the region of discord ; the third, Averno, of cruelty ; the fourth, Asiro, of evil memories ; the fifth, Gena, is a region of sulphur ; the sixth, Grabasso, is a place of trial ; the seventh, Baratro, is characterised by depth ; and the eighth, Abisso, is full of fiery furnaces and boiling pitch. The total circumference exceeds a thousand miles. Access is afforded by means of ten gates lying a hundred miles apart ; each gate has its special features and is reserved for one particular class of sinners. Mountains, rivers and lakes of fire are seen at the entrance. The first gate is called the Gate of Tears, and the others are the Gates of Pain, Terror, Chains, Sulphur, Serpents, Thirst, and so forth.

6. The comparison made in a former chapter of the symmetric plan of Dante's hell with its Moslem prototypes shows how little originality exists in the conception of the Italian troubadour.[1] The two meanings of *storey* and *gate*, given in Moslem exegesis to the Koranic word *bab*, he placidly accepts and simply adapts his facts to the double interpretation by representing hell as having ten gates besides eight regions or storeys. The same solution finally predominated among the Sufis, for the Murcian Ibn Arabi imagined hell as having seven strata and seven gates. The dimensions of hell are stated with similar precision, though with greater hyperbole, in the *hadiths*, which fix the distance between the gates as equal to what a man might cover on foot in seventy years.[2] Again, according to some *hadiths*, there are mountains and rivers of fire at the entrance to hell.[3] Lastly, it has repeatedly been shown that each stage of the Moslem hell had a name and special features of its own and was reserved for one category of sinners. Indeed, to judge by the names, the bard of Regio Emilia may well be suspected of having availed himself of the *hadith* of Ibn Jurayj.[4] For, having exhausted his stock of classical and Biblical names with Tartaro, Averno, Baratro and Abisso, he seems to have

[1] See *supra*, pp. 85–95.   [2] *Tadhkira*, 70.   [3] *Tadhkira*, 70.
[4] See *supra*, p. 88.

resorted to transcribing roughly the Arabic terms. Thus, while Ago appears to be derived from Haguia, Asiro is clearly copied from Asair, and Gena from Gehenam.[1]

V

LEGENDS ON THE WEIGHING OF SOULS

1. Throughout a whole cycle of legends, which D'Ancona groups with the political legends, there recurs a scene the immediate, though not remote, origin of which is Islamic. The protagonists of these legends are the Emperors Charlemagne and Henry III., and King Rudolph of Burgundy.

These princes are brought up before the Divine tribunal, and their sins are cast on to the balance by demons ; but, just as the scale is about to sink under the heavy weight, a saint, such as St. James, St. Denis or St. Lawrence, throws on the other scale all the good deeds of the prince, the sanctuaries he erected, the ornaments he presented to churches and abbeys, and so on. These outweigh the sins, and the soul is saved from hell.[2]

2. That the religious myth of the weighing of the souls on scales at Divine judgment had its early origin in Egypt is well known.[3] The myth reappeared in the Persian eschatology of the Avesta,[4] and it had penetrated into Arabia by Mahomet's time, as is shown, among other passages, by Ch. XXI, 48, of the Koran : " We shall set up true scales on the Day of Judgment. No soul shall be unjustly dealt with, though the works to be judged should weigh no more than a grain of mustard seed." The traditionists, needless to say, soon seized upon the theme and adorned it with realistic scenes, some of which are identical with those of the Christian legends.[5]

---

[1] Taking the Arabic name in the form used in vulgar speech, and changing the feminine into the masculine, e.g. Haguia=Hagu=Ago.

[2] D'ANCONA, 77 ; LABITTE, 110. The myth of the scales occurs in other, non-political, visions, such as the Vision of Turcill (D'ANCONA, 69, footnote). Cf. GRAF, II, 106, note 207.

[3] CHANTEPIE, Hist. des relig., 107. Cf. VIREY, Relig. anc. Egypte, 157–162.

[4] CHANTEPIE, 473.   [5] Tadhkira, 55, and IBN MAKHLUF, II, 22.

A Moslem is brought up before the Divine tribunal on the Day of Judgment. His sins, recorded in ninety-nine books, are read out to him and, after he has confessed, the books are placed on one of the scales, which naturally falls ; whereupon God Himself places on the other scale a scrap of paper containing the profession of faith made by the sinner in his lifetime. The scales are turned, and the Moslem is saved. According to other legends Mahomet intervenes by placing on the right hand scale a scrap of paper representing the prayers addressed to him by the sinner. Often the realistic effect is enhanced by the substitution of objects for the pieces of paper. Thus, a small bag containing a handful of earth, which the sinner once threw on the grave of a fellow-man that his soul might have peace, alone suffices to outweigh a heap of sins. In many legends the sinners are shown co-operating towards their mutual salvation : Those rich in virtue assist their needy brethren by lending them their surplus merits ; and often the anxious sinner is to be seen threading his way through the groups of souls in search of a friend who can oblige him with the one virtue he may lack, by the weight of which he hopes to turn the balance in his favour.

As it is inconceivable that in that obscure age Western Christianity should have had direct knowledge of the Egypto-Persian myth, the immediate origin of the Christian legends must be sought for in the Islamic tales. This hypothesis is confirmed by the fact that in both the *hadiths* and the Christian legends the same *Deus ex machina* effect is introduced.

3. The same explanation may throw light upon a point in mediæval art that has hitherto remained obscure. Mâle, in his work " L'art religieux du XIIIme siècle en France," calls attention to the fact that in the porches of the Gothic cathedrals of France St. Michael is represented with scales in his hand weighing the good and evil deeds of men.[1] Apart from a few vague phrases of St. Augustine and St. John Chrysostom to the effect that the deeds of men will be weighed " as in a balance," Mâle finds no authority for this scene and concludes, that the image must have been

[1] MÂLE, p. 420.

formed in the popular mind by spontaneous evolution from those allusions of the Saints, and may thus have reached the artists.

A more specific explanation is provided by the effect of Moslem influence in producing legends in Christianity similar to those existing in Islam. In the Bible and in Christian doctrine generally, St. Michael is the *princeps militiae coelestis*, and as such he is represented, clad in armour, in early mediæval monuments, notably in an eighth-century window of the Cathedral of Châlons-sur-Marne. In paintings and bas-reliefs of a later date, however, as in Van der Weyden's Day of Judgment in the Hospital of Beaune, and in that of Memling at Dantzig, he is always shown with the scales in his hand. The inference to be drawn is that the myth of the scales was introduced in the ninth or tenth century and, in the course of adaptation, the Archangel Gabriel (who in Islam was entrusted with the weighing) was replaced by the Archangel St. Michael, one of whose functions indeed, according to the doctrine of the Church is to lead the souls of the deceased to the Divine throne and introduce them into heaven.[1] This adaptation was not only unauthorised by the Catholic Church, but condemned by learned religious critics. Thus, the seventeenth century Spanish friar, Interián de Ayala, in his work " El pintor cristiano y erudito," says : " It will appear even stranger to see the Archangel Michael himself depicted with scales in his hand ; the origin of this, I must frankly confess, is unknown to me."[2]

4. Nor is this instance of the influence of Islam upon mediæval art by any means exceptional. Both Mâle and Friar Interián point out other scenes of the day of judgment as equally unauthorised by Catholic tradition,[3] and notably the scene of intercession. In the sculpture of several French cathedrals of the thirteenth century ; in the fourteenth century Day of Judgment at the Campo Santo of

---

[1] Cp. the offertory of the requiem masses : " Sed signifer Sanctus Michael representet eas in lucem sanctam . . ."
[2] INTERIÁN, I, 135. Interián, one of the founders of the Spanish Academy, died in 1730.   [3] MÂLE, 416. INTERIÁN, I, 66 ; II, 168.

Pisa ; in that of Fra Angelico at the Academy of Florence belonging to the fifteenth century—in all the Virgin Mary is shown, either alone or accompanied by St. John the Baptist, kneeling at the throne of Christ, the Judge, and interceding for the sinners. The scene is, of course, quite contrary to the spirit of that day of wrath, when there shall be neither intercession nor pardon. With the Moslem creed, however, it is in perfect agreement. Algazel—to quote the highest authority only—states that, after the Moslem sinners have been sentenced, God in His mercy will hearken to the pleading of the prophets and saints that stand highest in His favour.[1] As evidence he adduces many passages in the Koran and *hadiths* of the Prophet, in which the scene is described in picturesque detail.

Mahomet, the leader of the prophets, draws nigh to the seat of the Divine Judge casting, as he passes, a look of compassion on the unhappy throng of Moslem sinners. In vain have the other prophets interceded for them ; their sole hope now lies with him. Moved to pity by their entreaties and at the special request of Jesus, he prostrates himself before the throne of God and obtains the desired pardon.[2]

Lastly, the scenes in mediæval and renaissance pictures of the day of judgment in which the sinners are shown coming to life again naked, are denounced by Friar Interián as shameless and unchristian.[3] Those scenes, though indeed lacking all authority of the Church, are strictly in accordance with Moslem doctrine, which categorically states that on the day of judgment all men will meet before the throne of God naked and uncircumcised.[4] In fact, their very nakedness is a cause of physical suffering ; for, as the sun will on that day draw nearer to the earth, they will sweat exceedingly and suffer greatly from thirst. This detail was even objected to by the early Moslems, and Aysha, the Prophet's wife, pointed out how unseemly was such pro-miscuous nakedness. But Mahomet replied :

" Oh, Aysha ! On that dread day none will bethink him-

---

[1] *Ihia*, IV, 377 ; *Ithaf*, X, 485. *Tadhkira*, 61. [2] Cf. *Ithaf*, X, 491.
[3] INTERIÁN, II, 168–173.
[4] *Tadhkira*, 41. Cf. *Ihia*, IV, 368, and *Ithaf*, X, 454.

self of casting eyes upon his neighbour, for each one will be intent upon his own thoughts."[1]

Nevertheless, *hadiths* of a later date sought to lessen the crudeness of the scene by reserving such nakedness to infidels.[2]

VI

LEGENDS OF PARADISE

1. D'Ancona paid due heed to the materialism shown in the conceptions of paradise in almost all the Christian legends precursory of the Divine Comedy, and concluded that Dante, in tracing his spiritual and ethereal picture of paradise, was uninfluenced by those legends. The contrast between Dante and his Christian predecessors was referred to in the discussion of the Paradiso,[3] when it was suggested that the materialistic pictures of heaven appearing in the mediæval Christian legends were themselves based on Moslem models. Now is the occasion to prove that assertion.

To begin with, these Christian legends bear a general resemblance to the Moslem tales in that they often make no distinction between the earthly and the heavenly paradise.[4] This confusion, it will be remembered, is characteristic of Islamic stories, and particularly of some versions of the ascension of Mahomet. In these, a garden of bliss, watered by clear streams, is the scene of the theological paradise,

---

[1] *Tadhkira*, 41.

[2] Other picturesque scenes, which Mâle attributes to the working of the popular mind, may also have had a Moslem origin. Thus, the wicked are shown being dragged off in chains to hell by demons (Mâle, 422), just as described in the Koran and the *hadiths* (*Tadhkira*, 73). The personification of hell as a monster with ôpen fangs, which Mâle believes to be an imitation of the Leviathan of the Book of Job, is surely modelled upon the monster often quoted in the preceding pages. The avaricious shown in the porches of the cathedrals with their money-bag hanging from their neck are reminiscent of the sinners described in the *hadiths* on the Day of Judgment as likewise burdened with the *corpus delicti*, for instance, the drunkards, who carry a flagon slung from their neck, or the fraudulent merchants, who carry a balance (*Corra*, 12 and 41).

[3] See *supra*, pp. 140–141.

[4] GRAF, I, 69: " Il paradiso terrestre alle volte diventa tutt'uno col celeste." See *supra*, pp. 134–135.

which, although not specifically laid on earth, is not supposed to be in the firmament of the heavens.[1]

This Moslem conception of paradise as a garden reappears in some poetical legends of thirteenth-century Christian Europe. For instance, in the poem " Le vergier du paradis," published by Jubinal,[2] paradise is represented as a garden watered by limpid streams and shaded by trees ; the air is scented with rare perfumes and the sweet music of instruments and the song of birds enchant the ear ; within the bowers of this garden are castles of marvellous beauty, built of gold and precious stones. Were it not for some exclusively Islamic features, the picture might indeed have been evolved from the Celestial Jerusalem of Revelations.[3] Some of these features are of interest.

2. The protagonist of the legend of Turcill, in passing through the garden of paradise, sees Adam seated at the foot of a miraculous tree, close to the source of the four Biblical rivers.[4] He observes that "Adam appeared to be smiling with one eye, and weeping with the other ; smiling at the thought of those of his descendants who would find eternal life, and weeping at the thought of those destined to eternal damnation."

This episode, for which Graf quotes no precedent, is undeniably based upon a scene in the ascension of Mahomet[5] ; and the fact that the version in question is included in the collection of Bukhari and Muslim is proof that it was current in Islam before the ninth century.

3. But, apart from mere episode, in many Christian legends of paradise the general outline of the conception is of Moslem origin. This conception is mostly modelled upon one type ; paradise is conceived as the court of a feudal lord who receives his retainers at a brilliant gathering enlivened by music and dancing. The *Cour du paradis,*

---

[1] Cf. Versions A and B of Cycle 1 of the *Miraj.*
[2] D'ANCONA, 104. [3] Cf. GRAF, I, 19.
[4] GRAF, I, 67. It should be remembered that the legend dates from the thirteenth century.
[5] See *supra,* p. 10, Version A of Cycle 2. The scene, as told in the *hadiths,* agrees literally with that in the Christian legend. Cf. also *Kanz,* VI, 96, No. 1,466.

the work of an anonymous Provençal troubadour of the thirteenth century, describes the reception as follows[1] :

On All Saints Day the Lord holds a festive meeting at His court. St. Simon and St. Jude are sent to each dwelling in paradise to invite the blessed to the party ; they call in turn at the mansions of the angels, the patriarchs, the apostles, the martyrs, the confessors, the innocent children, the virgins and the widows. In these groups the blessed flock to the reception, where they sing songs of heavenly love and tread the same measures as are danced on earth ; Mary and Mary Magdalene lead the singing and dancing.

The *Visione dei gaudii de' santi*,[2] a legend of Dante's time, depicts the blessed as barons and paradise as a feudal castle with battlements and towers of crystal and precious stones. This picture is reproduced in the poem of the minstrel Giacomino of Verona, in which the saints are represented as knights militant under the banner of the Virgin, who in reward crowns them with wreaths of flowers of a perfume sweeter than musk or amber, and bestows upon them precious gifts of harness set with gold and emeralds and of chargers swifter than the hart or the wind chasing over the sea.[3]

In other legends, the festival in paradise is conceived on less worldly lines, more as a religious ceremony ; in place of the cavalcade of knights is a holy procession led by the Lord, and then follows a meeting, at which St. Stephen recites the Epistle, and St. John the Gospel.[4]

It is significant that long before the tenth century there existed in Islam a whole cycle of *hadiths* the very title of which—" The Court of Holiness "—suggests a resemblance to the Christian legends. As a matter of fact, the same general ideas underlie both. Paradise is conceived either as a courtly gathering where there is music and dancing, or, again, as a religious festival. The likeness extends down to actual detail, which would seem to be undeniable evidence of imitation.

[1] D'ANCONA, 88.   [2] D'ANCONA, 105.   [3] D'ANCONA, 105.
[4] D'ANCONA, 90, footnote 2.

This cycle of *hadiths* comprises, not only those legends upon which the Beatific Vision of the mystics was founded, but others created by the traditionists to satisfy the ruder tastes of the early Moslems, whose only interests ever lay in the direction of the miraculous.[1]

The *hadiths* of the " Court of Holiness " begin, like the Christian legends, with the invitation of the blessed to the reception at the heavenly court. The invitation is for Friday, the festive day of Islam, on which the elect, in addition to their continual bliss, are granted the special favour of gazing upon the face of the Almighty. Thus the enjoyment of the Beatific Vision is not constant, but weekly ; and in the " Cour du Paradis " the blessed only behold the Almighty once a year. The point is important in that it is quite unauthorised by Christian doctrine.

Early on Friday morn angel messengers call upon the blessed in their mansions and deliver a sealed invitation to each together with rich gifts of jewelry for his adornment. The reception is held in two castles, built of pearls, that stand in the gardens of paradise—the one destined for the men, under Mahomet, and the other for the women, under Fatima. Reclining on soft cushions, the guests listen to houris chanting hymns of praise to the Lord to the accompaniment of countless flutes that hang from the trees and are sounded by the softest of breezes. Enraptured by the music, the blessed feel an impulse to dance ; so, in order that they may be spared the physical exertion, they are provided with instruments fitted with wings, on which they sway hither and thither to the rhythm of the music. After the dancing follows the reception by God, Who speaks to each guest in turn, whereupon they retire each to his dwelling.

The analogy of this version to the " Cour du Paradis " is obvious. In other versions, the reception is followed by a religious ceremony.

The blessed beg to be allowed the pleasure of holy prayer, which was their delight on earth. God bids David ascend the

[1] The versions here summarised are to be found in the *Corra*, 102, 107, and 132 ; in SUYUTI, *Al-Laali*, I, 28–29, and *Dorar*, 30. Cf. also MS 159, Gayangos Coll., fol. 2–6, and MS " Junta de Ampliación de Estudios," fols. 148–156.

pulpit, and in an inspired voice he chants one of his Psalms. Thereupon Mahomet in even more impressive tones recites a chapter from the Koran. Finally God shows Himself to each of the guests, who then retire to their mansions.

A third version of the *hadith* appears to be the prototype of the Christian legends that represent the heavenly festivity as a brilliant cavalcade. After the prologue of the invitation common to all the readings, the story proceeds as follows :

After all the guests have mounted, the men on horses of the purest breed and the women on she-camels, they are led by Mahomet and Fatima to the court. Mahomet, mounted on Boraq, hoists the Green Standard of the Glory of God, which is borne by angels on a staff of light above his head. The prophets Adam, Moses, and Jesus join the procession, as it passes their castles. In other versions, Mahomet is surrounded by Abu Bakr, Adam, and Omar and preceded by the first muezzin Bilal, who rides at the head of the heavenly muezzins. The cavalcade follows the flowery banks of the river Kauthar till it reaches the golden walls of the castle of the King of Heaven. Gabriel climbs to the battlements and summons all the blessed to join in the festivity. They arrive in groups led by their respective prophets and take up their place behind Mahomet and his flock. Inside the castle walls the sward is perfumed and shaded by trees, whose branches are laden with fruit and peopled with countless birds of song. Here the reception is held in a manner similar to that already described.

The resemblance between this version and the Christian legends of the cavalcade of knights extends even to descriptive detail. Mary presents her knights with coursers such as never were seen on earth, red in colour, and swifter than the hart or the wind sweeping over the sea ; their trappings are of gold resplendent with emeralds. The terms of the Moslem legend are almost identical :

God saith to His angels, " Give My elect steeds of the purest breed, yet such as they have never ridden. And the

angels proffered them coursers of a ruby red, the trappings
of which are set with emeralds ; with their wings of gold
and hoofs of silver, they can outrun the swiftest racehorse
and fly faster than lightning. . . .[1]

VII

LEGENDS OF SEA VOYAGES

1. Through the Christian literature of the Middle Ages
from the eleventh century onwards runs a rich vein of legend,
which Dante students have explored in search of a possible
clue to the genesis of the Divine Comedy.   The theme, it
may be said, is also a visit to places, which, being inaccessible
to the ordinary mortal, may readily be identifiable with the
regions beyond the grave.   These legends, having three main
characteristics in common, may be grouped in one cycle.
They are tales of wonderful voyages to fantastic islands ;
the protagonists are either adventurers, or saints, or conquerors, who are invariably more mythical than historical ;
and the aim of these is generally a religious one—to spread
the Gospel, to do penance, to find the isle of earthly paradise
or the fountain of life, or to seek the immortal prophets,
Enoch and Elijah.[2]

These legends may be roughly subdivided into three
groups corresponding to the natures of the protagonist.
Tales of mere adventure are the voyages of Harold of Norway
and Gorm of Denmark ;   the Celtic voyages of Maldwin,
of the sons of Conall Dearg Ua-Corra, and of Snedhgus and
MacRiaghla.   Of the adventurous pilgrimages by sea the
most celebrated is the voyage of St. Brandan, a veritable
monastic odyssey, imitations of which are the stories of the
voyages of St. Barintus, St. Mernoc, St. Malo, St. Amarus,
and the Armorican monks.   Voyages of conquest are the
parallels to the voyage of Alexander the Great, such as the

---

[1] Cp. the text of D'ANCONA, 105, footnote 4, with *Corra*, 115, line 8 inf. ;
128, line 5 inf. ;   126, line 7 inf. ;   and *Al-Laali*, 28, line 1 inf.
[2] GRAF, I, 93–126.

legends of Hugh of Bordeaux, Baldwin of Seeburg, Ugger the Dane, Hugh of Auvergne, and Guerin the Mean.

2. By the tenth century, at the very latest—the epoch of flourishing trade in the Persian Gulf and Indian Ocean—Islam had produced and given widespread popularity to a whole cycle of similar legends ; and the hypothesis that their influence was responsible for the genesis of the Christian legends is strengthened by the fact that they show the same three characteristics mentioned above. They also are stories of wondrous adventure in fabulous islands. The protagonists are seldom historical persons and, like the heroes of the Christian legends, are either adventurers or conquerors, religious devotees or pseudo-prophets. Thirdly, the aim of most of these voyages is religious. The adventurers set out to seek Mahomet or spread the gospel of Islam ; to visit hell and the paradise of saints and martyrs ; or to find the abode either of the prophets Enoch and Elijah or of the fabulous pseudo-prophet Khidr, who is the protagonist of some of the legends.

Like their Christian counterparts, these Moslem legends may be grouped, in accordance with the nature of the protagonist in each, under three headings. The voyages of Sindbad the Sailor, of Hassan of Basra, of Azim, of Ganisa, and of the Prince of Karizme, are purely voyages of adventure. The heroes of the religious voyages are prophets or ascetics, who are either wholly mythical or are historical personages clothed in mythical garb, such as Khidr, Moses, Joseph, Jonah, and Boluqiya. To this group also belong the tales of the birth of Mahomet, the tales of Abd al-Mutallib the Wise, Yarab the Judge, Tamim Dari the Soldier, Abu Talib the Lawyer, Zesbet, Abu al-Fawaris, and Sayf al-Muluk. The third group comprises the expeditions that are partly warlike and partly religious ; typical of these is the Koranic legend of Dulcarnain, a mythical figure that in Moslem legend is strangely interwoven with the figure of Alexander the Great as depicted by the pseudo-Callisthenes.

3. This similarity in outline shown by the two legendary cycles is in itself significant of Moslem influence. But there

is further evidence. Victor Chauvin, in his monumental
work on the bibliography of Moslem fiction, has traced a
number of episodes and descriptive features from the Moslem
to Christian tales.[1] Thus, the legends of Herzog Ernst,
of Heinrich der Loewe, of Reinfried of Brunswick, of Hugh
of Bordeaux, and of Guerin the Mean, would all appear to
be derived from the Arabic story of the Prince of Karizme.
Hence Chauvin's conclusion that " the direct or indirect
influence of Oriental tales of marvellous voyages is to be
seen in several works of mediæval fiction."[2] In addition,
there is the testimony of the Dutchman, De Goeje, the
eminent Arabic scholar, whose inquiry into the close relationship between the " Voyage of St. Brandan," the most
typical of Irish tales, and the voyages of Sindbad the Sailor,
has won at least the partial adhesion of so great an authority
on Romance philology as Graf.[3] Thus, the problem may be
regarded as practically solved, and there only remains to
add a few data corroborative of De Goeje, and to point out
the hitherto unsuspected Arabic origin of some other
Christian legends.

4. A typical instance of imitation from a Moslem source
is provided by the " Voyage of St. Brandan." De Goeje
attributes its origin to the voyages of Sindbad the Sailor
and a few other tales of adventurous voyages that are
briefly recorded by Al-Idrisi. Even more likely sources,
however, would appear to have been the tales of Boluqiya
and of Dulcarnain, which, having been handed down by
Thaalabi, must have been known before the eleventh
century. Other Islamic tales of remote date also come into
consideration.

St. Brandan chances upon an uninhabited castle on an
island, and in the castle a table laden with the richest food,
of which he and his followers eat their fill.[4]

---

[1] CHAUVIN, Bibliographie, VII, 1–93.   [2] Ibid. 77.
[3] DE GOEJE, Légende St. Brandan. Cf. GRAF, I, 102 : " Non si può escludere
la possibilità che alcune di esse (immaginazioni) sieno orientali di origine."
[4] The present study of the legend of St. Brandan is based on the works
of GRAF, I, 97–110 ; DE GOEJE, loc. cit. ; LABITTE, 119–123 ; and
D'ANCONA, 48–53.

Boluqiya, on arriving at an island, likewise finds beneath a tree a table set with food of different kinds. A bird greets him from the branches of the tree and invites him to partake of the food, which has been prepared by the order of God for all His servants who come on foreign pilgrimage; and Boluqiya eats his fill.[1]

On another island, visited by St. Brandan and his monks, grow trees, from which they cut wood and make a fire to cook their food. But what appeared to them an island was, in fact, an enormous whale, which, upon feeling the heat of the fire upon its back, begins to move and the monks throw themselves into the sea and swim to safety.

This episode, as has been pointed out by De Goeje, and before De Goeje by Reinaud and D'Avezac, is identical with that of the island-whale which Sindbad and his companions come across on the first of their voyages. This fact, however, does not dispose of the difficulty; for the legend of St. Brandan, though none of its extant versions dates back further than the eleventh century, is by some supposed to be derived from earlier Irish sources. Hence it is that Schroeder even goes so far as to suppose that the episode of the whale passed from Ireland to the East, and Graf himself does not deny the possibility of this.[2] Weighty arguments can, however, be adduced against this theory. For one thing, the myth is contained in remote works of Oriental literature,[3] for both the Talmud and the Avesta mention a sea-serpent or tortoise on whose back the same scene is enacted; so that, as any direct imitation of these works by the author of the legend of St. Brandan is out of the question, it is reasonable to suppose that Arabic literature was the medium of communication. Is it possible that the tale of Sindbad the Sailor formed this connecting link? In default of any documentary evidence of the date of the Arabic tale, De Goeje has recourse to an argument which, though interesting, is not conclusive. " In the oldest forms

---

[1] *Qisas*, 225. The episode recurs in the voyages of Abd al-Mutallib the Wise. Cf. CHAUVIN, VII, 46.
[2] SCHROEDER, *Sanct Brandan* (Erlangen, 1871), Introduction, XI–XIV. GRAF, I, 103.   [3] DE GOEJE, 47, and GRAF, I, 105.

of the legend that I know," he says, " the island-whale is devoid of all vegetation. The tale of Sindbad and the *Navigatio* (of St. Brandan) alone mention trees as growing on the fish." Accordingly, he argues, as it appeared in the East in its simple as well as its more complex form, the tale originated there rather than in Ireland, where it appeared only in the latter form, and that at a comparatively late time. De Goeje's argument would have been strengthened had he been able to produce an Arabic document giving the myth in its more complex form before the tale of Sindbad appeared. Such a document does exist in the *Book of Animals*, written by Al Jahiz, of Basra, who lived from 781 to 869 A.D., or more than a century prior to the date attributed to the tale of Sindbad,[1] and certainly long before the composition of the Irish tales that have been regarded as the sources of the " Voyage of St. Brandan."[2] Al Jahiz, speaking of monsters that are supposed to live in the sea, mentions the sea-serpent or dragon, a certain crustacean of the sea called " sarathan," and an enormous fish, which undoubtedly is the whale. He is inclined to doubt the existence of the two first-mentioned animals.[3]

" To tell the truth," he says, " we have never heard of these " (the sea-serpents) " except in tales of magic and in sailors' yarns. To believe in the existence of the sea dragon is akin to believing in the existence of the phœnix. Never did I hear the dragon spoken of, but those present called the teller of the tale a liar. . . . As to the *sarathan*, I have never yet met anybody who could assure me he had seen it with his own eyes. Of course, if we were to believe all that sailors tell . . . for they claim that on occasions they have landed on certain islands having woods and valleys and fissures and have lit a great fire ; and when the monster felt the fire on its back, it began to glide away with them

[1] Cf. Asín, *Abenmasarra*, Appendix I, 133.

[2] According to Schirmer the Latin version is based on tenth or ninth century texts, and Zimmer even connects the legend with the Celtic story, *Imram Maelduin*, which on the strength of its archaic language he assigns to the ninth or eighth century. These hypotheses, which are not even shared by all Romance scholars, are far from having the positive value of a dated document such as the book of Al Jahiz.

[3] *Hayawan*, VII, 33–34.

and all the plants growing on it, so that only such as managed to flee were saved. This tale outdoes the most fabulous and preposterous of stories. . . . However, as for the fish, I state that it is as true as I am alive that I have with my own eyes seen the fish of enormous size called *Albala* (the whale) and it was killed with unerring aim."

Originating in Persia, the myth lived on in the neighbouring countries and, seeing that Al Jahiz gives it as a common theme of the sea legends of his time, must have passed into Islam at least as early as the eighth century. Thus, it is included in the popular tenth-century story of Sindbad the Sailor, and is handed down in various Arabic works to the twelfth century. Algazel refers to it in his *Ihia*, written at the beginning of that century. Speaking of the immensity of the ocean, he says, " in it live animals of so great a size that when the back of one of them appears upon the water it is taken for an island and sailors land upon it ; but should they perchance light a fire, the monster, feeling the heat, moves and the sailors become aware that it is alive."[1]

The further arguments adduced by Schroeder in support of his theory, that the myth of the whale arose in the north, are feeble. His assertion that the whale is only to be found in the northern seas we have just seen categorically denied by Al Jahiz. Surely the myth would be more likely to arise among a people to whose seas whales would only come from time to time rather than in the northern countries, where their appearance was too common an occurrence even to suggest such a fable.

The next island to which St. Brandan comes is inhabited by a multitude of birds which are gifted with speech and conceal certain angelic spirits beneath their plumage.

Boluqiya, it will be remembered, also meets a marvellous bird, endowed with the gift of speech, which invites him to partake of the food spread upon a table. It explains that it was one of the birds of paradise sent by God to offer Adam, after he was driven out of Eden, food from that very table. Later it is this same bird or another, also of white

[1] *Ihia*, IV, 318. Cf. *Ithaf*, X, 205.

plumage, that is charged with carrying Boluqiya on its wings from the island to his home. It is seen, then, that the Moslem legend also mentions birds of white plumage, that are gifted with speech and act as angels or messengers of God. Moreover, in the discussion of the legend of St. Macarius, Moslem precedents were shown to exist for the idea of supposing human souls incarnate in birds gifted with speech from the time of death until the day of judgment. Some *hadiths* even go further[1]; speaking precisely of white birds, endowed with the gift of speech, they say that they incarnate, not human souls, but angelic spirits, to wit, the angels that are entrusted with the duty of judging the soul after death. Again, several religious legends attest the Moslem belief that flocks of white birds, beyond all doubt angels incarnate, attended the burial of ascetics as if to receive their souls and lead them up to heaven.[2] The strong hold this myth had on the Moslem imagination explains why in all books on the interpretation of dreams birds are said to signify angels.[3]

Proceeding on his voyage, St. Brandan lands on another island, inhabited by holy monks whose only sustenance is the bread that falls from heaven ; these monks observe strict silence and are subject neither to illness nor old age.

This episode is simply an amalgamation of two scenes appearing in some versions of the expeditions of Dúlcarnain —the scene of the island of the monks and the island of the wise men.[4]

On the former island Dulcarnain finds ascetics so emaciated by the austerity of their holy life that they appear as black as coal ; the fish and herbs provided for them by God are their only nourishment, yet they assure Dulcarnain that they feel no desire for the things of this world. On the other island the wise men ask him whether with all his vaunted power he can vouchsafe them eternal life and freedom from sickness. To his answer that he cannot, they reply that God has granted them this, and many other things besides.

Another island in the voyage of St. Brandan is described as bearing enormous vines, from which hang bunches of

---

[1] *Sudur*, 32.   [2] *Sudur*, 108.   [3] DAMIRI, II, 110.   [4] *Kharida*, 93–94.

grapes of monstrous size ; the seeds alone are as large as apples and suffice to satisfy the hunger and slake the thirst of the saint and all his companions.

This incident is undoubtedly founded on the *hadiths* telling of the gardens of paradise, in which grow vines of monstrous size.[1]

" Does the vine grow in heaven ? " asked one of the first disciples of Mahomet, and upon the Prophet's answering that it did, the disciple inquired, " Of what size are the fruit ? " " As the distance covered by a raven in a month's uninterrupted flight," was the answer. " And what is the size of the seeds ? " " Of that of a large jar." " Then, with a single seed I and all my family could eat their fill ? " " And thy whole tribe as well," concluded Mahomet. Other *hadiths* even state the exact length of each bunch of grapes to be twelve cubits.

Continuing his pilgrimage, St. Brandan comes to an enormous column of the clearest crystal; rising from the bottom of the sea it appears to touch the sky, and around it is what seems to be a great pavilion formed of a silvery substance with large meshes.

Two very similar descriptions are found in the Islamic fables of Solomon, which depict a submarine dome and an aerial city.[2]

Solomon sees rising from the bottom of the sea a pavilion, tent, tabernacle, or tower, vaulted like a dome, which is made of crystal and is beaten by the waves ;' from a gate emerges a youth, who proceeds to relate to him his life of solitary devotion beneath the waters. The aerial city is erected by the genii at the order of Solomon, who bids them build him a city or palace of crystal a hundred thousand fathoms in extent and a thousand storeys high, of solid foundations but with a dome airy and lighter than water ; the whole to be transparent so that the light of the sun and the moon may penetrate its walls ; a white cupola, surmounting the highest storey and crowned by a brilliant banner, with a resplendent light lit up the route of Solomon's army during the night, when the king, floating through space

---

[1] *Tadhkira*, 87.   [2] *Qisas*, 190.

in his aerial castle as in an airship driven by the wind, sallied forth on an expedition.

Upon reaching the regions of the damned, St. Brandan and his companions find Judas sad, and naked but for a rag over his face, seated upon a rock in the midst of the ocean. Other similar Christian legends show Judas standing in a pool or pit through·which flow all the waters of the world ; or again, he is represented as being consumed internally with fire in spite of the waters that beat incessantly upon him. The picture is an adaptation from the Moslem legends of the torment of Cain, one of which, dating from the eighth century, reads as follows :

A man of the Yemen, named Abd Allah, with various companions set out on a voyage, in the course of which they came to a sea that was wrapt in darkness. For several days they sailed onwards until suddenly the veil of darkness lifted and they found themselves close to an inhabited coast. " I went ashore," said Abd Allah, " in search of water, but all the houses I came to were closed ; in vain I knocked at the doors, for no one answered. Of a sudden two horsemen appeared, mounted on snow-white steeds, who said to me : " Abd Allah ! follow yonder path and thou wilt come to a pool of water ; drink thy fill and be not afeared at what thou seest there." I inquired of them about the empty houses through which the wind whistled, and they told me they were the dwellings of the souls of the dead. Upon arriving at the pool, I found a man leaning head downwards and seeking to reach the water with his hand. When he saw me, he cried out : " Abd Allah, I pray thee, give me to drink," and I filled the cup to give him water, but lo ! my hand was stayed. I said to him, " Oh, servant of the Lord ! thou hast seen that I would fain have served thee. Tell me, then, who thou art ! " And he answered, " I am the son of Adam who first shed blood upon earth."

Another tale, also dating from the eighth century, is similar :

A shipwrecked sailor saves himself by clinging to a spar and is flung upon the shore of an island. Proceeding along the shore, he comes to a stream the course of which he follows to a spot where the water seems to flow from the bottom of the earth. There he finds, chained by the feet just out of reach of the water, a man who begs him to slake his thirst, saying he is the son of Adam that slew his brother and since that deed is chastised for every murder that is committed on earth.[1]

The last incident in the voyage of St. Brandan that is worthy of note is his meeting with the hermit Paul, who lives on a rock in the middle of the ocean, fed by a lark for the last hundred and forty years, and will there remain alive until the day of judgment.

Here, blended into one, we have two characters—the historical person of St. Paul the Hermit, who, fed by a raven until his death, lived in the desert of Thebes, and the mythical figure of Khidr, in the conformation of which Islam combined features of Elijah, Elishah, the Wandering Jew, and St. George. Khidr, like Elijah, is immortal, and in many legends is depicted as a sea-hermit, praying in the midst of a desert island, or on a rock beaten by the waves, where he is fed by a bird, which brings him food and water in its beak, or from a table sent down from heaven. There, it is said, he will live until the day of judgment and, having often been seen by shipwrecked sailors, he is regarded in Islam as the patron saint of mariners.[2]

St. Brandan now approaches the Isle of Paradise, which is the goal of his pilgrimage ; but, like Abd Allah of the Yemen, and like Dulcarnain in his search for the Fountain of Life, he first has to pass through a region of darkness. The German version of the voyage, moreover, contains two interesting features. The ground of the Isle of Paradise is, like the ground traversed by Dulcarnain, strewn with precious stones ; and from a fountain spring four rivers, of milk, of wine, of oil, and of honey, similar to the rivers

---

[1] *Sudur*, 73 and 74. For the nakedness of Judas, whose face alone is covered with a piece of cloth, cf. *Sudur*, 117, which depicts some of the damned in hell in the self-same fashion.

[2] *Qisas*, 135–143, contains several legends on Khidr. A richer collection is that included by Ibn Hijr in his *Isaba*, II, 114–137. Cf. also *Sudur*, 109, and *Kharida*, 92. Other Arabic legends represent Elijah and Enoch as praying on a rock or island. Cf. CHAUVIN, *Bibliographie*, 48, 52, 54, 59, and 63.

that water the gardens of paradise in the Koran (XLVII, 16-17).

5. It would thus seem that everything points to the same conclusion, namely, that an Eastern or, to be more precise, an Islamic origin must be given to this legend—the legend that Renan regarded as " the most perfect expression of the Celtic ideal and one of the most admirable creations of the human mind,"[1] and that Graf, though admitting the influence of the story of Sindbad the Sailor, nevertheless believes to be Gaelic in foundation. Other Romance scholars, however—owing to their lack of all documentary evidence, they could never go beyond mere suppositions—came nearer to the truth. Labitte, for instance, was struck by " le tour, l'imagination brillante et presque orientale qu'elle décèle "[2] ; and D'Ancona admits that Eastern fables are mixed among its other elements.[3] The very monotony of rhythm in the narration : the precise number of seven voyages, corresponding to the seven seas through which Boluqiya also sailed ; the fantastic adventures, which led St. Vincent of Beauvais and the Bollandists to describe these legends as *apocrypha deliramenta* ; and, lastly, the many episodes traced to Islamic sources by De Goeje[4] and in the above pages—all go to warrant the conclusion that, if the voyage of St. Brandan and other similar legends were indeed written by an Irish monk on a basis of Celtic tradition, the plethora of Islamic elements that were grafted on to the native stock was such as to change their original character.

6. The same conclusion may be drawn from an examination of the other tales of voyages that are more warlike expeditions than mere pilgrimages. In these legends traces of the Arabic stories of the fabulous Dulcarnain are frequently to be found.

---

[1] See GRAF, I, 37.   [2] LABITTE, 122.   [3] D'ANCONA, 50.
[4] The miraculous lighting of the altar lamps, witnessed by St. Brandan on the isle of the monks, is, as De Goeje has pointed out (*loc. cit.* 55), modelled upon the similar miracle performed each Easter Eve in the Church of the Holy Sepulchre at Jerusalem. But the author of the tale need not necessarily have seen the miracle himself, nor heard of it from an eye-witness, in 1,000 A.D., as De Goeje suggests. The news may have been transmitted to him through an Arabic medium, for as early as the eighth century Al Jahiz relates the miracle in his *Hayawan*, IV, 154.

Thus, in the legend of the Frisian sailors, narrated by Adam of Bremen in the eleventh century, the adventurers, after traversing a dark region of the ocean, arrive at an island the inhabitants of which hide in caves while the sun is on the horizon, that is to say, at midday, the time of the arrival of the strangers.[1]

This detail is characteristic of the country described in the legends of the voyage of Dulcarnain as being that in which the sun rises, " the inhabitants of which do not build houses, but take refuge in caves until the sun goes down, when they sally forth to seek their living."[2] The tenth century Moslem record is based on *hadiths* of a much earlier date, and they in their turn were written as gloss on a passage of the Koran (XVIII, 89), which alludes to the fabulous voyage of Dulcarnain to " the country where the sun shines on people to whom We have given no protection from its rays."

A more striking instance of imitation from the Arabic is seen, however, in the final episode of the Latin and German versions of the voyage of Alexander the Great to the earthly paradise.[3]

The guardian of paradise presents Alexander with a precious stone, the hidden virtues of which, he says, will cure him of his ambition. Alexander returns with the stone to where his army awaits him, and of all his followers a wise Hebrew alone is capable of solving the riddle. The stone, he finds, outweighs whatever quantity of gold is put in the balance, but, when covered with a little dust, it at once loses its weight and becomes as light as a feather. The aged Hebrew concludes his interpretation with the words : " This precious stone is an image of the human eye ; when alive, it is insatiable, but, when dead and covered with earth, it aspires to nought."

Graf, after tracing the story to its most ancient sources both in Greek and Hebrew lore, comes to the conclusion that its model is to be sought in a tale of the Babylonian Talmud, though that tale mentions a real human eye. A

[1] GRAF, I, 95.   [2] *Qisas*, 228.   [3] GRAF, I, 116–118.

more likely model, however, is provided by the Arabian story, recorded in the tenth century and attributed to Ali, the son-in-law of Mahomet[1] :

Alexander, or rather the Koranic Dulcarnain, with his army reaches the region of darkness that lies before the Fountain of Life, and, beyond this region, he beholds a palace rising to an enormous height. Advancing to the gate, he speaks to the youthful guardian, who hands him an object like a stone, saying, " If this be satisfied, thou also wilt be satisfied ; if it be hungry, then wilt thou be hungry too." Alexander returns to his companions with the stone and summons the wise men to discuss the riddle. They test the stone in the balance with first one, then two, and finally a thousand similar stones, and find to their amazement that it outweighs them all. Khidr, a counsellor of Alexander's, upon seeing that all the sages are unable to solve the riddle, thereupon intervenes and places on one of the scales an ordinary stone and, on the other, the miraculous stone covered with a handful of dust ; and, to the amazement of all, the scales now balance. To Alexander, Khidr then explains the riddle as follows : " God has granted thee the utmost power achievable by man, yet thou art not satisfied. For man is never satisfied until dust cover him and the earth fill his belly." According to another, longer, version, Khidr ends his explanation with the words : " The stone is the human eye, which, whilst alive, even though it should possess the whole world, is insatiable, and which only death can satisfy."[2]

VIII

LEGENDS OF SLEEPERS

1. Graf has reviewed all the legends on this theme that were common in Christian Europe from the thirteenth century onwards.[3] In the main they tell the same story. The protagonists are monks or princes who, after visiting the earthly paradise, return to their homes believing that their absence has lasted but a few hours or days ; whereas in reality long years, even centuries, have passed ; astonished

---

[1] *Qisas*, 231. [2] MS 61 Gayangos Coll., fols. 72–80. [3] GRAF, I, 87–92.

at the change in their surroundings, they try to make themselves known, only to meet with incredulity ; in the end they succeed in establishing their identity either by the testimony of some venerable old man, who vaguely remembers the story of their disappearance, or by the aid of books of record.

Of the three principal legends of this cycle, the Italian one of the monks of the Jihun dates from the fourteenth century :

Three monks set out to seek the earthly paradise, and after many adventures succeed in finding it.   They return under the delusion that they have been absent but three days, whereas three whole centuries have elapsed.   The monastery still stands, but the monks are strangers who do not recognise them.   With the aid of old records they manage to prove their identity, and forty days after recounting their experiences they turn into dust.

The German legend of the Cistercian monk, Felix, also dates from the fourteenth century :

Felix doubts that the bliss of heaven can last eternally without cloying the elect.   But one day, listening in the garden to the sweet song of a little bird of white plumage, he falls into a trance.   The clanging of the bell calling to Matins awakens him and he hastens towards the monastery to find that he is unknown to the porter, who, on hearing his explanations, believes him to be either drunk or mad and turns him away.   Nor do the monks recognise him, although one of them, a centenarian and infirm, does remember that when he was a novice a monk named Felix disappeared ; and it is found that the books record his supposed death.   A century had passed in what seemed to Felix a single hour.

Another Italian legend, which is later than the eleventh century, tells a similar story of a young prince :

Three days after his wedding, the prince sets out from his castle and is miraculously led to a garden of paradise, where he remains for three hundred years, which to him appear but three hours.   On his return, he finds his home strangely changed ; for his wife and parents, having given him up for

dead, had converted the castle into a monastery and his hall
into a church. On the tower, where formerly had flown
the standard of his family with the eagle, he sees a banner
with the cross. He makes himself known to the porter and
tells his story to the monks and people of the village, who
listen to him in awe. The story is recorded, but the prince,
upon eating the bread of man, ages and dies and is buried
by the side of his wife.

Occasionally, this theme is introduced into stories of
fabulous voyages, as in the legend of the Armorican monks,
which is an imitation of the voyage of St. Brandan[1] :

After visiting the isle of paradise, the monks return to
their monastery and find everything changed ; church and
town have disappeared, and a new king rules over a strange
people. They have been absent for three hundred years.

The Spanish legend of San Amaro, which is still current
in Spain, belongs to the same group :

After many wonderful adventures at sea, the saint visits
the earthly paradise and, on returning to the place where his
companions were to await him, finds a city built by them ;
and, in a monastery erected to his memory, he dies. His
absence, which he had believed to be but of an hour's duration, had lasted two centuries.

2. From the eighth century onwards there existed in
Islam two groups of legends, which deal with this subject
pretty much after the manner of the Christian legends.
The protagonists are either prophets—Hebrew or mythical—
or noble Christian martyrs, who, after a sleep of centuries,
which to them appear brief hours, return to their homes
where they finally succeed in proving their identity by
means either of witnesses of venerable age or of ancient
documents.

3. The tales of the first group were composed by companions of the Prophet as gloss on a passage of the Koran
(II, 261), in which the theme is outlined as follows :

Behold him who, passing one day by a ruined and deserted
city, cried out, " How shall God bring this dead city to life

---

[1] GRAF, I, 113 and 116.

again ? " God laid the hand of death upon this man for
a hundred years and then, bringing him to life again, asked
him : " How long hast thou lain here ? "   " A few hours,
or maybe a day," answered the man. And God replied :
" Thou hast lain there for a hundred years. Behold thy food
and thy drink, they are yet good ; and, lo ! there is thine ass.
We have proposed thee as a sign (of wonder) to the people.
Behold how the bones are brought to life again and are
clothed with flesh." And when (this miracle) was made
manifest (the man) exclaimed : " Verily, I see that God is
all-powerful."

Around this nucleus, which had its origin in a Talmudic
source, three legends appeared, one of which, dating from
the eighth century, reads as follows[1] :

Nebuchadnezzar destroys Jerusalem and its temple and
carries off the surviving Israelites into captivity at Babylon.
Jeremiah (in other versions, Esdras), who had sought refuge
in the desert, returns to find the city in ruins and he doubts
whether God will be able to rebuild the city and its temple.
God sends him into a profound slumber, which lasts for a
hundred years. In the meantime, the ass he was mounted
on dies, but the wine and figs he carried with him remain
intact. God shields the prophet from beasts and birds of
prey and renders him invisible to man. A hundred years
later, and thirty years after God has caused Jerusalem to
be rebuilt, Jeremiah is brought to life again and, when he
opens his eyes, he sees the bones of the ass lying scattered
on the ground. A voice from heaven calls upon them to
unite and clothe themselves with flesh and skin, and the ass
returns to life. God asks Jeremiah how long he thinks he
has slept and, when he answers " a few hours or a day,"
tells him that he has slept a hundred years.

The second tale dates from the seventh century :

Esdras, who had been carried off into captivity at Babylon
in his boyhood, escapes some years later and, mounted on
an ass, sets out for his native country. Passing on his way
through a deserted village on the banks of the Tigris, he eats
his fill of the fruit of the trees and, having drunk the juice
of the grapes, he stores the remainder in a pitcher and some
figs in a basket. He does not believe that God could ever

[1] *Qisas*, 215–216.

rebuild the ruined village and, having tied up his ass, he falls asleep. God sends death upon him for a hundred years and then brings him to life again. The angel Gabriel asks him how long he thinks he has been asleep, and he replies " A day or less." Gabriel tells him that he has slept a hundred years and bids him observe that the ass, the figs and the wine are intact. Thereupon Esdras returns to his native country and finds that his children and grandchildren have grown old, whilst his own hair and beard are still black.

The third legend is attributed to Ibn Abbas, and provides the conclusion to the two former versions :

Upon awakening from his hundred years' sleep, Esdras returns to his native village, where no one will believe his story. At last he finds an old woman who had been his father's servant and is now a hundred and twenty years of age, blind and paralytic. " Esdras," replies the old woman to his story, " was hearkened to by the Lord in his prayers. If thou art he, pray then to God that He restore my sight, that I may see thee." Esdras cures the old woman of her infirmities, and she leads him to the house where a son of his is still alive, although a hundred and eighteen years old. Even his grand-children are of great age. None will believe either him or the old woman, until finally his son recognises him by a birth-mark he bears between his shoulders.

According to a variant version, he is recognised by his knowledge of the Torah[1] :

During their captivity at Babylon, the Israelites lose their knowledge of the Mosaic Law. Esdras, on his return, is scoffed at as a liar and is only believed when he recites by heart and writes out the whole of the Torah and the text is found to agree literally with an old copy found buried in a vineyard.

4. The Islamic tales belonging to the second group of this cycle were also woven around a passage of the Koran (XVIII, 8–24), which in its turn was based upon a Christian legend of the East, the tale of the Seven Sleepers of Ephesus. The fact that this Islamic myth had its remote origin in Christianity renders it of little interest as far as our argument

[1] *Qisas*, 217.

is concerned, so that especially as Guidi has published an Italian version of the Oriental texts, both Christian and Moslem, we need give here only the outline of the Moslem tale, as it appears in the four versions handed down by Thaalabi and translated by Guidi [1]:

During the persecution under Dacian seven Christian nobles of Ephesus seek refuge in a cave where, after a frugal meal, they fall asleep for three hundred years. Their kinsmen give them up for lost, and record on a tablet the story and date of their disappearance. At the end of the three centuries God restores them to life, and they awake thinking they have slept but a day. Under this delusion, one of them sets out for Ephesus to purchase provisions and secretly bring back tidings of the persecution. As he proceeds, his astonishment increases at the changes he sees on every side. Over the gate of the city a banner bearing the inscription, " There is but One God, and Jesus is His Spirit," puzzles him greatly. In the city the people are all strange and, when he tenders a coin of the time of Dacian in payment of bread, he arouses suspicion and is led before the authorities on the charge of having found secret treasure. In vain does he attempt to vindicate his story, for the authorities refuse to listen to him until he can find someone who can identify him. He ultimately succeeds in reaching his own house, when a grandson of his, though blind and infirm with great age, recognises him. The tablet recording his disappearance is also found and thus his story is corroborated. The authorities and townsfolk seek out his companions, who now definitively die and are buried with great pomp.

5. The close resemblance of the Islamic tales of both the above-mentioned groups to the Christian mediæval legends related by Graf is too evident to be ignored. But, it will be asked, is this resemblance to be attributed to Moslem influence upon Christian folklore ? Graf, with all his erudition, makes no mention of the precedents that these Christian tales may have had in other literatures.[2] And, indeed, the question is not an easy one to answer. Guidi has shown[3]

---

[1] Guidi, *Sette Dormienti*.

[2] He merely mentions the legend of the Rabbi Joni as somewhat similar to the story of the monk Felix. GRAF, I, 180, note 31.

[3] *Loc. cit.* 444.

that the Islamic tales of Jeremiah and Esdras are derived from rabbinical stories, the protagonist of which is either Abimelech or the Rabbi, Joni Hamaggel. Now both of these probably lived before the third century of our era, but there is no evidence to prove that these Jewish tales, as such, ever spread to the West. On the other hand, the Islamic legends of the Seven Sleepers are based on a Syrian legend that appeared, also in the East, in the sixth century ; and this tale, we know, in that very century passed to the West, where it is found in a Latin version that St. Gregory, of Tours, included in one of his books on the saints.[1] But are we, on that account, to suppose that the Christian mediæval tales mentioned by Graf grew solely from the seed sown by St. Gregory and were uninfluenced by the Islamic legends ? If so, how can it be explained that that seed should have taken over six centuries to germinate and did not produce its crop of legends until the thirteenth century ?

That is the problem, in so far as the influence of the myth of the Seven Sleepers on the similar Christian tales of the thirteenth century is concerned. But there still remains the other group of Islamic legends, of which the protagonists are Jeremiah and Esdras. The resemblance of these to the Christian tales is no less striking ; and here there can be less doubt about the direct Moslem influence, for there is nothing to show that the early rabbinical models ever passed to Christian Europe.

IX

LEGENDS OF THE RESPITE FROM TORTURE

1. Until the sixth century the question whether the sufferings of the sinners in hell were to be regarded as eternal or not was still debated by the Fathers of the Church. Indeed some doctors, mainly of the Eastern Church, favoured temporality.[2] Western opinion prevailed, however, and by the Council of Constantinople the doctrine of everlasting

---

[1] *De gloria martyrum*, ch. 95.   [2] Cf. TIXERONT, II, 199.

punishment was definitely established as part of the Catholic dogma. It is, then, all the more strange to find, in the eleventh century, legends popular in Western Christendom treating mainly of a respite from, or mitigation of, the sufferings of the damned.[1] The myth first appeared in the vision of St. Paul. But, as was pointed out in the discussion of that legend, the primitive Greek version spoke of a *yearly* respite, whereas in the Latin versions, dating from the twelfth century, the respite is *weekly*.[2] The difference is significant, as explaining the genesis of the later forms of the legend from Moslem models ; for, whilst the doctrine of a weekly respite lacks foundation in Christian tradition, and particularly in that of the West, it was indeed fully justified in the dogma of Islam.

2. Even more striking influence of Islamic influence is shown by another Christian tale, told in substantially the same terms by St. Peter Damian, in the eleventh century, and Conrad of Querfurt and St. Vincent of Beauvais, in the twelfth.[3]

A cavern situated in the volcanic region of Pozzuoli, to the west of Naples, or on the volcanic island of Ischia in the gulf of the same city, and washed by black and evil-smelling waters, was supposed to be the mouth of hell. At sunset every Saturday, birds of a sulphur-blackened plumage and fearsome aspect were believed to rise from the waters of that cave and fly away to the neighbouring mountains. There they would stay stretching and pruning their wings until the early morn of the following Monday, when they would return and enter the waters of the cave. These birds were generally believed to be the souls of the dwellers in hell, who thus enjoyed a respite from their tortures.

3. It was a doctrine of Islam,[4] quoted even by Graf, that the torture of both believers and infidels ceased for the day and night on Friday, during which time the soul is allowed to visit its tomb and there receive the prayers offered up on its behalf. The belief, which inspired many very popular

---

[1] GRAF, I, 241–260, *Il reposo dei dannati.*   [2] *Supra*, p. 185.
[3] GRAF, I, 250–251.   [4] See *Sudur*, 76 and 128.

legends,[1] is based on the sanctity of the day and is as old as the Moslem religion ; indeed from the first century of the Hegira onwards it was held for certain that Moslems who died during the day or night of Friday were exempt from the private judgment of the soul that is peculiar to Islam.[2]

That the souls of the wicked are incarnate in birds of black plumage is a belief attributed to Mahomet himself, just as the myth that holds the saintly soul or angelic spirit to be incarnate in white birds has been shown to be of Moslem origin.[3]

" The souls of the host of Pharaoh are imprisoned in hell in the body or belly of birds of a black hue ; these birds sit on nests of fire in the bottommost depths of the seventh earth and eat and drink fire."[4]

That these black birds rise to the surface, in respite from their torture, and precisely from the waters on the seashore, is told in a Moslem legend so strikingly similar to the Christian tale as actually to appear to be its model or prototype. The legend in question is attributed to Al-Awzai, a writer of the eighth century, and is related by Ibn Abu Aldunya, of the ninth century[5] :

A man of Askalon inquired of Al-Awzai, " Oh, Abuamer ! We see birds of a black plumage rise from the sea and when they' return at night, behold ! their plumage is white." And Al-Awzai said to him, " Dost thou not know what those birds are ? " And he answered, " Yes." And Al-Awzai proceeded, " In the entrails of those birds are the souls of the host of Pharaoh ; they are exposed to the fires of hell, which burn and blacken their plumes. After a while they lose those plumes, but, when they return to their nests, once again they are burnt in the fire. Thus shall they continue to the day of judgment, when a Voice shall say : Cast the host of Pharaoh into the bottommost pit."

4. Closely related to this subject of respite from torture is that of the mitigation of suffering when a debt is paid.

---

[1] Cf. *Ihia*, IV, 352, and *Ithaf*, X, 366.   [2] Cf. *Tadhkira*, 35.
[3] *Supra*, pp. 181 and 209.   [4] *Sudur*, 97.   [5] *Sudur*, 110.

Graf quotes, among others, the legend related by Cæsar of Heidenbach in the thirteenth century.[1]

After his death a soldier appears before a certain man and tells him that he is in hell for an act of robbery. He begs the man tell his children of his wish that the property be restored to its rightful owner, so that his punishment may be lightened, but the children turn a deaf ear to the other's pleadings.

It was a Moslem belief, borne out by numerous *hadiths*, that debts left behind on earth either delayed or hampered the soul in its ascension to heaven[2] :

Thus, at a certain funeral Mahomet decreed that no prayers should be said for the deceased until his debts had been paid. On another occasion, he addressed the children of the deceased thus, " Your father stands at the gates of heaven, detained by a debt. If ye wish, ye may yet ransom him ; if not, ye must leave him to be dealt with by the wrath of God." In other *hadiths*, Mahomet is represented as ordering a son of the deceased to pay the debts in order to obtain a remission of his father's suffering.

Around these *hadiths* there grew up legends very similar to the Christian tale described above. One such legend, dating from the ninth century, runs as follows :

To two ascetics, who lived in the eighth century, there appeared a man who, seated on boards floating in the bottom of a pit, cried out to them in a hoarse voice, saying he was a citizen of Antioch who had just died and was held prisoner in that pit until a debt of his were paid. He added, " My children live at Antioch unmindful of me and of my debt." The two ascetics proceed to Antioch and pay the debt, and the next night the deceased again appears to them and thanks them for their act of charity.[3]

5. In conclusion, it was a common belief in mediæval Europe that prayers, fasting and almsgiving served to obtain mitigation, not merely of the expiatory suffering in purgatory, but even of the punishments of hell.[4] This belief persisted in the face of the opposition of the Church, which adhered the more rigidly to the doctrine of everlasting damnation

---

[1] GRAF, I, 251.   [2] *Sudur*, 111, and 116.   [3] *Sudur*, 111 and 112.
[4] GRAF, I, 255–257.

as being the one feature distinguishing hell from purgatory. But the rigidity of the official theology was set off by what Graf happily terms the theology of sentiment, as expressed in many popular legends. These, Graf is of opinion, were the spontaneous outcome of the feelings of pity to which the masses are ever prone. That such feelings may lead to popular reactions, unconsciously heterodox, against the strictness of doctrine based on intellectual exegesis, is undeniable ; but the growth of the belief in question may have been stimulated by contact with Moslem eschatology, which on this point was much more benign than the official Christian doctrine.

Islam, as is well known, condemns only the infidel and the polytheist to eternal punishment ; the true believer, however sinning, will one day see an end to his suffering. And even this temporary torture may be alleviated by the prayers of those on earth. Suyuti, with many other authors, has left us a collection of authoritative texts on this point.[1] These show that prayer, almsgiving, pilgrimage, fasting, and even such pious or merely beneficent works as the erection and endowment of mosques, hostels, schools, or the construction of bridges and irrigation works, all serve to influence the lot of the soul ; but special importance is attached to the offering up of prayers on Fridays on the tomb of the deceased. Thus Islam, in adopting the milder views of a minority of Eastern churchmen, may have been the medium through which this belief was transmitted to the West after it had been unanimously rejected as heretical by the Councils, the Fathers, and the Doctors of the Roman Church.

X

Legends of the Debate Between Angels and Devils for Possession of the Soul

1. A common subject of Christian mediæval legend is the inquest held on the soul immediately after death by angels and devils as a preliminary to final judgment. Graf, in

[1] *Sudur*, 126–131.

Demonologia di Dante,[1] and Batiouchkof, in *Le débat de l'âme et du corps*,[2] have analysed these legends, the main elements of which are the following :

   i. Every soul has one or more angels and devils to guard and tempt it during life.

  ii. At death these angels and devils fight for possession of the soul.

 iii. Often the debate is conducted with the aid of two books, one recording the sins, and the other the virtues of the soul.

 iv. In other legends, the virtues and vices appear in person to bear witness.

  v. Or again, the members of the body accuse the soul of the sins they committed.

 vi. The balance is also used to decide the debate.

vii. Finally, the angels or devils carry off the soul to heaven or hell.

2. Christian doctrine furnishes but scant authority for these features, especially the more striking ones enumerated under iv, v and vi. These are precisely the elements that were most common in Islam, which had derived them from other Oriental religions, particularly the Zoroastrian religion.

The belief in a guardian angel, based as it is on the Gospel and conserved in patristic writings, formed part of the Christian faith both in the East and West. From the fifth century onwards it was, though not dogma, commonly believed that, in addition, everyone had a devil to tempt him. That, at death, the angel and devil fought for the soul, was again merely a popular belief, the earliest documentary evidence of which is to be found in a seventh century vision of the after-life composed by St. Boniface, the apostle of Germany. It reappears in the ninth century Germanic poem *Muspilli*[3] ; and it is noteworthy that both these legends are enhanced by the introduction of elements iv and v personifying the virtues and vices and the members

---

[1] In *Miti*, II, 103–108. [2] In *Romania*, year 1891, p. 41 *et seq.*
[3] Cf. GRAF, II, 104–5.

of the body, features of Islamic or Zoroastrian origin,[1] which then make their first appearance in Christian eschatology.

3. Islam, in contrast to Christianity, contained in its early *hadiths* the sources of all the elements detected in the mediæval legends. These tales, with the exception of those dealing with the balance[2], are briefly summarised on the following pages:

1. *Hadiths on Topic* i

Algazel records the following *hadith* without mentioning the companion of the Prophet who related it :

" At his birth each man has an angel allotted to him by God, and a devil by Satan, who whisper good and evil suggestions into his right and left ear respectively."[3]

A *hadith* by Jabir ibn Abd Allah, of the seventh century :

In this tale Mahomet says that God has appointed a guardian angel to each man and two other angels to record his good and evil deeds. At his death these angels return to heaven, whence they will descend to bear witness on the day of judgment.[4]

A *hadith* by Al-Hasan, of the seventh century, says :

" To every man lying on his death-bed there appear his guardians, who show him his good and evil deeds. At the sight of the former, he smiles ; at the sight of the latter, he frowns."[5]

A *hadith* by Salman, also of the seventh century, reads :

" A man who lay on his death-bed told the Prophet that a black and a white figure had appeared before him. The Prophet inquired, " Which stood the nearer to thee ? " and the man replied, " The black figure." " Then," said the Prophet, " great is the evil and little is the good."[6]

Finally, a *hadith* by Wahb ibn Al-Ward, of the eighth century, says :

" To everyone at his death there appear the two angels who during his life were the guardians of his deeds. . . ."[7]

---

[1] The Zoroastrian origin of all the legends of this group is evident. Cf. CHANTEPIE, *Hist. des religions*, 473.   [2] See *supra*, Ch. V.
[3] *Minhaj*, 19.   [4] *Sudur*, 49.   [5] *Sudur*, 34.   [6] *Ibid.*   [7] *Ibid.*

2. Hadiths dealing mainly with the fight for the soul

A *hadith* by Ibrahim, son of Abd ar-Rahman ibn Awf, of the seventh century :

Abd ar-Rahman, who had been given up for dead, tells how, as he lay prostrate, two demons of fearsome aspect appeared before him, saying, " Rise, for we will lead thee to the Supreme Judge." On their way they met two angels of mercy, who cried out, " Whither would ye lead him ? Leave him to us, for God has destined him to enter heaven."[1]

A seventh-century *hadith* of the Caliph Muawya, but attributed to Mahomet :

A murderer, moved to repentance, proceeds to a monastery to end his days in prayer. But death overtakes him on the way. The angels of wrath and of mercy appear on the scene and fight for his soul. The dispute is decided by the soul being allotted to the nearest dwelling. This, upon measurement, is found to be the monastery, and the murderer is saved.[2]

Hadith of Abu Hurayra, also of the seventh century :

A person relates his experiences during a trance. A man of beautiful features and sweet-smelling breath had hardly placed him in his grave, when a woman of repulsive mien and evil odour appeared and accused him of his sins. She then disputes with the other for his soul. During the dispute he withdraws at the woman's bidding and, in a mosque near by, finds a man reciting the same verses of the Koran that he used to delight in reciting. These verses are adduced in his favour, and the man of the beautiful countenance claims him as saved.[3]

Legend of Daud ibn Abu Hind, of the eighth century :

Daud, as he lies sick, sees a black figure of monstrous shape appear, whom he takes to be a demon come to carry him off to hell. At that moment two men in white tunics descend through the ceiling, who, after warding off the other, seat themselves at the foot and head of Daud's bed ; they feel his palate and toes and conclude that both show signs of a life of prayer.[4]

[1] *Sudur*, 31–32. [2] *Sudur*, 28. [3] *Sudur*, 31. [4] *Sudur*, 32.

The legend of the seventh-century traditionist, Shahr ibn Hawshab, is similar :

Two white angels seat themselves on the right of the sick-bed, and two black angels, on the left, and dispute over the soul. An examination of the dying man's tongue, which shows traces of having uttered a certain prayer, finally settles the dispute in his favour.[1]

3. Legends introducing the books of record

These legends are all based on the passages of the Koran[2] treating of the two books in which angels record the good and evil deeds of each man. These books were mentioned in one of the tales of Group i, and many other similar legends might be quoted. Thus, a hadith attributed to Ibn Abbas[3] tells of the recording angels and describes minutely the pens, the ink, and the sheets they use.[4]

4. Legends treating mainly of the personification of virtues and vices

This feature, though also of Zoroastrian origin, attained its full development in the eschatological lore of Islam.

A hadith quoted from earlier traditionists by Ibn Abu Aldunya, of the ninth century, says :

" No man dies, but his good and evil deeds appear in person before him, and he turns his eyes away from the evil towards the good deeds."[5]

A hadith attributed to Mahomet says :

" At the death-bed of the believer attend his prayers, his fasting, the alms he gave. . . ."[6]

A hadith quoted by a companion of the Prophet reads :

At the judgment of the soul the Koran will appear in its defence before the angels Munkar and Nakir. It will ask

---

[1] *Sudur*, 33.
[2] Koran, XVII, 73 ; LXXXIII, 8–9 ; 19–20 ; LXXXIV, 7–10.
[3] *Kharida*, 180.
[4] It is noteworthy that the feature of the two books of record does not appear in the legendary lore of the West until the time of Bede, or eighth century of our era. GRAF, unmindful of the Koranic precedents, considers that the myth was evolved from the Gospel metaphor of the " liber vitae," to which, by way of contrast, was added a book of sins.
[5] *Sudur*, 34.   [6] *Sudur*, 49.

the soul, " Dost thou know me ? I am the Koran which thou didst recite and which delivered thee from evil. Fear not."[1]

Other similar *hadiths* relate as follows[2] :

To the righteous soul there appears in the grave a man of great beauty, dressed in fine garments and scented with rare perfumes, who says, " I am thy good deed." To the wicked soul appear its vices, in evil shape.

His prayer places itself on the right of the virtuous soul ; his fasting, on the left ; the Koran, at his head ; the virtue of walking to the Mosque, at his feet ; his fortitude in adversity, at the side of the tomb. The punishment of the soul, which then appears in person, is driven off by these virtues.

5. *Legends in which the members of the body are personified*

A typical legend of this group, though attributed to Mahomet, is recorded in the tenth-century *Corra* :

An adulterer is brought before the Divine Judge, and the thigh relates the sin it committed. The accused indignantly denies the charge, but God imposes silence on the lying tongue. Each of the members then confesses its share in the sin, and their evidence is borne out by the recording angels and the earth. At God's bidding the angels seize the sinner and cast him into the pit.[3]

6. *Legends of feature* vii.

All the legends of this group are variants of the *hadith* of the Prophet relating the death of the upright man and the sinner.[4] A brief outline is here given :

The angel of death extracts the soul from the body gently or violently, according as it is righteous or sinning. The angels guard the body as it is lowered to the grave. The devil, upon seeing a soul escape him, turns in anger upon his host of demons, who explain that they were powerless, as the soul was free of sin. The soul is then led through the

---

[1] *Sudur*, 50.
[2] *Sudur*, 23–24.
[3] *Corra*, 29–30. The influence on the Christian legends of this *hadith*, which must have been widely known in the first two centuries of the Hegira, can hardly be denied ; for, although unauthorised by either Christian or Zoroastrian doctrine, the scene reappears in *Muspilli* described in the same terms.   [4] *Sudur*, 22 and 23.

astronomical heavens to the Throne of God. A similar, but antithetical, story is told of the death of the sinner.[1]

4. Summarising the partial comparisons contained in this third part of our work, we may divide the Moslem features appearing in the mediæval Christian legends precursory of the Divine Comedy into two categories.[2] The first category is formed of those Islamic features that reappeared in Dante's poem and accordingly were treated at greater length in the first and second parts of this work. These, with the Christian legends in which they appear, may briefly be enumerated as follows :

Division of hell into seven regions (*St. Macarius, Edda*), or eight storeys (*Bard of Regio Emilia*). Typical tortures of hell, such as the tunics of fire (*St. Patrick*) ; fiery sepulchres (*St. Patrick*) ; molten metal and sulphur (*St. Patrick* and *Tundal*) ; immersion of the sinners in a lake (*St. Macarius, St. Patrick,* and *Alberic*) ; graduation of the fire (*St. Paul*) ; demons armed with prongs (*Tundal*) ; torture by the monster (*Tundal*) ; attraction and repulsion of the damned by its breathing (*Tundal, St. Patrick,* and *St. Paul*) ; sinners hanging head downwards (*St. Patrick, Alberic,* and *St. Paul*) ; or crucified to the ground (*St. Patrick*) ; or devoured by serpents (*St. Macarius, St. Patrick,* and *Alberic*) ; or laden with burdens (*Edda*) ; or forced to swallow their illicit gains (*Turcill*) ; the torture of ice (*Tundal, St. Patrick,* and *Alberic*) ; the picture of the giant held in chains (*St. Macarius*) ; and Lucifer bound in the bottommost pit of hell (*Alberic*).

The second category consists of Moslem features detected in the Christian legends, but not appearing in the Divine Comedy. These features, not having been mentioned in the

---

[1] Islamic precedents exist also for other subjects dealt with in the Christian legendary cycle and discussed by Batiouchkof (*op. cit.*). Cf. *Sudur*, 24, 25, and 136.

[2] Needless to say, the themes of the Christian legendary lore have not been exhausted in the above survey. D'ANCONA (83–95) and GRAF (I, 256–7) quote legends belonging to the political and comic or burlesque cycles. The Moslem counterparts of the former may be found in *Sudur*, 30, 31, and 121 ; and of the latter, in *Tadhkira*, 80, and *Sudur*, 118, 120, and 123.

two former parts of this work, have been dealt with in this part at greater length. The more important among them are the following :

The myth of the balance (*Ch. V*) ; the slippery bridge (*Tundal, St. Patrick, St. Paul, Abbot Joachim*) ; the torture of the sepulchre (*Hugh of Brandenburg, St. Brandan*) ; the intercession at the final judgment (*Ch. V*) ; the nakedness of sinners (*Ch. V*) ; the torture by the mad cow (*Tundal*) ; the vision of heaven granted to the sinners in order to increase their suffering (*Tundal*) ; the devil with the hundred hands (*Tundal*) ; the damned incarnate in birds of black plumage (*Edda*, and others in *Ch. IX*) ; the saintly souls and angels incarnate in white birds (*St. Macarius, St. Brandan*) ; Adam in paradise, smiling and crying at the same time (*Turcill*) ; the life of glory conceived as a courtly or religious festival (*Cour du Paradis, Vergier du Paradis, Visione dei gaudii de' santi*). Finally, the main characteristics of the cycles examined in the last four chapters : the voyages, particularly the voyage of St. Brandan with its scenes, such as the table decked with food, the enormous vines, the torture of Judas, the description of the sea hermit, the island-whale ; the legends of sleepers ; the tales of respite from torture ; the legends of the debate for the soul, with the striking features of the books of record, the personification of virtues and vices, and the accusation by the members of the body.

In view of the abundance of Islamic features present in the pre-Dante Christian legends, there is but one conclusion to be drawn : The many poetic conceptions of the after-life current throughout Europe before Dante's time had grown from contact with Islam rather than from the native stock, for several of those poetic myths or their descriptive features had no foundation in Christian doctrine but owed their origin to other religions of the East, whence they were transmitted in a new and richer form by Islam.

5. The doubt that had assailed the mind at the end of the second part of our work is thus dispelled. The natural inference to be drawn at that stage of our inquiry from the

great number of analogies detected in the Divine Comedy and the eschatological literature of Islam was that there existed some relation connecting the poem with that literature. To that hypothesis, however, it was possible to object the hypothesis put forward by the Dantists, that the conception of the divine poem could only have been influenced, and that indirectly, by the precursory Christian legends. But, once it has been shown that these legends also bear unmistakable signs of Moslem influence, that objection falls to the ground, and Dante now appears connected to Islam by a double tie—the indirect relation of the Islamic features present in his Christian precursors, and the direct relation of the Islamic elements contained in the Divine Comedy.

One question arises at this culminating point of our investigation : could Dante have known of the Moslem works on the after-life, and, if so, by what channels ? The answer to this question will complete the chain of reasoning.

PART IV

*PROBABILITY OF THE TRANSMISSION OF
ISLAMIC MODELS TO CHRISTIAN EUROPE
AND PARTICULARLY TO DANTE*

of the after-life, that is to say, the *ideas* or doctrines common to both eschatological conceptions. But, when these doctrines appear clothed in the same artistic form, when the ideas are represented by the same symbols and described with similar details, then the hypothesis of chance coincidence can no longer be maintained.

The difference is obvious. The ideas or doctrines are limited in number. Being the outcome of a trend of thought followed by mankind throughout the ages, they all necessarily fall within a few main categories. Not so the images. These, which are but the reflexion of the *actual* forms of *material* objects, are as numerous and varied as the objects themselves. It is morally impossible, therefore, that two conceptions of one and the same idea actually agreeing in detail should be formed in two minds, unless there existed a connecting link between the two. Such a miracle would be all the more unlikely, as the coincidence would be one, not of the conceptions of two particular minds, but of the artistic fancy of an individual, and the imaginings of a collective body such as Islam. In other words, it would be necessary to admit the possibility of Dante's having, by his sole mental effort, conceived in a few years the same fantastic picture of life beyond the grave as took the Moslem traditionists, mystics and poets centuries of artistic endeavour to elaborate. The claim to so marvellous an originality would require to be substantiated by evidence showing how this miracle came to be accomplished by Dante Alighieri. The burden of proof would thus be on the Dantists, and it would be for them to explain the enigma of the coincidences between Dante's poem and the Islamic legends, were it not that there did indeed exist a link between the two and evidence of that contact that is indispensable to all imitation.

3. This evidence may be furnished under three headings. It may be shown, firstly, that the Christian peoples of mediæval Europe, by their contact with Moslems, acquired a knowledge of their beliefs and conceptions of the after-life ; secondly, that Dante may well have drawn, directly or indirectly, upon Moslem sources for the material of his

poem ; and, lastly, that there are indications of his having been influenced by those sources.

II

COMMUNICATION BETWEEN ISLAM AND CHRISTIAN EUROPE DURING THE MIDDLE AGES

1. Islam, after the conquest of the countries bordering on Arabia, spread rapidly throughout the north of Africa, Spain, the south of France and southern Italy, and extended its dominion over the Balearic Isles and Sicily. The effect of war in imparting to the belligerents an intimate knowledge of each other is notorious ; but in times of peace, too, contact between the two civilisations of Christianity and Islam was established across their eastern and western frontiers through the medium of commerce.

From the eighth to the eleventh century an active trade was carried on between Moslem countries of the East and Russia and other countries of northern Europe. Expeditions left the Caspian regularly and, ascending the Volga, reached the Gulf of Finland and so through the Baltic to Denmark, Britain, and even as far as Iceland. The quantities of Arabic coins found at various places in this extensive commercial zone bear witness to its importance.[1] In the eleventh century trade was conducted by the easier sea route across the Mediterranean, chiefly by means of Genoese, Venetian or Moslem vessels. Large colonies of Italian traders settled in all the Moslem ports of the Mediterranean, and merchants, explorers, and adventurers sailed at will across its waters. Benjamin of Tudela has left us trustworthy evidence, in his " Itinerary " of the twelfth century, of the busy intercourse between Christians and Moslems at that time.

To the stimulus of trade must be added the impulse of the religious ideal. Pilgrimages to the Holy Land, which had been suspended owing to the early conquests of Islam,

[1] Cf. BABELON, *Du Commerce des Arabes dans le nord de l'Europe avant les croisades*, pp. 33–47, and *passim.*

were renewed and, with the establishment under Charlemagne of the Frank Protectorate over the Christian churches of the East, were assured by conventions and assisted by the foundation of hostels and monasteries in Moslem lands. During the ninth, tenth, and eleventh centuries the number of pilgrims grew, until some of the expeditions comprised as many as twelve thousand ; these expeditions were the forerunners of the Crusades.[1]

The influence of the Crusades in bringing Islam and Christian Europe together need hardly be insisted upon. The Christian States founded after the first Crusade may be likened to a European colony implanted in the heart of Islam, between the Euphrates and Egypt. The civil administration and the army of these States were formed on the Moslem model, and even the habits, food, and dress of the Orientals were adopted by the Frankish knights, who poured into Syria in Crusades from all parts of Europe even as far distant as Scandinavia.[2]

The failure to destroy Islam by the sword begot in its turn the idea of the pacific conquest of souls, and led in the thirteenth century to the establishment of the Missions to Islam. The Franciscan and Dominican Friars who formed this new tie of spiritual communication were obliged to make a thorough study of the language and religious literature of Islam, and to reside for many years amongst Moslems.[3]

2. More important and more interesting, however, from our point of view than any of these general channels of communication, is the contact of the two civilisations in Sicily and Spain. Beginning in the ninth century with piratical raids upon the coasts of the Atlantic and Mediterranean, the Normans gradually formed settlements in Moslem towns of the Peninsula (such as Lisbon, Seville, Orihuela and Barbastro) and in Sicily.[4] The latter island, indeed, which had become permeated with Islam, was conquered in the eleventh century and ruled by a dynasty of Norman Kings

[1] BREHIER, L'église et l'orient au moyen âge, pp. 20–50.
[2] Ibid. pp. 89–100 ; 354.   [3] Ibid. p. 211.
[4] DOZY, Recherches, II, 271. Cf. AMARI, Storia dei musulmani di Sicilia, III, part 2, 365, 445 et seq. SCHIAPARELLI, Ibn Giobeir, 322 and 332.

until the thirteenth century. Throughout that period the Sicilian population was composed of a medley of races professing different religions and speaking several languages. The court of the Norman King, Roger II, at Palermo, was formed of both Christians and Moslems, who were equally versed in Arabic literature and Greek science. Norman knights and soldiers, Italian and French noblemen and clergy, Moslem men of learning and literature from Spain, Africa, and the East lived together in the service of the King, forming a palatine organisation that in all respects was a copy of the Moslem courts. The King himself spoke and read Arabic, kept a harem in the Moslem manner, and attired himself after the Oriental fashion. Even the Christian women of Palermo adopted the dress, veil, and speech of their Moslem sisters.

But the time when Palermo most resembled a Moslem court was the first half of the thirteenth century, during the long reign of Frederick, King of Sicily and Emperor of Germany. A philosopher, free-thinker and polyglot, the Emperor, even as his predecessors had done in war and peace, surrounded himself with Moslems. They were his masters and fellow-students, his courtiers, officers and ministers ; and he was accompanied by them on his travels to the Holy Land and throughout Italy. His harems, one in Sicily and the other in Italy, were under the charge of eunuchs ; and even the tunic in which he was buried bore an Arabic inscription. The Popes and other Kings of Christendom raised public outcry against the scandal of the court of such an Emperor, who, though representing the highest civil authority of the Middle Ages, was Christian only in name.

This patron of literature and learning formed a unique collection of Arabic MSS. at the University of Naples, which he founded in 1224 ; and he had the works of Aristotle and Averrhoes translated, and copies sent to Paris and Bologna. Not only did he gather to his court Hebrew and Moslem philosophers, astrologers and mathematicians, but he corresponded with men of learning throughout Islam.

It was at the court of Frederick that the Sicilian school of poetry, which first used the vulgar tongue and thus laid the foundations of Italian literature, arose. The Arab troubadours assembled at his court were emulated by the Christians ; and the fact is significant inasmuch as it affords an instance of contact between the two literatures, Christian and Moslem.[1]

3. Important as Norman Sicily was as a centre of Islamic culture, it is nevertheless eclipsed in this respect by mediæval Spain. Here were to be found the same phenomena as in Sicily, but on a much larger scale and with the precedence of centuries. For Spain was the first country in Christian Europe to enter into intimate contact with Islam. For 500 years, from the eighth to the thirteenth century, when the Florentine poet came into the world, the two populations, Christian and Mahometan, lived side by side in war and peace.

The Mozarabs formed the first link between the two peoples. As early as the ninth century the Christians of Cordova had adopted the Moslem style of living, some even to the extent of keeping harems and being circumcised. Their delight in Arabic poetry and fiction, and their enthusiasm for the study of the philosophical and theological doctrines of Islam, are characteristically lamented by Alvaro of Cordova in his *Indiculus luminosus.*

The contact thus established in the early centuries of the Islamic conquest became, as may be imagined, more pronounced in the course of time. With intervals of intermittent strife, the intermingling of the two elements of the population steadily continued. And thus we find the Mozarabs of Toledo, the ancient capital of the Visigoths, using the Arabic language and characters in their public documents as late as the twelfth century, after the reconquest of the city. The suggestion that these Christians, who had become half Arabs, communicated to their brethren in the north of Spain, and even in other parts of Europe a

[1] AMARI, III, 2, pp. 589–711 ; 888–890.

knowledge of Islamic culture, may, therefore, be readily accepted. The hypothesis is strengthened by the fact of the constant emigration of Mozarabs northwards from Andalusia.[1]

To the Mozarab influence must be added another factor in the communication of Moslem culture—that of the slaves of Christian origin. Drawn from northern Spain and all parts of Europe, even as far as Russia, large numbers of slaves served in the court and in the army of the Emirs of Cordova. Many, no doubt, remained in their adoptive country where they had acquired both rank and fortune; but some, it may well be believed, would return to their native country in their old age.[2]

To attempt to enumerate the many other channels of communication between Christian Europe and Moslem Spain, we should require to re-create in our imagination the wonderful picture of Moslem society in Spain. As the centre of Western culture, Moslem Spain irresistibly attracted the semi-barbarous peoples of Christian Europe. From all parts came travellers, bent on study as well as trade, and eager to behold the wonders of this new classic civilisation of the Orient.

To paint the picture in detail it would be necessary to include the Jewish traders as other instruments of communication. With their flourishing international trade and their aptitude for languages and the sciences, they knit ties both material and spiritual between Moslem Spain and the chief cities of Christian Europe. Nor should we omit the part played by prisoners of war returning often after many years' absence to their native country; nor the effects of the frequent visits of Christian Ambassadors to the Moslem courts of the Peninsula.[3]

---

[1] Simonet, *Hist. mozárabes*, pp. 216–219, 252, 273, 292, 346, 368, 384, 690. Throughout the tenth century Arabicised monks and soldiers flocked to Leon, where their superior culture secured them high office at the court and in the ecclesiastical and civil administration of the kingdom. Cf. Gomez Moreno, *Iglesias mozárabes* (Madrid, 1917, Centro de Estudios Históricos), pp. 105–140.

[2] Ribera, *Discurso Acad. Hist.*, pp. 40–45.

[3] Ribera, *Disc.*, 46, Note 1.

4. With the gradual reconquest of Spain by the armies of the Christian kings, the Mudejars, their subdued Moslem subjects, took the place of the Mozarabs in transmitting Islamic culture. The undeniable superiority of this culture commanded the respect of the Christians, and the kings were prompt to adopt the policy of attracting the Mudejar element, thereby contributing to the more rapid and easy assimilation of Moslem civilisation. Further political alliances through marriage between the royal houses of Castile or Aragon and the reigning Moslem families were frequent.

Thus Alphonso VI, the conqueror of Toledo, married Zaida, the daughter of the Moorish King of Seville, and his capital resembled the seat of a Moslem court. The fashion quickly spread to private life; the Christians dressed in Moorish style, and the rising Romance language of Castile was enriched by a large number of Arabic words. In commerce, in the arts and trades, in municipal organisation, as well as in agricultural pursuits, the influence of the Mudejars was predominant, and thus the way was prepared for literary invasion, that was to reach its climax at the court of Alphonso X or the Wise.[1]

Toledo had throughout the twelfth century been an important centre for the dissemination of Arabic science and *belles-lettres* in Christian Europe. In the first half of that century, shortly after the city had been captured from the Moors, Archbishop Raymond began the translation of some of the more celebrated works of Arabic learning. Thus, the whole encyclopædia of Aristoteles was translated from the Arabic, with the commentaries of Alkindius, Alfarabius, Avicenna, Algazel and Averrhoes; as also the master works of Euclid, Ptolemy, Galen, and Hippocrates, with the comments upon them of learned Moslems, such as Albatenius, Avicenna, Averrhoes, Rhazes, and Alpetragius. Translated into the Romance language of Castile with the help of learned Mudejars and Hebrews, these works were in turn

[1] RIBERA, *Orígenes Justicia*, 19–84. FERNÁNDEZ Y GONZÁLEZ, *Mudéjares,* 224, *et passim.*

rendered into Latin by Christian doctors drawn from all parts
of Christendom.[1]

5. Alphonso the Wise, who had been educated in this
environment of Semitic culture, on ascending the throne
personally directed the work of translation, and gathered to
his court as collaborators wise men of the three religions,
an instance demonstrative of the tolerance of his time.
Besides contributing new works on physics and astronomy,
he also devoted considerable attention to subjects that would
appeal more to the popular mind. His father, Ferdinand the
Saint, had encouraged the compilation of the *Libro de los
doce sabios* and *Flores de filosofia*, in which Oriental influence
is first seen ; and Alphonso caused similar books, such as
Calila y Dimna, *Bocados de Oro*, and *Poridad de poridades*
to be translated and works on Oriental pastimes compiled.
From Arabic sources he wrote his *Grand e General Estoria*,
and he ordered the translation of Talmudic and cabbalistic
works, and, lastly, of the Koran.[2]

The advance of the Reconquest opened up a new field of
action, and Murcia and Seville, after their recapture, became
centres of philosophy and literature that rivalled Toledo.
During the lifetime of his father, Alphonso had been
Governor of Murcia, where he had a school built specially
for Muhammad ar-Riquti, in which the Moslem sage lectured
to Moors, Jews, and Christians alike.[3] Before 1158, another
learned Moslem, Abd Allah ibn Sahloh, had taught mathe-
matics and philosophy to Moors and Christians at Baeza,
and in his school discussed theological questions with the
Christian clergy.[4] Encouraged, no doubt, by these precedents, the king decided to give official sanction to the
fusion of the two civilisations, of Christendom and Islam.
He founded at Seville a general Latin and Arabic college,
at which Moslems taught medicine and science side by side

[1] JOURDAIN, *Recherches sur les anciennes traductions latines d'Aristote*,
pp. 95–149.
[2] JOURDAIN, pp. 149–151. FERNÁNDEZ Y GONZÁLEZ, 154–159. AMADOR
DE LOS RÍOS, *Hist. crít. de la liter. esp.*, III, ch. 9–12.
[3] AL-MAKKARI, *Analectes*, II, 510. Cf. *Ihata*, II, fol. 153 v°.
[4] *Ihata*, III, fol. 85.

with Christian professors.[1] This in itself is eloquent of the close relationship between the two elements of the population in the first half of the thirteenth century.

III

TRANSMISSION OF THE MOSLEM LEGENDS ON THE AFTER-LIFE TO CHRISTIAN EUROPE AND DANTE

1. Anyone of the channels mentioned may have served as the means of communication, even to the farthest ends of Europe, for the news of the legends on the after-life that were popular throughout Islam.[2] It has been shown that the legends that sprang up in Ireland, Scandinavia, France, Germany and Italy—the so-called precursors of the Divine Comedy—were most probably based on Islamic models. These may have been introduced into Christian Europe by pilgrims, Crusaders, merchants or missionaries; or, again, by Norman adventurers, slaves, men of learning or simple travellers. Once the possibility of a connecting link has been established, the hypothesis of imitation tends to become

---

[1] AMADOR DE LOS RÍOS, III, 496. BALLESTEROS, *Sevilla en el siglo XIII*, docs. Nos. 67 and 109. LA FUENTE, *Hist. de las Universidades*, I, 127–130.

[2] BLOCHET in his *Sources orientales de la Divine Comédie*, omits or disregards the nearest and most constant channels of communication between Eastern and Western culture. To him the main channels are the trade routes from Persia to the North-East of Europe via Byzance; the intellectual relations between Ireland and Italy, and Italy and Byzance; and, finally, the Crusades. Moslem Spain is hardly once mentioned as a means of communication. This appears to be due to the fact that, in Blochet's opinion, the pre-Dante legends (such as the Voyage of St. Brandan, the Visions of St. Paul, St. Patrick, Hincmar, Charles the Bald, and Tundal, and the Tale of the Three Monks of the East) are derived rather from the Persian ascension of Ardâ Virâf than from Arabic and Islamic sources. He admits, indeed, that the *Mîraj* may also have influenced these legends, but only as transmitted by the Crusaders from the East. The vast majority, however, of Islamic elements in the precursory legends have been shown to be derived from *hadiths* of the future life and only very few from the *Mîraj*. Still less can there be any question of direct relation between the precursors and the Persian legend. Blochet, moreover, contents himself with pointing out analogies between the precursory legends and the Eastern sources, but hardly ever furnishes documentary evidence; though, even if he did so, it would still be more natural to account for the resemblance as due to the effect of Islamic religious literature, rather than any direct contact with Persia. JOURDAIN (*Recherches*, 208 *et seq.*) long ago pointed out how insignificant was the influence of Byzance and the Crusades on the transmission of science and philosophy to Western Christendom, compared with that of the Hispano-Arabic centre.

that moral certainty that historical demonstration requires and is content to accept.

It must be borne in mind that the majority of the Christian legends prior to the Divine Comedy originated later than the tenth century, whereas the *hadiths* on the after-life date much further back. That these *hadiths* were of popular origin is, moreover, evident. Until the ninth century they were transmitted solely by word of mouth, a fact that helped to spread them and rendered the creation of new legends easier.[1] Not until the formation by the two great critics, Bukhari and Muslim, of the collections of authentic *hadiths* can the era of invention be considered closed. Their popularity did not, however, diminish on that account. Moslems everywhere, of all ages and every social rank, acted as transmitters, often undertaking long journeys to hear new tales and so increase their stock of religious lore ; for, apart from the attraction that the fantastic nature of the theme held for the masses, it was considered an act of faith to learn these tales and share in their dissemination. No wonder, therefore, that the teachers of *hadiths* prior to the ninth century were reckoned by thousands.

2. It may be said that from the earliest times Spain was the country most addicted to the study of these legends ; for the intolerance of the Faqihs alone produced a superabundance of traditional lore. Indeed, in the ninth century, it was regarded as the home of the traditions of the Prophet and of all these it was but natural that the story of the *Miraj*, or ascension of Mahomet, should have the widest diffusion, as narrating an important part of the biography of the Prophet—the story of the performance of his supreme miracle, which has been accepted as a dogma, and is solemnly commemorated to this day throughout Islam.

Knowledge of these Moslem tales would, sooner or later, inevitably filter through the slender barrier separating the two peoples in their conception of the hereafter.[2] Indeed,

---

[1] The early Moslems, who were Arabs by race and, like the Prophet, illiterate, felt the same aversion for writing as did Mahomet ; and at first it was thought unlawful to record the *hadiths* in writing.

[2] Cf. *Supra*, pp. 79–81.

18

poor as are the records of the beliefs of Islam left us by
mediæval Christian writers, there is evidence that the
Christians in Spain were, from the first centuries of the
conquest, aware of these legends, and especially of the legend
of the *Miraj*.

3. At the very outset of the ninth century, in the apologetic writings of the Mozarabs of Cordova, mention is made
of Moslem *hadiths*. Alvaro òf Cordova, in his *Indiculus
luminosus*; St. Eulogius, in his *Memoriale Sanctum*; and
the Abbot Esperaindeo, in his *Apologetico contra Mahoma*,
repeatedly allude to tales " leves et risu dignas " describing
the life and miracles of the pretended prophet.[1] In his
Apologeticus Martyrum St. Eulogius interpolates a brief
biography of Mahomet. Founded largely upon spurious
data, it is in the main a baseless fabrication that, nevertheless,
shows a considerable knowledge of the Koran and the
hadiths.[2]

4. This biography of Mahomet, St. Eulogius found at the
Monastery of Leire in Navarre, which proves that as early
as the ninth century the legend had penetrated to the north
of Spain. This explains why Spain should have been the
country from which it first passed into Western literature.
Indeed, in 1143 a Latin version of the Koran was written
by the Archdeacon of Pamplona, Robert of Reading, an
English ecclesiastic who had formerly worked at the college
of translators founded at Toledo by Archbishop Raymond.
Together with this version, the archdeacon wrote a treatise
entitled " Summa brevis contra haereses et sectam Sarracenorum " and derived from Arabic sources.[3] It is unlikely
that a polemical work of this kind would omit to mention
the *Miraj*, which by its very extravagance would readily
lend itself to refutation ; but is impossible to make any
definite assertion on the point, as the treatise in question
has not been preserved complete.

---

[1] SIMONET, 377, notes 2 and 3. Cf. *Indic. lum.* in *España Sagrada*, XI,
249.   [2] EULOGIUS, *Apologeticus*, fol. 80 v°.
[3] JOURDAIN, *Recherches*, 100–103. Cf. WÜSTENFELD, *Die Übersetzungen
arabischer Werke*, 44–50.

5. Another document of the same century still exists however—the "Historia Arabum," written in Latin by Archbishop Rodrigo Jimenez de Rada of Toledo.[1] In the prologue the author states that his compendium will start from the time of Mahomet, and that his data upon the origin, teaching and government of the Prophet will be taken " ex relatione fideli et eorum scripturis." Nor should this have been difficult, seeing that he wrote in Toledo, where at the time many Arabic books on religion, science, and lighter literature were then being translated.[2] In Chapter V of this " Historia Arabum," which is entitled " De sublimatione Mahometi in regem et de jussionibus mendaciter excogitatis," the author relates the raising of Mahomet to the dignity of king, after the taking of Damascus ; and he adds that Mahomet then began to impose upon the Arabs with stories in which he professed to be a prophet, with the object of obtaining a firmer hold upon his subjects. He then inserts a literal version of the legend of the *Miraj*, culled from what he terms the " second book " of Mahomet. This can be no other than the canonical collection of *hadiths* on the Prophet, second from an authoritative point of view only to the Koran, which latter the Archbishop would consider to be the first book of Islam. Indeed this version is almost identical with Versions A and B of the second cycle given in the first part of the present work, as recorded in the collection of authentic *hadiths* compiled by Bukhari and Muslim.

From the " Historia Arabum " it passed to the " Cronica General " or " Estoria d'Espanna," which King Alphonso the Wise himself compiled or had compiled in the Romance language of Castile between 1260 and 1268, and where it appears with some slight additions,[3] no doubt made from

---

[1] AMADOR DE LOS RÍOS, *Hist. crit. de la liter. esp.*, III, 415 *et seq.*, mentions a Castilian version of 1256. The text here used is the Latin text from ERPENIUS, *Historia saracenica.*

[2] It should be remembered that Alphonso the Wise had ordered the Koran to be translated. Another translation was made in the 13th century by a canon of Toledo, named Marco. Cf. JOURDAIN, *Recherches*, 149.

[3] See the *Primera Crónica General* of Alphonso the Wise, pp. 270–272, chapters 488 and 489, entitled " De como Mahomat dixo que fallara a Abrahan et a Moysen et a Ihesu en Iherusalem " and " De como Mahomat dixo que subira fasta los syete cielos."

other Arabic sources current at the time. The greater interest attaching to the " Cronica," and the fact that it was written in Romance would ensure the wider diffusion of the legend.

6. Indeed not long afterwards, towards the end of the thirteenth century, another document appeared showing how widespread the legend was among Christian Spaniards. This was the " Impunaçion de la seta de Mahomah," written during his captivity at Granada by St. Peter Paschal, Bishop of Jaen and Friar of the Order of Mercy.[1] Born at Valencia in 1227, of captive or Mozarab parents, he not unnaturally was a master of Arabic, a fact that would stand him in great stead in his mission of redeeming prisoners. Appointed tutor to the son of the King of Aragon, he accompanied his charge to Toledo when the latter was raised to the dignity of Archbishop, and there he devoted himself to fostering and extending throughout Castile the Order of Mercy, which was then in its infancy. His work in this connection led him to undertake a journey to Rome, where his learning and religious zeal excited the admiration of Pope Nicholas IV. On his return, he stayed a while at Paris, and at the university there gained fame as a theologian. Appointed Bishop of Jaen in 1296, he was taken prisoner by the Moors of Granada in the following year and was martyred in 1300. During the four years of his captivity he wrote, among other books, the apologetic work against Islam mentioned above.[2]

The knowledge of Islam he displays is considerable. At every step he quotes the Koran and authentic versions of the *hadiths* ; the latter he calls " Alhadiz," and occasionally " Muslimi," in reference to the canonical collections made by the critic Muslim. He also mentions a book on paradise and hell, which is, no doubt, one of the compendiums of *hadiths* common among the Moslems of Spain ; and refers

---

[1] Recently published under the title " El Obispo de Jaén sobre la seta Mahometana," by Fr. PEDRO ARMENGOL in vol. IV of the *Obras de San Pedro Pasqual* (Rome, 1908). The Catalan Dominican RAYMOND MARTIN also mentions the *Miraj* in his *Explanatio simboli apostolorum*, written in 1256-1257. Cf. Edit. MARCH, p. 41 : " . . . non sicut Machometus qui jactavit se ad celos ascendisse, sed de nocte et nullo vidente."

[2] Cf. AMADOR DE LOS RÍOS, *Hist. crit. de la liter. esp.*, IV, 75-85.

to other " Libros escriptos de los Moros," which must also
have been collections of legends on the after-life.[1] More
interesting, however, are his quotations from a book the
title of which he variously transcribes as " Elmiregi,"
" Miragi," " Miraj " or " Elmerigi." This is evidently the
Miraj or ascension of Mahomet, or, as the Saint has it,
" the book in which he told how he rose to the heavens " ;
" the book which tells how Mahomet rose as he says to
heaven, where is God, and how he spoke with God and saw
paradise and hell and the angels and devils and the tortures
of hell and the delights of paradise."[2] But he does more
than merely quote from this book. In Chapter 8 of the
first part of the " Impunaçion " he inserts the entire legend
of the *Miraj*, adding a burlesque commentary in refutation
of its fabulous episodes and miraculous visions ; these the
Saint airily disposes of as " mere fancy, vanities, lies, humbug
and idle talk."[3] The version of which he availed himself
belongs to the third cycle, in which the Nocturnal Journey
and the ascension of Mahomet are fused into one story. The
ascension proper, however, is related according to Version C
of the second cycle, where in spirituality the visions of
paradise approach nearer to Dante's conception. Finally,
there are introduced into the general scheme of the legend
many *hadiths* dealing with the day of judgment, the " Sirat "
or purgatory, the topography of hell, and life in paradise,
the resemblance of which to the descriptions of Dante has
been duly demonstrated.

7. If, therefore, the legend of the *Miraj* was well known in
Spain, at any rate as early as the thirteenth century, is it
unlikely that it should also reach Italy, bound as that country
was by ties of close and constant communication with Spain ?[4]
St. Peter Paschal, who knew the legend well, resided for a

---

[1] Cf. ARMENGOL, IV, 3, 4, 28, 29, 37, 41, 49, 143, etc.
[2] Cf. ARMENGOL, IV, 28, 53, 55, 66, 143. Incidentally it is also mentioned
in the *Tratado contra el fatalismo musulman* (III, 54–91) on pp. 55, 72,
and 83.　　　　　[3] Cf. ARMENGOL, IV, 90–138.
[4] How close these ties were is shown by the mere fact that shortly after
the reconquest of Seville Italian nobles and merchants occupied whole
streets and quarters of their own. Cf. BALLÉSTEROS, *Sevilla*, ch. III,
Los extranjeros, 42–46.

time in Rome during the Pontificate of Nicholas IV, *i.e.*, between 1288 and 1292, and, though it would be idle to base an argument on this mere fact, it may at least serve as a typical example of the hidden channels through which the legend might have reached the Florentine poet. At that time the plan of his divine poem, the first part of which, the Inferno, was finished in 1306, was maturing in Dante's mind. Moreover, in 1301, Dante himself visited the Papal Court as the Ambassador of Florence to Pope Boniface VIII.[1]

8. But there are other surer channels by which the legend could have been transmitted. Dante received his literary training from Brunetto Latini, a scholar of encyclopædic knowledge and a notary of Florence, who rose to fill the highest offices of state.[2] More than a master, Brunetto was a literary adviser and friend for whom the young poet felt the greatest respect and admiration, and whose counsel and guidance were a source of constant inspiration to him. The affectionate discourse Dante feigns to hold with his master on meeting him in hell is eloquent testimony of the spiritual tie that Dante himself admits bound him to Brunetto Latini and his work.[3] This connection has long been apparent to the commentators on the Divine Comedy[4]; and some Dante students have even sought in the writings of Brunetto, particularly in the allegorical and didactic poem of the "Tesoretto," the model and idea that inspired the Divine Comedy. Although the hypothesis has been rejected by the Dante students themselves,[5] there yet remains the important fact of the link between the studies of the pupil and the oral and written doctrine of the master.

The written doctrine is contained in the "Tesoretto" and the "Tesoro," which respectively are a small and large encyclopædia of mediæval learning. To obtain the mass of data required for the latter work Brunetto, without ignoring

---

[1] Cf. ROSSI, I, 118 and 138.
[2] SCARTAZZINI in his comment on *Inf.*, XV, 23–54, gives a bibliography of the person and works of Brunetto Latini. The work here consulted is SUNDBY, *Della vita e delle opere di Brunetto Latini*.
[3] *Inf.*, XV, 58 and 60; 79–87; 119–120.
[4] Cf. SCARTAZZINI, *loc. cit.*, *Inf.*, XV, 32.
[5] Cf. VOSSLER, II, 118–120; D'ANCONA, 101, note 1.

classical and Christian sources, drew, as did all his contemporaries, upon the Arabic works on science then available. Sundby, the learned Dane who half a century ago investigated the sources of the "Tesoro," restricted his research to the works that were then more easy of access, that is to say, the Christian and classical writers. But many of the passages, the origin of which he admits he does not know, may easily be traced to Arabic models.[1] Thus the classification of philosophy given at the beginning of the work is copied from Avicenna[2]; the version of the *Nichomachean Ethics* of Aristotle that Brunetto used, appears to have been a translation of an Arabic text from Spain ; and the Bestiaries or collections of animal legends, of which he availed himself, were mostly of Arabic origin. Lastly, Brunetto's own references to Oriental authors form a strong argument in favour of a like origin being attributed to other passages which it has been impossible to connect with any previous Christian or classical works.[3]

9. In addition, the Tesoro contains a biography of Mahomet, in which, coupled with a puerile belief in certain legends deriding the Prophet, Brunetto shows considerable knowledge of the doctrine and customs of Islam.[4] As the Italian Codices of the Tesoro have not yet been edited, it is difficult to say whether the legend of the *Miraj* is contained in this biography, among the fables attributed by Brunetto to Mahomet. But, even if it were not included, the hypothesis that Brunetto may have known of the legend and communicated it by word of mouth to his disciple cannot be rejected as improbable.

For Brunetto Latini was in a position to acquire his knowledge of Arabic culture at first hand, when in 1260 he was

---

[1] SUNDBY, 29–41.

[2] Cf. SUNDBY, 86–88, and CARRA DE VAUX, *Avicenne*, 177–180, and note the classifications given by Avicenna in his *Rasail*, 2–3 and 71–80.

[3] SUNDBY, 136, and *passim*, acknowledges that he does not know the origin of some passages ; on p. 111 he admits that Brunetto availed himself of Arabic texts of the physician Ishaq ibn Hunayn. D'ANCONA (*Il Tesoro di B.L. versificato*) points out the Arabic origin of some episodes of the story of Alexander the Great as told in the *Tesoro* (cf., p. 141). The very title of *Tesoro* is reminiscent of Arabic literature. BROCKELMANN quotes over sixty works bearing that title, some far earlier than the thirteenth century, when the fashion spread to Christian Europe.

[4] Cf. D'ANCONA (*Tesoro*, 176–227).

sent as Ambassador of Florence to the court of Alphonso the Wise, the patron and director of the famous Toledan school of translators.[1]

The details of this mission are not known, but the mere facts of Brunetto's having stayed at Toledo and Seville, where the court resided at the time, is significant. It is easy to imagine how deep would be the impression produced on so cultured a mind, ever eager to acquire more knowledge, by these two brilliant centres of learning. Living at the court of a king, whose learning was unique in mediæval Europe, and in the midst of a hybrid society that was influenced by classical, Christian and Oriental traditions alike, he cannot fail to have been impressed ; and it is unlikely that his ambassadorial duties should not have left him leisure to satisfy his curiosity as a scholar. At the Toledan School of Translators, and the inter-denominational University of Seville, Christians and Moslems were continually engaged on the production of literary and scientific works, and only four years before had rendered into Romance Castilian the " Historia Arabum," which contained the very legend of the *Miraj*. As a matter of fact, on his return to France, Brunetto almost immediately wrote his two main works, the " Tesoretto " and the " Tesoro." The latter, as has been seen, contains traces of the influence of Arabic works, and nowhere could these have been more readily available than in Toledo and Seville ; the former is even supposed to have been dedicated to Alphonso the Wise.

Everything thus would seem to bear out the suggestion that the master of Dante Alighieri received more than a merely superficial impression from his visit to Spain,[2] and may well have been the medium through which some at least of the Islamic features apparent in the Divine Comedy were transmitted to the disciple.[3]

---

[1] SUNDBY, 6–10. Brunetto mentions the date of his mission in the first verses of his *Tesoretto* (1–25).

[2] AMADOR DE LOS Ríos, IV, 17–23.

[3] Apart from the legend of the *Miraj*, Brunetto may have obtained philosophical and theological information in Spain about the eschatology of Ibn Arabi, whose *Ishraqi* and mystical school of thought lived on in the works and teaching of other Murcian Sufis.

The documentary evidence, however, consisting in the likeness shown between the divine poem and the Islamic sources, is in itself sufficient, even though it may not be possible to demonstrate through what hidden channels communication actually took place.[1] For do not the characteristics of each style of architecture found on a monument of varied design betray the influence of its respective school, even though history may have left no actual record of the association between these schools ? Documentary evidence, should it exist, would not strengthen the expert's conviction ; it would but confirm the inferences he had already drawn.

[1] A knowledge of Islamic lore may have been transmitted to Dante by a learned Rabbi, such as Emmanuel Ben Salomo, of the Zifroni family, a poet and philosopher of Rome and a friend of Dante ; or Hillel of Verona. [The importance in this connection of the Italian Rabbis, who were perhaps better informed of the Moslem sources than the Christians of Dante's time, has lately been pointed out by BECK, in Zeitschrift für Romanische Philologie (Berlin, 1921, vol. XLI, p. 472) and VAN TIEGHEM, in Revue de Littérature Comparée (Paris, April/June, 1922, p. 324). Other critics of the thesis have suggested further likely channels of communication. Thus, CABATON, in Revue de l'Histoire des Religions (Paris, 1920, p. 19) recalls the fact that Dante's friend, the poet Guido Cavalcanti, had visited Spain on a pilgrimage to Santiago de Compostela. NALLINO, in Rivista degli Studi Orientali (Rome, 1921, vol. VIII, 4, p. 808), mentions the following as likely means of contact between Dante and Islam : The captive Moslems of all ranks of society living in Tuscany, and particularly at Pisa ; or, the Italian troubadours who flocked to the Court of Alphonso the Wise ; or, again, the innumerable Italian traders who came and went between Italy and Spain and the Moslem ports of Africa and the East. He adds : " If the Pisan merchant Leonardo Fibonacci could acquire in the Aduanas of the Moslem ports the knowledge of Algebra that he introduced into Europe early in the 13th century ; and if other, nameless, travellers could be the bearers of the popular Oriental tales that later passed into Italian literature ; is it unlikely that among other fantastic tales the legendary story of Mahomet should be thus transmitted, a story that was in perfect keeping with the mentality of the people in mediæval Europe ? " Finally, the critic GABRIELI, on pp. 55–61 of his pamphlet, " Intorno alle fonti orientali della Divina Commedia," in Arcadia, III (Rome, 1919), though generally adverse to the theory, makes two interesting suggestions. As possible means of transmission he names the Spanish Franciscan Lull and the Florentine Dominican Ricoldo de Monte Croce. Lull, who had a vast knowledge of Islamic culture and knew and imitated the doctrines of Ibn Arabi, repeatedly visited Italy between 1287 and 1296, residing two whole years in Rome as well as in Genoa, Pisa, and Naples. Even more likely appears the intervention of Ricoldo, who lived in the East from 1288 to 1301, preaching the Gospel in Syria, Persia and Turkestan, whence he returned to the Monastery of Santa Maria Novella at Florence and there died in 1320, at the age of 74. In Chapter XIV of his famous work Contra legem sarracenorum, or Improbatio Alchorani, he treats of the legend of the Miraj. Dante is known to have had dealings with the Dominican friars of Santa Maria Novella ; indeed, it appears that during his youth he attended their cloister schools, where letters and sciences were also taught to laymen.—Note added since the publication of the Spanish original.]

THE ATTRACTION FELT BY DANTE TOWARDS ARABIC CULTURES
CONFIRMS THE HYPOTHESIS OF IMITATION

1. The possibility that the Moslem models of the Divine
Comedy may easily have reached Italy and the Florentine
poet from Moslem sources having been sufficiently proved,
one question alone remains to be answered. Was the
mentality of Dante, as revealed in his works, antagonistic
to the ready assimilation of these models ? For, obviously,
no contact, however close, could beget imitation if diversity
in language, religion, race, philosophy and art had inspired
the Florentine poet with an aversion to the culture of the
Arabs. In answer to this question, it may at once be said
that all the evidence points to the contrary.

2. In the first place, Dante Alighieri was in matters of
learning and literature open to influence from all quarters.
Dante students have one and all laid stress upon this mental
receptivity. Ozanam repeatedly dwells upon the passionate
desire for knowledge that urged on the poet in his search for
truth and beauty.[1] D'Ancona has explained how Dante
studied and mastered a vast range of subjects ; how in his
mind inspiration was reconciled with a respect for tradition,
and inventive faculty with erudition.[2] Umberto Cosmo,
more recently, asserts that in its receptiveness the mind of
Dante might be likened to a sea that receives its waters
from all parts. Dante, he says, gathered intellectual
nourishment from the whole culture of his time, and in his
mind were reflected and recast in a new, personal form the
sentiments and ideas of the past and the present.[3]

Opinions of such weight would seem to establish *a priori*
that the culture of Islam, dominant in thirteenth-century
Europe, must have been known to Dante. It is inconceivable that he, leading a life of such mental activity,
should have ignored Moslem culture, which at the time was

[1] OZANAM, 437, 467.
[2] D'ANCONA, 108, 113.
[3] Cf. *Rassegna dantesca*, in " Giorn. stor. della letter. italiana " (1914,
Nos. 2–3), pp. 385, 390.

all-pervading ; that he should not have felt the attraction
of a science that drew men of learning from all parts of
Christian Europe to the court of Toledo, and of a literature
the influence of which was paramount in Christian Europe,
which it initiated in the novels, the fables and the proverbs,
as well as the works on moral science and apologetics, of the
East.[1]

The prestige enjoyed by Islam was largely due to the
Moslem victories over the Crusaders.[2] Roger Bacon, a contemporary of Dante, attributed the defeats of the Christians
precisely to their ignorance of the Semitic languages and
applied science, of which the Moslems were masters.[3] In
another field of learning, Albertus Magnus, the founder of
scholasticism, agreed with Bacon on the superiority of the
Arab philosophers[4] ; and Raymond Lull even recommended

---

[1] That the lyrical and epic poetry of the then rising Christian literatures
were also influenced by Hispano-Moslem models has been shown by my
master RIBERA in his *Discursos de ingreso en las Academias Española y de
la Historia* (Madrid, 1912 and 1915). He has also traced the connection
between Hispano-Moslem music and that of the French troubadours, in
La música de las Cantigas (Madrid, 1922) and *La música andaluza medieval
en las canciones de trovadores y troveros* (Madrid, 1923). How profound
and extensive the influence of Arabic poetry was has also been shown by
S. SINGER, in *Arabische und Europäische Poesie im Mittelalter* (Berlin,
1918), and by BURDACH, in *Ueber den Ursprung des Mittelalterlichen
Minnesangs* (Berlin, 1918) ; these authors give the Arabic sources of
poems such as *Floire et Blanchefleur*, *Aucassin et Nicolette*, and legends
such as that of the Grail, Parsifal, and Tristan.—*Note added.*

[2] Typical of the vogue for Arabic is the following text, taken from the
Liber Adelardi Batensis de quibusdam naturalibus questionibus (MS. Bibl.
Escur., III, o, 2, fol. 74). Adelard of Bath was one of the learned English-
men who worked at the Toledan School of Translators. The text is from
the prologue and is addressed to a nephew.
" Meministi, nepos, quod, septennio iam transacto, cum te in gallicis
studiis pene puerum juxta Laudisdunum una cum ceteris auditoribus in
eis dimiserim, id iter nos convenisse *ut arabum studia ego pro posse meo
scrutarer* . . . Quod utrum recte expleverim re ipsa probari potest. Hac
precipue oportunitate quod *cum sarracenorum sentencias te sepe exponentem
auditor tantum noverim earumque non pauce satis utiles mihi videantur,*
pacienciam meam paulisper abrumpam, teque edisserente, ego siccubi mihi
videbitur obviabo. *Quippe et illos impudice extollis et nostros detractionis
modo inscitia invidiose arguis . . .*"

[3] *Opus majus* (Edit. Jebe, 1733), p. 246:
" Latini nihil quod valet habent nisi ab aliis linguis . . ." *Ibid.* p. 476.
" Et iam ex istis scientiis tribus patet mirabilis utilitas . . . contra inimicos
fidei destruendos."

[4] In so delicate a matter as the question of the union of the active intellect
with man, he declares (*Opera omnia*, III, 3, *De Anima*, 166) :
" Nos autem dissentimus in paucis ab Averroe . . ." " His duobus
suppositis, accipimus alia duo ab Alfarabio . . ." " In causa autem quam

the imitation of Moslem methods in preaching to the people.[1]

Rarely can public opinion have been so unanimous in admitting the mental superiority of an adversary. This view was upheld by Moslem men of learning, who adjudged the European races to be unfit for civilisation. This curious assertion was actually made by two Moslem thinkers of Spain in the eleventh century, Ibn Hazm of Cordova, and Said of Toledo. In their respective works, the Critical History of the Religions and the History of the Sciences, they declared that the peoples of Northern Europe were by nature unfitted for the cultivation of the sciences and arts, which flourished in Moslem Spain.[2]

3. In view of the universal admiration for Islamic culture, it is not astonishing to find a certain leaning towards it on the part of Dante.

It was at one time believed that Dante had a knowledge of Semitic languages, especially of either Arabic or Hebrew, the inference being based on two solitary verses of the Divine Comedy. Modern opinion, however, favours the view that in these verses the poet merely intended to introduce meaningless phrases, though it is admitted that the words attri-

inducemus et modo, *convenimus* in toto cum Averroe et Avempace, in parte cum Alfarabio."
and he rejects the opinion of the Latin scholars (*Ibid.* p. 143), " Sed isti, absque dubio, numquam bene intentionem Aristotelis intellexerunt."

[1] Cf. *Blanquerna*, II, 105, 134, 158–160 in RIBERA, *Lulio*, II, 193–197.
[2] IBN HAZM, *Fasl*, I, 72:
" . . . the countries in which there are none of the arts and sciences mentioned (i.e., medicine, astronomy and the mechanical arts), such as the countries of the Sudan and of the Slavs and among the majority of peoples, both nomad and settled . . ."
SAID, *Tabaqat*, 8:
" The other peoples (apart from the Chinese and Turks) that do not cultivate the sciences, resemble rather beasts than men ; as regards those that live in the lands of the far North, bordering on the uninhabited part of the globe, the prolonged absence of the sun renders the air cold and the atmosphere in which they live less clear ; accordingly they are men of a cold temperament and never reach maturity ; they are of great stature and of a white colour, with long and lank hair. But they lack all sharpness of wit and penetration of intellect, and among them predominate ignorance and stupidity, mental blindness, and barbarism. Such are the Slavs, Bulgars and neighbouring peoples. (*Ibid.* 9) As to the Galicians and Berbers, they are ignorant, rebellious and hostile people."
It should be borne in mind that by " Galicians " are meant the Christian inhabitants of the North East of Spain and Portugal, and by " Slavs " and " Bulgars " all the peoples of the North and East of Europe.

buted to Nimrod contain Semitic elements.[1] Be this as
it may, if it cannot be proved from Dante's writings that he
knew the Semitic languages, neither can it be proved that
he was ignorant of them. It may at least be supposed that
he knew of their qualities and aptness as a means of social
intercourse ; and, indirect as his knowledge may have been,
it was sufficient to enable him to compare them with the
Romance languages, to the disadvantage of the latter. For,
treating in his work, *De vulgari eloquio*, of the multitude of
languages spoken in the world, he, although a native of
Florence and by race and language a Latin, does not allow
himself to be prejudiced in favour of his mother tongue ;
rather does he show proof of his characteristic breadth of
mind when he admits " that there are many other nations
speaking tongues more pleasant to the ear and more expres-
sive than those of the Latin peoples."[2]

4. It need hardly be added that such attraction as Dante
felt towards Oriental culture does not imply a liking for the
Moslem faith, for the sincerity of his Christian belief is
beyond all doubt. His sympathies were merely literary, and
scientific ; and his mental attitude is revealed in two typical
passages of the Divine Comedy. Avicenna and Averrhoes he
places in the limbo,[3] but Mahomet, in hell.[4] And even
Mahomet is not punished as the founder of Islam, but as a
sower of discord and an author of schism ; he is placed
along with men the effect of whose actions cannot be compared with the profound upheaval—religious, social and
political—that Islam caused in the history of the world and,
to her unutterable loss, in the history of the Church. The
leniency of this punishment is significant of Dante's sympathies for Arabic culture. In his eyes, Mahomet is not so
much a repudiator of the Trinity and Incarnation as a
conqueror whose violence cut asunder the ties uniting
mankind. Incomplete as his picture may be, it does not
display the absurdity marked in the mediæval fables of the

---

[1] The different opinions and bibliography on this point may be found in
SCARTAZZINI (*Inf.* VII, 1 ; XXXI, 67).
[2] *De vulgari eloquio*, I, ch. VI.   [3] *Inf.*, IV, 143, 144.
[4] *Inf.*, XXVIII, 22-63.

Prophet. The Christian historians of Dante's age outvied one another in weaving the most extravagant and contradictory tales about Mahomet. According to some, he was a pagan ; to others, a Christian. He was given in turn the names of Ocin, Pelagius, Nicholas, and Mahomet. Some depict him, rightly, as illiterate ; others, as a magician, or even a scholar of Bologna. He is represented as having been a Spaniard, a Roman, and even a member of the family of Colonna. Some historians, again, confuse the Prophet with his mentor, the Nestorian monk Bahira, and make of him a deacon or cardinal who, aspiring to the Papacy, set out for Arabia from Constantinople, Antioch or Smyrna.[1] Before the gross ignorance displayed in such crude misrepresentations, the sober picture drawn by Dante stands as a silent rebuke to his contemporaries. One is tempted to think that Dante was content to depict Mahomet as a mere conqueror, not because he was unaware of the other sides to his character, but because the portrayal of these would have been incompatible with the absurd image stereotyped on the minds of his readers.

That the restraint shown by Dante is not due to ignorance is abundantly borne out by one fact. The poet shows Ali suffering the same torture as his cousin and father-in-law, Mahomet. The role played by Ali in the history of Islam is nowadays a matter of general historical knowledge. It is well known that the Caliphate did not pass to his sons or their descendants, who were hunted down by the Ommeyad and Abbaside Caliphs ; but they soon found eager partisans who, under the name of Shiites, dominated Persia, Syria, Egypt and Barbary down to the twelfth century. The history of the bloody struggles provoked by this undoubted schism down to the time of Saladin, fully justifies the placing of Ali, the unwitting cause of the great split, among the authors of schism. But, natural as this may now appear, it was quite beyond the understanding of the Christian historians of Dante's age. To them the figure of Mahomet himself was an enigma, let alone that of his cousin Ali.

[1] See D'Ancona (*Tesoro*, 186–277).

Accordingly, the early commentators on the Divine Comedy are at a loss to account for his appearance alongside of the Prophet.[1] The contrast between the ignorance of the Christian writers and the thorough knowledge displayed by Dante in itself argues a considerable acquaintance on his part with Islamic lore.

But there is still further evidence. The figure of Ali is sketched with a sober realism that is no mere creation of the poet's imagination, in fact it is strictly in accordance with historical data.[2] The assassin Ibn Muljam, the Moslem chroniclers state, with one stroke of the sword cleft open Ali's skull, or, according to others, struck him in the forehead with a dagger, which split open his head and penetrated into the brain. The tragic scene must have vividly impressed the early Moslems, for legends soon arose according to which Mahomet, or Ali himself, prophesied the sad fate awaiting the latter. " Thy assassin—said Mahomet to him—will strike thee there—and pointed to his head—and the blood from the wound will flow down to here—and he touched his chin."[3]

5. In addition to a knowledge of Islamic tradition, Dante displays a general sympathy with Moslem philosophers and men of science. In his minor prose writings he frequently quotes, and occasionally makes use of, the works of the astronomers, Albumazar, Alfraganius and Alpetragius, and the great philosophers, Alfarabius, Avicenna, Algazel and Averrhoes.[4] Thus, Paget Toynbee has shown how some of the passages in the Convito and the Vita Nuova are based upon the astronomical theories of Alfraganius or the ideas of Averrhoes on the lunar spots. In his De vulgari eloquio (I, 6)

---

[1] Cf. FRANCESO DE BUTI's commentary of the fourteenth century (in D'ANCONA, Tesoro, 268) :

" Ali, secondo ch'io truovo, fu discepolo di Maometto : ma per quel ch'io credo, elli fu quel cherico che l'ammaestrò, lo quale elli chiama Ali forse perchè in quella lingua così si chiama il maestro: ... Di queste istorie m'abbi scusato tu, lettore, chè non se ne può trovare verita certa."

St. Peter Paschal, on the other hand, to whom Arabic sources were available, knew about Ali and his death (Cf. ARMENGOL, IV, 10 and 61).

[2] Inf., XXVIII, 32–33.

[3] Tarikh al-Khamis, II, 312–314. Isaba, IV, 270. Al-Fakhri, 90.

[4] Convito, II, 14, 15 ; III, 2, 14 ; IV, 13, 21. De Monarchia, I, 4.

Dante himself admits having read books on cosmography, and the most common of these at that time were Arabic.

This accounts for the benevolent treatment accorded by Dante to men like Saladin, Avicenna, and Averrhoes, whom he places in the limbo—a treatment that, judged upon theological principles, is indefensible. No one, and certainly not Dante, could have been unaware of the hostility shown by Saladin to everything Christian, and of how he had over-run Palestine and wrested the Holy City from the grasp of the Crusaders. Neither the military qualities nor the magnanimity of Saladin can be regarded as natural virtues sufficient in themselves to warrant the exemption from eternal punishment of one who did such grievous harm to the faith of Christ. The same may be said of Avicenna and Averrhoes. However blameless their conduct may have been, their learning excluded all possibility of their defence on the plea of utter ignorance of Christ that, according to the doctrine guiding Dante, could alone have justified their deliverance from hell. Averrhoes, moreover, stood in the eyes of the Christian Europe of the time as the embodiment of rationalistic unbelief.[1]

6. Dante's sympathies for Islamic science in general, and for Averrhoes in particular, furnish the key to another enigma, as has recently been shown in a clever study by Bruno Nardi.[2] This was the hitherto incomprehensible presence in Dante's paradise, side by side with St. Thomas Aquinas, of Sigier of Brabant, the champion of Averrhoism, who died under the ban of the Church. How, it was asked, could this defiance of public opinion be justified ? For, it should be noted that the poet not only exempts this heretic from the punishment of hell, but even exalts him to the mansion of the theologians, and, with a crowning presumption bordering upon sarcasm, places in the mouth of his irreconcilable adversary, St. Thomas, words of praise for the outcast that are equivalent to a rehabilitation of his memory.

[1] Cf. Asín, El Averroismo teológico de Santo Tomás de Aquino, 299–306.
[2] Sigieri di Brabante nella Div. Com. e le fonte della fil. di Dante (Rivista di fil. neoscolastica, 1911–12). Cf. BRUNO NARDI, Intorno al tomismo di Dante e alla quistione di Sigieri (Giornale Dantesco, XXII, 5).

7. Nardi, to solve this problem, reopens the question of the sources of Dante's philosophy, hitherto regarded as exclusively Thomist. By a close comparison of Dante's works with the writings of other scholastics of the neo-Platonic school and the systems of Avicenna and Averrhoes, he shows that Dante, far from appearing as an unconditional Thomist, was a scholastic, but of eclectic tendencies, who accepted theories from all thinkers ancient and mediæval, Christian and Moslem, and embodied them in a system of his own that was intermediate between the philosophy of St. Thomas and that of Avicenna and Averrhoes, although more akin to the latter. The main points in Dante's philosophy that Nardi has shown to be of Arabic filiation relate to cosmology, theodicy and psychology : God is Light, whose rays grow weaker as they travel further from their Centre. The Intelligences of the Celestial Spheres reflect these rays and thereby imprint the various forms upon Matter. Creation must, therefore, be conceived as a gradually decreasing emanation of the Divine Light, and is brought about, not by God directly and exclusively, but through the medium of the Celestial Spheres. The intellective part of the human soul is distinct from the vegetative-sensitive part ; the former alone is created. Intellection begins by Divine illumination and needs the help of Faith before it can attain to super-sensible Truth.

Nardi proceeds to show how these ideas of Dante, although found in part in the Augustinian tradition, are rather derived from the neo-Platonic philosophy of the Arabs and, more particularly, from the systems of Alfarabius, Avicenna, Algazel and Averrhoes.

V

THE CLOSE RESEMBLANCE BETWEEN DANTE AND THE MYSTIC, IBN ARABI OF MURCIA, FURNISHES FURTHER PROOF OF THE THESIS OF IMITATION

1. The conclusions arrived at by Nardi are more than sufficient to indicate that, as in his artistic representation of the after-life, so in his trend of thought Dante betrays

signs of Arabic influence. Should further proof of our thesis be required, the poet's philosophical system might be traced back to its actual sources in Islam, which are to be found not so much among the philosophers as in the works of the Illuministic Mystics, and of the Murcian Ibn Arabi in particular. The Illuministic, or *Ishraqi* and pseudo-Empedoclean school, was founded by Ibn Masarra of Cordova ; and from Spain its ideas were transmitted to the so-called Augustinian scholastics, among others to Alexander Hales, Duns Scotus, Roger Bacon, and Raymond Lull. As has been shown in the discussion of the Paradiso, an essential part of *Ishraqi* teaching—the metaphysical doctrine of light —reappears in the Divine Comedy, where it is illustrated, moreover, by the same symbols as are used by the Moslem mystics. Creation, too, is conceived as an emanation of Divine light, the teleological cause of which is love, and its primary effects, universal and formless matter.[1] Thus a new vista is opened up. Seen in this wise, Dante would appear to have been but one more follower of the Illuministic school, and pre-eminent by his art alone. It has been demonstrated above that almost all of the artistic forms used in Ibn Arabi's picture of the realms beyond the grave were reproduced a century later in the Divine Comedy. The suggestion now presents itself that many of the Illuministic theories of Dante were derived from the same Ibn Arabi, the leading exponent of *Ishraqi* ideas, rather than from the other Arabic philosophers with whose systems Nardi compares them.

2. The solution of this problem is beyond the limits of the task at present before us, which is restricted to the search for evidence of a leaning on Dante's part towards Islamic culture. Nevertheless, it may be of interest to establish a general parallel between the two thinkers, Dante and Ibn Arabi. This should bear, not so much upon the ideas common to both, as upon the images and symbols by which they gave expression to these ideas and the literary devices to which both writers resort to expound their views. As

[1] Cf. Asín, *Abenmasarra*, 120, 121.

already stated, coincidence in imaginative detail more readily suggests imitation than sympathy in doctrine, although, naturally, conviction is strengthened when both ideas and images agree.

As regards the images, Ibn Arabi uses the same symbols as Dante to express the metaphysics of light, an essential part of the thought of both. God is pure light, and his manifestation *ad extra* is described by similes of light—diffusion, illumination, reflexion and irradiance—which are all typical of Dante's imaginings. The metaphor of the mirror, used by Dante to exemplify the influence of superior upon inferior beings, appears, like that of the flame of the candle, frequently in the works of Ibn Arabi. The geometrical symbol of the circle and its centre, representing the cosmos and its Divine principle, recurs even more often in Ibn Arabi than in Dante, and gives rise to similar paradoxes in the works of both writers. As light is the symbol of God and His manifestations, so is darkness of matter. Opacity and transparency respectively characterise the body and the mind in both Dante's and Ibn Arabi's conception.

3. A comparison of the expository methods of the two authors will prove still more interesting. The cabbala of letters and numbers is seen from all his works to be an obsession of Dante. Secret virtues are attributed to special numbers, or the numerical values of certain letters are associated with their ideological values. The flavour of occultism thus imparted to Dante's style is exactly like that found in all the works of Ibn Arabi, whose worship at the cabbalistic shrine argues the sincerity of his conviction. Entire chapters of his *Futuhat* and whole books are devoted to this superstition ; and he even goes so far as to base many of his philosophical demonstrations on the numerical relations thus established.

Another superstition common to the two writers is their belief in astrology. It is needless to dwell upon the many passages in the Divine Comedy and the *Convito* that testify to the blind faith shown by Dante in the absurd subtleties of astrology. Ibn Arabi, in his whimsical conceits, indulges in still wilder flights of fancy.[1]

The literary artifice of personifying abstract entities is seen in Dante's *Vita Nuova*, where the vital, the animal, the visual and natural spirits reason and discourse with one another. Ibn Arabi has no equal in the use, or rather abuse, of prosopopoeia. God and His names, the spirits of Being and of Nothingness, Matter and Shape, engage at each step in the *Futuhat* in lengthy discussions, like persons of flesh and blood.

Finally, whole passages in the *Vita Nuova* and the Divine Comedy, which purport to be autobiographical, are devoted to the description and mystical interpretation of dream visions. Ibn Arabi also narrates a multitude of dreams, hidden in which he discovers the loftiest metaphysical thought.

4. Of all the visions thus described by Dante, one is of particular interest.[2]

Dante in a dream sees a youth robed in white, seated near him in a pensive attitude. The youth sighs, as he raises his eyes to him, and to Dante's question why he is so sad, replies : " Ego tamquam centrum circuli, cui simili modo se habent circumferentiae partes ; tu autem non sic." The poet calls upon him to explain the meaning of this symbol, but the youth replies : " Non dimandar più che utile ti sìa."

Common in the extreme among Moslem mystics is the dream vision of God appearing to them in the image of a youth. A *hadith* attributed to the ninth-century traditionist, Tabrani, tells how Mahomet first saw the vision.

I saw the Lord my God in a dream—begins the *hadith*— seated on a stool, a beardless youth of great beauty. . . .[3]

Ibn Arabi himself claims to have seen similar visions, in which his Divine beloved, God, appeared to him in human form.[4]

" These apparitions," he says, " left me in such a state that for days I could take no food. Each time that I sat

---

[1] *Futuhat*, I, 64–117.   [2] *Vita Nuova*, § XII.
[3] SUYUTI, *Al-Laali*, I, 15–17.   [4] *Futuhat*, II, 429.

down to eat He appeared standing at the end of the table, gazing upon me and saying in words that I actually heard, ' and wilt thou eat in My presence ? ' and eat I could not. In truth I felt no hunger, for His presence filled and well-nigh intoxicated me. . . for throughout those days His vision haunted me wheresoe'er I went."

True, none of these visions contains the same cryptic words that Dante places in the mouth of the youth. But these words undeniably have their interpretation in the metaphysics of Ibn Arabi. In his geometrical symbolism, God is the independent centre of a circle and His creatures the points on the circumference, that are dependent for their existence on the centre. God, then, is the centre of gravity towards which all creatures are drawn by the love inspired in them by the infinite beauty of the Divine essence.[1]

It may be argued that this interpretation does not neces-sarily furnish the key to the enigma of Dante's vision, but it does offer an explanation. In the obscure words attributed to the youth Dante would indeed seem to express the love he felt in his heart towards God, the centre of creation. This is the very doctrine he unfolded later in the Divine Comedy, where he asserts that the entire universe is swayed by the love of God, which is the principal and the final goal of all movement.[2]

5. Coincidences of literary artifice even more striking will be found by comparing the *Cancionero* and the *Convito* with two books of Ibn Arabi, " The Interpreter of Love " and its commentary, " The Treasures of Lovers."[3] Indeed, it will be seen that the literary principles underlying the works of both authors are the same. The intermingling of verse with prose, which is characteristic of the *Convito*, is to be found in almost all the works of Ibn Arabi, but no two works of the poets coincide so remarkably as " The Interpreter

---

[1] *Futuhat*, II, 895.
[2] *Par.* I, 1 ; XXXIII, 145. See NARDI, *Sigieri*, 39–41, and compare with *Futuhat, loc. cit.*
[3] NICHOLSON has translated the former into English under the title of *Tarjuman al'Ashwâq* (London, 1911). An edition of the latter, referred to hereunder as *Dakhair*, appeared at Beyrout in 1894.

of Love " and the *Convito*. Both poets represent their work to be autobiographical, and the theme and mode of expression in each are almost identical.

In the *Convito* Dante declares his intention to interpret the esoteric meaning of fourteen love songs which he had composed at an earlier date and the subject of which had led to the erroneous belief that they dealt with sensual rather than intellectual love. The poet desires to clear himself of the accusation of sensuality, and thus has written the *Convito* as a commentary on those songs and in explanation of the allegory underlying the literal meaning.

The literal sense is the love of the poet for a fair and virtuous maiden, learned yet modest and devout, of a winning grace and courteous manner, whose bodily and moral perfections the poet extols in an outburst of impassioned verse. Beneath this cloak of voluptuousness Dante avers there is hidden the love for the Divine science of philosophy, personified by the maiden. Her eyes represent the demonstrations of wisdom ; her smiles, its persuasions ; the rays of love that descend from the heaven of Venus upon the lover are the philosophical books ; and the love-sick sighs he heaves are symbolic of the anguish of the mind tortured by doubt and the longing for truth.[1]

Finally, Dante explains how he came to write the original songs. One day after the death of his beloved Beatrice, Dante is walking alone, when of a sudden he meets a gentle maiden of great beauty and learning, with whom he falls in love ; not daring to declare his passion, he seeks solace in the ecstatic contemplation of his idol and sings his emotions in melancholy rhymes.[2]

An identical occurrence and motive inspired Ibn Arabi to compose the love poems contained in his " Interpreter of Love " and write the commentary upon it known as the " Treasures of Lovers." In the prologue to the commentary the author furnishes an explanation, of which the following is a summary :

---

[1] *Convito*, II, 13, 16 ; III, 8, 12.　[2] *Convito*, II, 2.

When I resided at Mecca in the year 598 (1201 A.D.) I made the acquaintance of a number of worthy people, pre-eminent among whom was the learned doctor Zahir ibn Rustam, a native of Ispahan, who had taken up his abode at Mecca. This master had a daughter, a tall and slender maiden. Virtuous, learned, devout and modest, she was a feast for the eyes and bound in chains of love all who beheld her. Were it not that pusillanimous minds are ever prone to think evil, I would dwell at greater length upon the quali-ties with which God had endowed both her body and her soul, which was a garden of generous feeling.

It was from her that I drew the inspiration for the poems, telling of the sweet fancies of a lover. In them I sought to convey some of the passionate feelings treasured in my heart and to express the tender longings of my soul in words that should suggest how dearly I loved her and how the thought of her filled my mind in those bygone days as it haunts me even now. Thus every name mentioned in this work refers to her, and hers is the dwelling of which I sing. But also, in these verses I make constant allusion to spiritual revela-tions and to relations with the Intelligences of the Divine spheres. This is customary in our allegorical style, for to our mind the things of the future life are preferable to those of this world ; moreover, she herself knew full well the hidden meaning underlying my verse. God forbid that the reader should attribute unworthy thoughts to the writers of poetry such as this—men whose aims are loftier and who aspire but to the things of heaven.

My reason for composing this allegorical commentary upon my songs was that my pupils had consulted me about them. They had heard learned moralists of Aleppo deny that holy mysteries lay hidden in my poems and allege that, in trying to affirm this, I merely sought to conceal the sensual love which I had felt. I therefore set to work to write this com-mentary upon all the amorous poems I had composed during my stay at Mecca in the months of Recheb, Shaban, and Ramadan. In all these poems I constantly allude to spiritual mysteries and to the teachings of philosophy and ethics. If, to express these lofty thoughts, I used the language of love, it was because the minds of men are prone to dally with such amorous fancies and would thus be more readily attracted to the subject of my songs.

Ibn Arabi then introduces a fragment from his book of songs, in which he enumerates the more usual among his poetic metaphors and interprets their general allegorical meaning. He adds:

" All these figures of speech should be regarded as symbolic of sublime mysteries and Divine illuminations vouchsafed to me by the Lord God. Turn thy thoughts, oh ! reader, from the mere words and seek the hidden meaning that thou mayest understand."

Having thus duly warned the reader, Ibn Arabi begins his commentary with the fictitious story of the vision of a beautiful maiden.

" One night," he says, " I was in the temple of the Caaba, walking, as required by rite, round and round the holy dwelling. My mind felt at ease and a strange peace overcame my soul. To be alone, I went out of the temple and started to walk along the roadway. As I walked, I recited aloud some verses, when, of a sudden, I felt a hand softer than velvet touch me on the shoulder. I turned and lo ! a Greek maiden stood before me. Never had I ·beheld so beautiful a countenance, nor heard so soft a voice ; never had I met a woman more endearing or with speech so refined, who expressed such lofty thoughts in more subtle language. Verily she surpassed all the women of her day in delicacy of mind, in literary culture, in beauty and in learning. . . ."

Prefacing his work with the narration of this fictitious episode in his life, which he alleges led to the composition of his songs, the author proceeds to give the allegorical meaning of each verse. His beloved, he explains, is the symbol of Divine wisdom[1] ; her virgin breasts, the nectar of its teachings ; the smile on her lips, its illuminations.[2] Her eyes are the emblems of light and revelation.[3] The mournful sighs of the lover represent the spiritual longings of the soul.[4] Among a host of other subjects, the author deals with the origin and destiny of the human soul, the nature and phenomena of love, and the essence of spiritual beauty. In matters of faith, he discusses the relations between reason and belief, the hidden trinal sense of the conception of God,

---

[1] *Dakhair*, 78, 84, 85.   [2] *Dakhair*, 21.   [3] *Ibid.* 33.   [4] *Ibid.* 44, 45, 49,

the transcendental value of universal religion in comparison with other religions, and Islam as a religion of love.

6. The coincidence here shown between the *Convito* of Dante and the *Treasures* of Ibn Arabi may prove of further interest, as furnishing an answer to the vexed question of the origin of that form of lyrical poetry known in Italy as *dolce stil nuovo*. In this new school of poetry, of which Guido Guinicelli, Guido Cavalcanti and Dante were the contemporary creators, the theme of each song is love. The emotion of the poet at the sight or remembrance of his beloved is described in two forms—either it is a mystical adoration, a sweet beatitude of the soul that in ecstasy longs for spiritual union with its beloved and thus strives heaven ward ; or else it is an affliction of the heart torn by anguish, a morbid fever that consumes the life blood of the lover, a dread disorder of the mind that pervades his whole being and makes him long for the approach of death as a relief from the torture he is suffering. In subtle inquiry into the emotional processes of love, Cavalcanti stands supreme, more especially when dealing with love as an affliction. His songs are tragic outbursts of this mode of feeling which is found to a less degree in Guinicelli and Dante, who treat love rather as a gentle melancholy, or as an ecstatic contemplation or mystical and semi-religious aspiration.

Another characteristic of the *stil nuovo* poetry is the analysis and philosophic interpretation of the emotions. The psycho-physiological faculties and spirits controlling the heart are distinguished and even personified. This scholastic manner, which robs the poetry of much of its charm, is used to excess in Cavalcanti's " Donna mi prega."

The mere possession of the woman they love is far from being the sole desire of these poets. On the contrary, their elect appears to them rather as an ethereal image, a being who is worthy of Platonic love. Indeed to them real love lies, not in marriage, but rather in a perpetual state of chastity ; and the figure of their beloved they idealise either as an angel of heaven or the symbol of Divine wisdom or philosophy. In either conception, she is the instrument by which God inspires the lover with noble feelings and sublime ideas. And so, earthly and heavenly love are merged in one.

Vossler has pointed out the absence in either classical or Christian literature of anything that might serve to account for this hybrid theory of a love that is at once earthly and spiritual; this curious and new form—to quote his own words—of Platonism, which yet is not directly derived from Plato.[1] There is nothing in the doctrine of the Church, in Ovid, or in Aristotle, to explain such an idealistic and romantic conception of woman, so spiritual a love, which, as Vossler says, must have appeared grotesque to the philosophers and theologians of the Middle Ages. Vossler's efforts to find an explanation are more remarkable as examples of ingenuity and erudition than they are convincing. The ideas expressed by the Italian poets of the *dolce stil nuovo* he traces back through the songs of Provençal troubadours to the chivalry and psychology of the Germanic race.

7. But Vossler's argument, based on complicated transformations of social psychology, is brought to nought by one outstanding fact: far earlier than the first of those many stages, Islam in the East and in Spain had furnished works, both of prose and poetry, treating of love in the same romantic spirit.

The common prejudice—common both by its wide diffusion and the absence of all logical foundation—denying all idealism to the conception of love of the Arabs, and Moslems in general, is quite contrary to fact. The Yemen tribe of the Banu Odhra, or "Children of Chastity," were famous for the manner in which they upheld the tradition of their name. "I am of a race that, when it loves, dies," said one of them. Jamil, one of their most celebrated poets, died mad with love for his lady, Butayna, upon whom he had never dared lay hands. Two other poets of the same tribe, the lovers Orwa and Afra, died together consumed by the

[1] VOSSLER, I, 199–236. Cf. ROSSI, *Il dolce stil novo*, 35–97, and ROSSI, *Storia*, I, 85–89 and 112–115.

flame of a lifelong passion, which left them in a state of chastity to the end. The romanticism that prefers death to the defilement of the chaste union of the souls is a feature of all the melancholy and beautiful songs of these poets.[1] The example of abstinence and perpetual chastity set by the Christian monks of Arabia may well have influenced the Banu Odhra. The mysticism of the Sufis, directly inherited from the Christian hermits, also drew its inspiration from the lives and writings of the romantic poets of Arabia.[2] Régardless of the fact that neither the Koran nor the life of Mahomet himself furnishes the slightest ground for so idealistic an interpretation of love, they do not hesitate to attribute to the Prophet the saying : " He who loves and remains chaste unto death, dies a martyr." Ibn Arabi adopts this motto[3] ; and the doctrine is followed by many Sufis who, although married, stand as heroic examples of perpetual chastity. Thus idealised, the wife is no longer the sexual mate of the Sufi, but rather his companion or sister in asceticism ; and his love for her is part of his love for God.

This new trend of thought is promptly reflected in the literature both of the East and the West. Ibn Daud of Ispahan, in his *Book of Venus* of the ninth century, analyses and defends romantic love. Ibn Hazm of Cordova, who lived in the eleventh century, has left us in his book called the " Necklace of the Dove," but better known as the " Book of Love," and in a smaller work, " Characters and Conduct," a whole treatise dealing with the passion of love and breathing the purest romanticism.[4] He regards the essence of love as consisting not in the commerce of the bodies but in the union of the souls. Moreover, his " Necklace " abounds in authentic stories of Spanish Moslems, drawn from all ranks of society, whose love is Platonic and who render silent homage to their beloved and worship her with an almost mystical adoration. At times, in his anguish, the

---

[1] IBN QOTAIBA, *Liber poësis et poëtarum*, 260–4, 394–9.
[2] Cf. ASÍN, *Abenmasarra*, 13–16, and *Logia et agrapha D. Jesu*, 8.
[3] *Muhadara*, II, 205.
[4] Cf. IBN HAZM, *Tawq al-Hamama ;* and ASÍN, *Caracteres.*

lover writes letters bathed in tears or even written in his blood. Many, in a paroxysm of despair, meet with a tragic end in madness or death.

But this romantic form of love, as sung by the poets of the Banu Odhra and described and classified in the books of Ibn Daud and Ibn Hazm is perhaps rather than ascetic continence an ultra-refinement of an erotic sensibility that has been worn out by excess. Accordingly, it appears at three epochs and in three centres that in this respect had reached the zenith of hyperæsthesia—in the Yemen, where the pre-Islamic poets had exhausted the theme of sensual love, and at the highly civilised courts of Baghdad and Cordova, where decadence had begun to set in.

8. We are thus still far from the Platonic conception of woman, idealised as an angel and a symbol of philosophy. The origin of this strange conception would seem to be due to an attempt to idealise the sensual coarseness of the Koranic paradise. The houris of the Koran, although celestial, are intended solely to be instruments of carnal delight. This idea was incompatible with the spiritual longings of the later Moslem mystics, who had been profoundly influenced by the asceticism preached and practised by the Christian monks. But it was impossible to eliminate from the Koran the verses proclaiming those sensual joys. The mystics, therefore, in their legends of the after-life replaced the houris by one celestial bride, a spiritual being whose love is chaste and whom God has appointed to each of the blessed.[1] In all those legends, this heavenly spouse is depicted as a guardian angel, who serves to inspire her lover with a desire for spiritual perfection and a greater love for God during his life on earth.

Later, when to the asceticism inherited from the Christian monks the Sufis applied a pantheistic and neo-Platonic form of metaphysics, the idealisation of sexual love reached the acme of subtlety and abstruseness. This has been shown by the erotic poems of Ibn Arabi, in which the beloved is a mere symbol of Divine wisdom and the passion felt for her

---

[1] Cf. *supra*, pp. 131-134.

allegorical of the union of the mystic soul with God Himself. The psychological phenomena attendant upon love he analyses with a surprising delicacy and penetration, and shows himself far superior, especially in the *Futuhat*, to any of the Italian poets of the *dolce stil nuovo*.[1] Not content with distinguishing between the different degrees of feeling that separate love from sympathy, from affection, from passion and from desire, he probes into the subconscious states of the heart and mind, and interprets them in a mystical sense. The sighs, the tears and mental anguish of the lover ; his languor and melancholy ; his bewilderment and his secret grief mingled with jealous anger ; his fits of brooding and dejection, of ecstasy and rapture—the whole gamut of the psychology of love is closely analysed in the pages of the *Futuhat*, which is at the same time a metaphysical exegesis of the passion. For, after admitting a threefold aim in love, viz., the union of the sexes, the union of the souls, and the spiritual union with God, he has the sublime audacity to assert that it is God who appears to every lover in the image of his beloved.[2] In order that we may learn to love Him, He assumes the form of the fair Zaynab, of Suad, of Hind, of Layla—of all those beauties of whose charms the poets sing, little suspecting that in their songs of love they are praising the only Beauty of the World, God, incorporate in those sensual forms.

9. Let us at this juncture glance backwards and collect the threads of the argument presented in this last part of our work.

The numerous symptoms of a leaning towards Islamic culture that have been discovered in the writings of Dante are proof that his mind, far from being averse from the influence of Moslem models, was rather inclined towards their assimilation. In a previous chapter it was shown how likely the transmission of these models from Moslem Spain to Italy and the Florentine poet was. In the first

---

[1] *Futuhat*, II, 426–481. The Arabic, and more particularly Averrhoist, origin of the psychology of Cavalcanti had suggested itself to Salvadori and Vossler. Cf. ROSSI, *Il dolce stil novo*, 94, note 66.

[2] *Futuhat*, II, 431.

two parts of this work the great wealth of Moslem feature in the Divine Comedy was demonstrated after minute examination. In the third part it was seen how the majority of pre-Dante Christian legends are also derived from the literature of Islam. It would seem, therefore, that the chain of reasoning is complete, and that no serious objection can be raised to the assertion that imitation did indeed exist, once we have established as facts the *resemblance* between the model and the copy, the *priority* of the former to the latter, and *communication* between the two.

Nor is it possible any longer to deny to Islamic literature the place of honour to which it is entitled in the stately train of the forerunners of Dante's poem. For this literature, in itself, furnishes more solutions to the many riddles that surround the genesis of the poem than all the other pre-cursory works combined.

But at every step of the long journey we have travelled in the research into the Islamic models of the Divine Comedy, the figure of one writer has stood out as the most typical and the most likely to furnish in his works the key to what is still obscure in Dante. We refer to the figure of the Spanish mystic and poet Ibn Arabi of Murcia. His works in general, and particularly his *Futuhat*, may indeed have been the source whence the Florentine poet drew the general idea of his poem. There also Dante could have found the geometrical plans of the architecture of hell and paradise, the general features of the scenery in which the sublime drama is laid, the vivid picture of the life of glory led by the chosen, the Beatific Vision of the Divine Light, and the ecstasy of him who beholds it. Moreover, it would be difficult to find two thinkers whose poetical and religious tempera-ments are so alike as those of Dante and Ibn Arabi ; for the resemblance extends not only to their philosophical thought, derived from the illuministic school of Ibn Masarra, but also to the images by which their ideas are symbolised and the literary means by which they are expressed. Nowhere is this seen more clearly than in the *Convito* and the *Treasures*. Conceived and composed in the self-same manner, these works were written with the same personal object ; and both authors follow the same method in the allegorical interpretation of the amorous theme of their songs. The share due to Ibn Arabi—a Spaniard, although a Moslem—in the literary glory achieved by Dante Alighieri in his immortal poem can no longer be ignored.

The gigantic figure of the great Florentine need not thereby lose one inch of the sublime height it has reached in the eyes of his compatriots and of all mankind. Blind admiration of genius is not the most appropriate form of homage. Nor could the worship of his memory, inspired by a mere spirit of patriotism, satisfy a man who placed above his love for Italy and the Latin race, the lofty ideals of humanity and religion ; who laid proud claim to the title of a citizen of the world ; and who breathed into the exquisite form of his divine poem an universal and eternal spirit of morality and mysticism that was the natural expression of the deepest Christian feelings.

In the end we find that it is that perennial source of poetry and spirituality, the Divine religion of Christ, that furnishes the real key to the genesis of Dante's poem and its precursors, both Christian and Moslem. For Islam, be it once more said, is but the bastard offspring of the Gospel and the Mosaic Law, part of whose doctrines on the after-life it adopted. Lacking the restraining influence of an infallible authority whereby the fancy of its believers might have been checked, it assimilated elements from other Eastern sources and thus came to deck and overlay with all the trappings of Oriental fancy the sober picture of the life beyond the grave that is outlined in the Gospel. Dante could, without altering the essence of Christian teaching on that life, draw for the purposes of his poem on the artistic features furnished by the Moslem legends. In so doing he was but reclaiming for Christianity property that was by rights its own, heirlooms that had lain hidden in the religious lore of the East until restored to the stock of Western culture greatly enhanced by the imaginative genius of Islam.

BIBLIOGRAPHICAL INDEX

Abu-l-Ala al Maarri, *Risalat al-ghufran* = رسالة الغفران التى
كتبها ابو العلاء المعرى الى الشيخ المحدث على بن منصور ....
ابن القارح. Cairo, Emin Hindie, 1907.

Albertus Magnus = *Opera omnia quae hactenus haberi potu-
erunt.* Lugduni, 1651.

Al-Fakhri = كتاب الفخرى فى الاداب السلطانية والدول الاسلامية
لابن الطقطقى. Cairo, 1317 Heg.

Algazel, *Ihia* = كتاب احياء علوم الدين للغزالى. Cairo, 1312
Heg.

Algazel, *Ithaf* = كتاب اتحاف السادة المتقين بشرح اسرار احياء
علوم الدين للسيد مرتضى. Cairo, 1311 Heg.

Algazel, *Minhaj* = منهاج العابدين للغزالى. Cairo, 1313 Heg.

Algazel, *Mizan al-Amal* = كتاب ميزان العمل للغزالى. Cairo,
1328 Heg.

Algazel, *Qistas* = القسطاس المستقيم للغزالى. Cairo, 1900.

Al-Horayfish = كتاب الروض الفائق فى المواعظ والرقائق للخريفيش.
Cairo, 1328 Heg.

Al Jahiz, *see* Jahiz.

Al-Kibrit, see Ash-Sharani.

Al-Laali = كتاب اللالى المصنوعة فى الاحاديث الموضوعة للسيوطى.
Cairo, 1317 Heg.

Al-Makkari = *Analectes sur l'histoire et la littérature des Arabes
d'Espagne par Al-Makkari,* publiés par Dozy. Leyden,
Brill, 1856–60.

Al-Nasafi, *Tafsir* = تفسير القران المسمى مدارك التنزيل وحقائق
التاويل. Edited marginally apud Khazin, *Tafsir.*

Alphonso the Wise = *Primera Crónica general, o sea Estoria de
España que mandó componer Alfonso el Sabio....;* publicada
por Ramón Menéndez Pidal. Madrid, Bailly-Bailliere, 1906

Al-Yawaqit, see Ash-Sharani.

Amador de los Ríos, José = *Historia crítica de la literatura española*. Madrid, Rodriguez, 1881–3.

Amari, Michele = *Storia dei musulmani di Sicilia*. Florence, Le Monnier, 1854–68.

Armengol = *Obras de S. Pedro Pascual, en su lengua original, con la traducción latina y algunas anotaciones*, por el P. Fr. Pedro Armengol. Roma, Imprenta Salustiana, 1906–8.

Ash-Sharani, *Al-Kibrit* = كتاب الكبريت الاحمر فى بيان علوم الشيخ الاكبر للشعرانى. Edited marginally apud *Al-Yawaqit*.

Ash-Sharani, *Al-Yawaqit* = كتاب اليواقيت والجواهر فى بيان عقائد الاكابر للشعرانى. Cairo, 1321 Heg.

Ash-Sharani, *Mizan* = كتاب الميزان للشعرانى. Cairo, 1321 Heg.

Asín Palacios, Miguel = *Abenmasarra y su escuela. Orígenes de la filosofía hispano-musulmana*. Madrid, Imprenta Ibérica, 1914.

Asín Palacios, Miguel = *Algazel: Dogmática, moral, ascética*. "Colección de estudios árabes," vol. VI. Saragossa, Comas, 1901.

Asín Palacios, Miguel = *Los caracteres y la conducta. Tratado de moral práctica por Abenházam de Córdoba*. Traducción española. Madrid, Imprenta Ibérica, 1916.

Asín Palacios, Miguel = *El Averroísmo teológico de Sto. Tomás de Aquino*. In "Homenaje a D. Francisco Codera," pp. 271–331. Saragossa, Escar, 1904.

Asín Palacios, Miguel = *La mystique d'Al-Gazzali*. Extr. from "Mélanges de la faculté orientale de Beyrouth," VII, 1914.

Asín Palacios, Miguel = *La psicología, según Mohidín Abenarabi*. Extr. from vol. III of "Actes du XIVᵉ Congrès international des Orientalistes." Paris, Leroux, 1906.

Asín Palacios, Miguel = *Logia et agrapha D. Jesu apud mos lemicos scriptores, asceticos praesertim, usitata* collegit, vertit, notis instruxit. In "Patrologia orientalis," vol. XIII, 3. Paris, Didot, 1915.

Asín Palacios, Miguel = *Mohidín*. In "Homenaje a Menéndez y Pelayo," vol. II, pp. 217–256. Madrid, Suárez, 1899.

Averrhoes, *Kitab falsafat* = كتاب فلسفة ابن رشد. Cairo, 1313 Heg.

20

Avicenna, *Rasail* = تسع رسائل فى الحكمة والطبيعيات لابن سينا.
Constantinople, 1298 Heg.

Avicenna, *Risala at-tayr = Traités mystiques....d'Avicenne.*
Texte arabe avec la trad. en français par M. A. F. Mehren.
IIe Fascicule. Leyde, Brill, 1891.

Babelon, Ernest = *Du commerce des Arabes dans le nord de l'Europe avant les Croisades.* Paris, 1882. Tirage à part de "l'Athénée Oriental," année 1882, No. 1er.

Bacon, Roger = *Opus majus.* Edit. Jebe, 1733.

Badai az-Zohur = كتاب بدائع الزهور فى وقائع الدهور لابن اياس.
Cairo, 1309 Heg.

Ballesteros, Antonio = *Sevilla en el siglo XIII.* Madrid, Pérez Torres, 1913.

Batiffol, Pierre = *La littérature grecque.* In "Anciennes littératures chrétiennes," vol. I. Paris, Lecoffre, 1898.

Batiouchkof = *Le débat de l'âme et du corps.* In *Romania,* Paris, 1891.

Blochet, E. = *Les sources orientales de la Divine Comédie.* In "Les littératures populaires de toutes les nations," voł. XLI. Paris, Maisonneuve, 1901.

Blochet, E. = *L'ascension au ciel du prophète Mohammed.* Extr. from "Revue de l'histoire des religions." Paris, Leroux, 1899.

Brehier, Louis = *L'église et l'orient au moyen âge: Les Croisades.* Paris, Lecoffre, 1907.

Brockelmann, Carl = *Geschichte der arabischen Litteratur.* Weimar, Felber, 1898–1902.

Bukhari = *Le Recueil des traditions mahométanes.* Edit. L. Krehl and T. Juynboll. Leyden, Brill, 1908.

Buxtorf = *Lexicon chaldaicum.* Basle, 1639.

Carra de Vaux = *Avicenne.* In "Les grands philosophes." Paris, Alcan, 1900.

Carra de Vaux = *Fragments d'eschatologie musulmane.* In "Compte rendu du troisième Congrès scient. intern. des catholiques." (Scienc. relig.) Brussels, Schepens, 1895.

Chantepie de la Saussaye = *Manuel d'histoire des religions* French translation by Hubert et Lévy. Paris, Colin, 1904.

Charles, R. = *The apocalypse of Baruch.* London, 1896.

Charles, R. = *The assumption of Moses.* London, 1897.

Chauvin, Victor = *Bibliographie des ouvrages arabes ou relatifs aux Arabes, publiés dans l'Europe chrétienne de 1810 à 1885.* Liège, Vaillant-Carmanne, 1892–1913.

Clair-Tisdall = *The sources of Islam.* Translated by W. Muir. Edinburgh, 1901.

Colección de textos aljamiados by Gil, Ribera and Sánchez. Saragossa, Guerra y Bacque, 1888.

Corra (Corrat Aloyun) = قرة العيون ومفرح القلب المحزون لابن الليث السمرقندى. Edit. marginally in *Tadhkira.*

Cosmo, Umberto = *Rassegna dantesca* in "Giornale storico della letteratura italiana," Turin, 1914.

Dakhair, see Ibn Arabi.

Damiri = كتاب حياة الحيوان الكبرى لكمال الدين الدميرى. Cairo, 1292 Heg.

D'Ancona, Alessandro = *I precursori di Dante.* Florence, Sansoni, 1874.

D'Ancona, Alessandro = *Il Tesoro di Brunetto Latini versificato.* In "Atti della R. Accad. dei Lincei," 1888 (clas. di scienc. mor.), IV.

Dante = *Opere minori di Dante Alighieri.* Edited in 3 vols. by Pietro Fraticelli. Florence, Barberà, 1908–12.

Dardir = حاشية الدردير على قصة المعراج للغيطى. Cairo, 1332 Heg.

De gloria martyrum, by St Gregory of Tours. Paris, 1563.

De Goeje, M. J. = *La légende de St Brandan.* In "Actes du VIIIe. Congrès intern. des Orient." Sect. I, pp. 43–76. Leyden, Brill, 1891.

De Haeresibus = *Joannis Damasceni opera omnia* (I, 110–15). Paris, 1712.

Dharir = كتاب نزهة الناظرين فى تفسير ايات من كتاب رب العالمين لعبيد الضرير. Cairo, 1317 Heg.

D'Herbelot = *Bibliothèque Orientale,* Maestricht, 1776.

Diyarbakri = *Tarikh al-Khamis.* تاريخ الخميس فى احوال انفس نفيس للدياربكرى. Cairo, 1302 Heg.

Dozy, R. = *Recherches sur l'histoire et la littérature de l'Espagne pendant le moyen âge.* 2nd edition. Leyden, Brill, 1860.

Ducange = *Glossarium mediae et infimae latinitatis.* Paris, Didot, 1840–50.

Erpenius = *Historia saracenica...latinè reddita opera ac studio Thomae Erpenii.* Lugduni Batavorum, Typographia Erpeniana, 1625.

Eulogius = *Apologeticus sanctorum martyrum Eulogii presbyteri.* Edited by Ambrosio de Morales. Compluti, Iñiguez de Lequerica, 1574.

Fasl, see Ibn Hazm.

Fernandez y Gonzalez, Francisco = *Estado social y político de los mudéjares de Castilla.* Madrid, Muñoz, 1868.

Firuzabadi, *Tafsir* = تنوير المقباس من تفسير ابن عباس للفيروزابادى. Cairo, 1316 Heg.

Fraticelli = *La Divina Commedia di Dante Alighieri, col commento di Pietro Fraticelli.* Florence, Barberà, 1914.

Freytag = *G. W. Freytagii Lexicon arabico-latinum.* Halis Saxonum, Schwetschke, 1830.

Futuhat, see Ibn Arabi.

Ghiti = المعراج الكبير للغيطى. Cairo, 1324 Heg.

Gomez Moreno = *Iglesias mozárabes.* Madrid, Centro de Estudios Históricos, 1917.

Graf, Arturo = *Miti, leggende e superstizioni del medio evo.* Turin, Loescher, 1892-3.

Gubernatis = *Matériaux pour servir à l'histoire des études orientales en Italie.* Paris, Leroux, 1876.

Guidi = *Testi orientali inediti sopra i Sette Dormienti di Efeso.* In "Atti della R. Accad. dei Lincei," 1884, pp. 343-445.

Hamadhani = *Kitâb al-Boldân.* Edit. De Goeje in *Bibliotheca Geographorum,* v. Lugduni Batavorum, Brill, 1885.

Hirschfeld = *Researches into...the Quran.* London, 1902.

Historia Arabum = *Roderici Ximenez, archiepiscopi toletani, Historia Arabum.* Edit. in *Erpenius.*

Huart, C. = *Littérature arabe.* Paris, Colin, 1902.

Ibn Arabi, *The Book of the Nocturnal Journey towards the Majesty of the Most Magnanimous* = كتاب الاسراء الى مقام الاسرى. See *supra,* pag. 45, n. 5.

Ibn Arabi, *Dakhair* or "The Treasures of Lovers" = كتاب ذخائر الاعلاق شرح ترجمان الاشواق لابن عربى. Beyrouth, 1312 Heg.

Ibn Arabi, *Futuhat* = كتاب الفتوحات المكية لابن عربى. Bulaq, 1293 Heg.

Ibn Arabi, *Muhadara* = كتاب محاضرة الابرار ومسامرة الاخيار لابن عربى. Cairo, 1305 Heg.

Ibn Arabi = *Tarjuman al'Ashwâq* or "The Interpreter of Love." *See Dakhair.*

Ibn Batutah = *Voyages d'Ibn Batoutah.* Texte arabe, accompagné d'une traduction par Defrémery et Sanguinetti. Paris, Imprim. impériale, 1853–9.

Ibn Daud, *Book of Venus* = كتاب الزهرى لابن داوود الظاهرى. Ms. Bibl. Khed. Cairo, IV, 260.

Ibn Hazm, *Fasl* = كتاب الفصل فى الملل والاهواء والنحل لابن حزم الظاهرى. Cairo, 1317–21 Heg.

Ibn Hazm = *Tawq al-Hamama.* Edit. Dimitri Pétrof. Leyde, Brill, 1914.

Ibn Hijr, *Isaba* = كتاب الاصابة فى تمييز الصحابة لابن حجر. Cairo, 1323–7 Heg.

Ibn Makhluf = كتاب العلوم الفاخرة فى النظر فى امور الاخرة لابن مخلوف. Cairo, 1317 Heg.

Ibn Qaim al-Jawziya, *Miftah* = كتاب مفتاح دار السعادة ومنشور ولاية العلم والارادة لابن قيم الجوزية. Cairo, 1323 Heg.

Ibn Qotaiba = *Liber poësis et poëtarum.* Edited by De Goeje, Leyden, Brill, 1904.

Ihata = الاحاطة فى اخبار غرناطة لابن الخطيب. Ms. 34 Bibl. of the Royal Academy of History of Madrid.

Ihia, see Algazel.

Interián = *El pintor cristiano y erudito,* por Fr. Interián de Ayala. Barcelona, 1883.

Isaba, see Ibn Hijr.

Ithaf, see Algazel.

Jahiz, *Hayawan* or "Book of Animals" = كتاب الحيوان للجاحظ. Cairo, 1323–5 Heg.

Jourdain, Amable = *Recherches critiques sur l'origine des traductions latines d'Aristote.* Paris, Joubert, 1843.

Kanz = كتاب كنز العمال فى ثبوت سنن الاقوال والافعال للهندى. Haidarabad, 1894.

Kasimirski = *Le Koran. Traduction nouvelle faite sur le texte arabe.* Paris, Charpentier, 1862.

284 BIBLIOGRAPHY

Kharida = خريدة العجائب وفريدة الغرائب لـعـمـر بن الوردى.
Cairo, 1314 Heg.

Khazin, *Tafsir* = تفسير القران الجليل المسمى لباب التاويل فى معانى التنزيل للخازن. Cairo, 1318 Heg.

Kitab falsafat, see Averrhoes.

Labitte = *La Divine Comédie avant Dante.* In *Œuvres de Dante Alighieri.* Paris, Charpentier, 1858.

La Fuente, Vicente de = *Historia de las universidades, colegios y demás establecimientos de enseñanza en España.* Madrid, Fuentenebro, 1884–9.

Landino = *Comedia del divino poeta Danthe Alighieri, con la dotta et leggiadra spositione di Christophoro Landino.* Venezia, 1536.

Lane, E. W. = *An account of the manners and customs of the modern Egyptians.* London, 1890.

Lane, E. W. *An Arabic-English Lexicon.* London, Williams and Norgate, 1863–74.

Mâle = *L'art religieux du XIIIᵉ siècle en France.* Paris, Colin, 1902.

Martin, François = *Le livre d'Henoch, traduit sur le texte éthiopien.* Paris, Letouzey, 1904.

Miftah, see Ibn Qaim al-Jawziya.

Minhaj, see Algazel.

Mizan, see Ash-Sharani.

Mizan al-Amal, see Algazel.

Modi = *Dante papers; Virâf, Adaaman and Dante.* Bombay, 1914.

Nardi, Bruno = *Intorno al tomismo di Dante e alla quistione di Sigieri.* Extr. from "Giornale Dantesco," XXII, 5. Florence, Olschki, 1914.

Nardi, Bruno = *Sigieri di Brabante nella Divina Commedia e le fonti della filosofia di Dante.* Extr. from "Rivista di filosofia neoscolastica," 1911–12. Florence, San Giuseppe, 1912.

Nicholson = *A Literary History of the Arabs.* London, T. Fisher Unwin, 2nd Ed. 1914.

Nicholson = *Tarjuman al 'Ashwâq.* London, 1911.

Ozanam = *Des sources poétiques de la Divine Comédie.* In *Œuvres complètes d'Ozanam,* vol. 5. Paris, Lecoffre, 1859.

Perrone = *Praelectiones theologicae quas in Collegio Romano S. J. habebat* Joannes Perrone. Parisiis, Roger et Chernoviz, 1887.

Pétavius = *De theologicis dogmatibus.* Paris, 1643–50.

Porena, Manfredi = *Commento grafico alla Divina Commedia per uso delle scuole.* Milan, Sandron, 1902.

Qazwini, *El Cazwini's Kosmographie* = كتاب عجائب المـخلوقات. *herausgegeben von* Ferdinand Wüstenfeld. Göttingen, Dieterich, 1849.

Qisas, see Thaalabi.

Qistas, see Algazel.

Qummi, *Tafsir* = تفسير غرائب القرآن ورغائب الفرقان للعلامة نظام الدين الحسن....القمـى النيسابورى. Edit. marginally in Tabari, *Tafsir.*

Rasail = كتاب اخوان الصفا وخلان الوفا. Bombay, Najbatolajbar Press, 1305–6 Heg.

Rasail, see Avicenna.

Risala, see Abu-l-Ala al Maarri.

Revue des traditions populaires. Paris, E. Lechevalier et E. Leroux, 1886.

Ribera, Julián = *Discurso de recepción en la R. Academia de la Historia.* Madrid, Imprenta Ibérica, 1915.

Ribera, Julián = *Orígenes del Justicia de Aragón.* "Colección de estudios árabes," vol. II. Saragossa, Comas, 1897.

Ribera, Julián = *Orígenes de la filosofia de Raimundo Lulio.* In "Homenaje a Menéndez y Pelayo," vol. II, 191. Madrid, Suárez, 1899.

Roeské = *L'enfer cambodgien.* In "Journal Asiatique." Paris, Leroux, 1914.

Rossi, Vittorio = *Storia della letteratura italiana per uso dei licei,* vol. I, *Il medio evo.* 5th ed. Milan, Vallardi, 1911.

Rossi, Vittorio = *Il dolce stil novo.* In "Lectura Dantis." Florence, Sansoni, 1906.

Said = *Kitab Tabaqât al-Umam, ou Les Catégories des Nations, par Aboû Qâsim ibn Sâid l'Andaloûs,* publié avec notes et tables par le P. Louis Cheikho, S. J. Beyrout, Imprimerie Catholique, 1912.

Scartazzini = *La Divina Commedia commentata da G. A. Scartazzini.* 7th ed. Milan, Hoepli, 1914.

Schiaparelli = *Ibn Giobeir: Viaggio in Ispagna, Sicilia, Siria e Palestina, Mesopotamia, Arabia, Egitto, compiuto nel secolo XII.* Prima traduzione da C. Schiaparelli. Rome, 1906.

Simonet, F. J. = *Historia de los mozárabes de España...* Madrid, Tello, 1897-1903.

Sundby = *Della vita e delle opere di Brunetto Latini.* Transl. by Renier. Florence, Successori Le Monnier, 1884.

Suyuti, *Dorar* = كتاب الدرر الحسان فى البعث ونعيم الجنان. On margin of كتاب دقائق الاخبار فى ذكر الجنة للسيوطى. والنار لابن القاضى. Cairo, 1326 Heg.

Suyuti, *Sudur* = كتاب شرح الصدور بشرح حال الموتى والقبور للسيوطى. Cairo, 1329 Heg.

Tabari, *Tafsir* = كتاب جامع البيان فى تفسير القران تاليف الامام ابى جعفر محمد...الطبرى. Bulaq, 1323 Heg.

Tacholarus = كتاب تاج العروس فى شرح القاموس للسيد مرتضى. Cairo, 1307 Heg.

Tadhkira = مختصر تذكرة القرطبى للشعرانى. Cairo, 1308 Heg.

Tarikh al-Khamis, see Diyarbakri.

Tecmila = *Apéndice á la edición Codera de la "Tecmila de Aben Al-Abbar."* Edited in "Miscelanea de estudios y textos árabes." Madrid, Imprenta Ibérica, 1915.

Thaalabi, *Qisas* = كتاب قصص الانبياء المسمى بالعرائس للثعلبى. Cairo, 1324 Heg.

Thomae Aquinatis = *Summa contra gentes.* Romae, Forzani, 1888.

Thomae Aquinatis = *Summa theologica.* Romae, Forzani, 1894.

Tisserant, Eugène = *Ascension d'Isaie.* Paris, Letouzey, 1909.

Tixeront, J. = *Histoire des dogmes.* 3rd ed. Paris, Lecoffre, 1906-12.

Torraca, Francesco = *I precursori della "Divina Commedia."* In "Lectura Dantis," Florence, Sansoni, 1906.

Vigouroux = *Dictionnaire de la Bible.* Paris, Letouzey et Ané, 1912.

Virey, Philippe = *La religion de l'ancienne Égypte.* Paris, Beauchesne, 1910.

Vossler, Karl = *Die Göttliche Komödie. Entwickelungsgeschichte und Erklärung.* Heidelberg, 1907-9. Quoted from the Italian translation by Stefano Jacini, *La Divina Commedia studiata nella sua genesi e interpretata.* Bari, Laterza, 1909–14.

Wicksteed, the Rev. P. H., M.A. = *The Paradiso of Dante Alighieri*, "The Temple Classics," Edit. J. M. Dent, London, 1912.

Wüstenfeld, F. = *Die Übersetzungen arabischer Werke in das lateinische seit dem XI Jahrhundert.* Göttingen, Dieterich, 1877.

Yaqut = *Dictionary of Learned Men.* Edited by Margoliouth in "Gibb Memorial" VI, 1 and 5. Leyden, Brill, 1907 and 1911.

INDEX

The Blessings of RAMADAN — Javed Ali

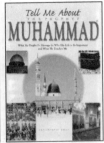

Tell Me About THE PROPHET MUHAMMAD — What the Prophet's Message Is, Why His Life Is So Important and What He Teaches Me

Tell Me About THE PROPHET MUSA — Mepferd

Tell Me About CREATION — Scientific evidence demonstrating that all living things have been created by God — HARUN YAHYA

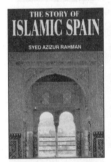

THE STORY OF THE PROPHET YUSUF

THE MOST BEAUTIFUL NAMES OF ALLAH — SAMIRA FAYYAD KHAWALDEH

The Travels of Ibn Battúta — H.A.R. GIBB

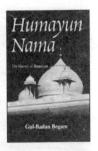

Humayun Nama — The History of Humayun — Gul-Badan Begam

THE STORY OF ISLAMIC SPAIN — SYED AZIZUR RAHMAN

ISLAM AT THE CROSSROADS — MUHAMMAD ASAD

DECISIVE MOMENTS —IN THE— HISTORY —OF— ISLAM — MUHAMMAD ABDULLAH ENAN

Islamic Medicine — EDWARD G. BROWNE

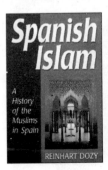

Spanish Islam — A History of the Muslims in Spain — REINHART DOZY

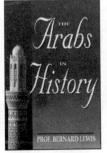

THE Arabs IN History — PROF. BERNARD LEWIS

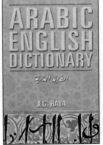

ARABIC ENGLISH DICTIONARY — J.G. HAVA

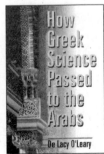

How Greek Science Passed to the Arabs — De Lacy O'Leary

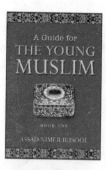

A Guide for
THE YOUNG
MUSLIM

BOOK ONE

ASSAD NIMER BUSOOL

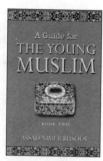

A Guide for
THE YOUNG
MUSLIM

BOOK TWO

ASSAD NIMER BUSOOL

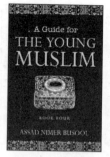

A Guide for
THE YOUNG
MUSLIM

BOOK FOUR

ASSAD NIMER BUSOOL

THE ARABIC
ALPHABET
THROUGH
THE BEAUTIFUL NAMES OF ALLAH

ASSAD NIMER BUSOOL

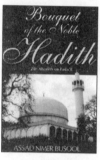

Bouquet
of the Noble
Hadith
290 Ahadith on Fada'il

ASSAD NIMER BUSOOL

Forty
Hadith

On the
Importance of
Knowledge,
Learning and
Teaching.

ASSAD NIMER BUSOOL

SERMONS
OF THE PROPHET
MUHAMMAD
ABU NASR MUHAMMAD IBN BAYAN

A HISTORY OF
ARABIC
LITERATURE

CLEMENT HUART

THE
ISLAMIC ART
AND
ARCHITECTURE
SIR THOMAS ARNOLD

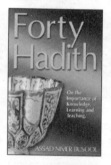

After Death,
Life!

Thoughts to alleviate
the grief of all Muslims facing
death and bereavement

Ruqaiyyah Waris Maqsood

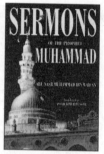

Introducing
Islam
A Simple Introduction to Islam

Maulana Wahiduddin Khan

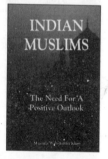

INDIAN
MUSLIMS

The Need For A
Positive Outlook

Maulana Wahiduddin Khan

PRINCIPLES OF
Islam
Maulana Wahiduddin Khan

THE MORAL
Vision
Islamic Ethics for Success in Life

Maulana Wahiduddin Khan

Tabligh
Movement

Maulana Wahiduddin Khan

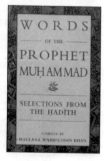

WORDS
OF THE
PROPHET
MUHAMMAD

SELECTIONS FROM
THE HADITH

COMPILED BY
MAULANA WAHIDUDDIN KHAN